MW01200322

THE *LAST*
EMPRESS
OF *FRANCE*

THE *LAST* EMPRESS *OF FRANCE*

THE REBELLIOUS LIFE OF EUGÉNIE DE MONTIJO

PETIE KLADSTRUP AND EVELYNE RESNICK

HANOVER
SQUARE
PRESS

ISBN-13: 978-1-335-01249-4

The Last Empress of France

Hanover Square Press
22 Adelaide St. West, 41st Floor
Toronto, Ontario M5H 4E3, Canada
HanoverSqPress.com

Printed in U.S.A.

CONTENTS

INTRODUCTION

"Women are still an undiscovered country."
—Tina Howe, playwright

OUR WORK ON THIS BOOK STARTED WITH A TELEPHONE CALL. "I'VE JUST BEEN READING about Empress Eugénie," said Petie, "and I'm astonished by all she did."

"Yes," said Evelyne. "I've always found her far more interesting than her husband."

Eugénie? Eugénie who? Who was this woman and why would anyone be interested? In reading about France, there's almost never a mention of her. Eugénie de Montijo, the last empress of France, was an extraordinary ruler whose accomplishments were key to transforming France and making it a modern country.

She got French women the right to be educated and earn degrees. She created the haute couture industry almost entirely on her own. She opened numerous professions to women. She established a medical college and an agricultural school for women. And she championed research by Louis Pasteur and other scientists.

Not only that, Eugénie was the only woman of her time to wield genuine political power when she was named regent by her husband Napoléon III, allowing her to run the country in his absence. Contemporaries such as Queen Victoria of the United Kingdom and Empress Elisabeth of Austria were largely figureheads.

The empress was a feminist long before the term was born, railing against "sex-prejudice" and the misogynistic Code Napoléon that the first Napoléon established, a group of laws relegating females to second-class citizenship.

She had a fiery personality that matched her red hair. She rode as if she were a centaur, swam and sailed in the worst of storms (nearly drowning more than once), danced with a smuggler in his cave, and roller-skated in the halls of the royal palace. She welcomed openly gay men and women into her entourage.

Hardly a day passed that Eugénie did not leave the Tuileries Palace in plain clothes and an unmarked coach to carry food and supplies to hospitals and orphanages. She financed rehabilitation centers for women and visited cholera and smallpox wards despite warnings from doctors, acts that attracted media attention and turned her into an icon adored by the public.

Her rebelliousness and visibility, however, made her an easy target for those who felt women had no place running a country. "She's nothing more than an ornament of the throne," complained one government minister. "And *he* is a fool!" Eugénie shot back.

She was fearless when fighting for her beliefs. She upset Catholic Church hierarchy by declaring that Muslims, Jews and Christians worshipped the same god. She supported Dreyfus and said France's treatment of him was "shameful."

While her sharp tongue and independent spirit offended many, they also won her a legion of admirers, among them German chancellor Otto von Bismarck who declared, "She's the only man in Paris."

Yet, the limited image of her that comes to us today is a narrow one gleaned largely from the official, romantic paintings by Franz Xaver Winterhalter: a "fashion plate" in picture-book hats and frothy gowns, carefree and light-hearted to the point of frivolous.

But frivolous was one thing Eugénie was not. For her, fashion was not a "superficial distraction," as Robin Givhan wrote about

Nancy Pelosi in *The Washington Post*. Like her, fashion "was testimony to her attention to detail, to her understanding of symbolism, to her awareness of just how useful aesthetics can be as a form of communication . . ."

Eugénie's frothy gowns were nearly all designed by Charles Frederick Worth, who became known as the "father of haute couture," and they were clearly "a form of communication"—nothing less than carefully selected advertisements for the arts and crafts of France. In wearing them, Eugénie's eye was also on politics. Her gowns were made with fabrics from Lyon, whose silk weavers had been bitter opponents of the regime. When she added dresses of their silk to her wardrobe, she won them over. She also captivated the British, then traditional foes of the French, when she appeared in a tartan-patterned dress on her first official visit to the United Kingdom. Later she beguiled onlookers when she wore an Egyptian dress during her trip to open the Suez Canal.

Under Eugénie's visible patronage the garment trade grew dramatically during the Second Empire to become the major employer in Paris and a key element of France's economy. People everywhere began to recognize Paris as the world's capital of luxury and style and Eugénie as its face. With her innate sense of marketing and with help from her husband, she sold French culture to the world by supporting writers, painters, sculptors and musicians as well as makers of luxury products.

Eugénie's interests, however, ranged far beyond culture and fashion. She was fascinated by science and technology and used her private funds to back Louis Pasteur in his research. She also supported her cousin Ferdinand de Lesseps in his plan to build the Suez Canal.

And yet, despite all her achievements, she remains "Eugénie who?" barely a footnote to history. School textbooks ignore her accomplishments, if they mention her at all, and even the Second Empire gets short shrift. It is forgotten or dismissed by historians—nearly all male—who view it as little more than a pale shadow of Napoléon Bonaparte's First Empire, referring to the Second as "the Carnival Empire," a circus with Napoléon III as ringmaster and Eugénie a trapeze artist in an eye-catching costume.

On the rare occasions when she is remembered, Eugénie is usually disparaged as the femme fatale who manipulated the emperor, leading him to make disastrous foreign policy decisions, such as the Mexican incursion and the Franco–Prussian War when the provinces of Alsace and Lorraine were stripped from France. Even today some French respond to her name by saying, "Eugénie who? Oh, don't talk to us about *her*. We lost Alsace and Lorraine because of her," even though the reality is that France regained them in large part because of her.

Which is why we were so intrigued by this woman, her contradictions and the question of how such a key figure could be almost lost to history. Was it rank chauvinism, a male centric view of the past that persists even today? Was it the "unhappy ending" to her time as empress? We wanted to see where she lived and worked to understand her and her life. We wanted to go to the heart of who Eugénie was and uncover the reality of the woman who had once ruled France. What we found is that although born two centuries ago, Eugénie de Montijo is very much a woman for today, one who deserves to be acknowledged and celebrated for her groundbreaking achievements.

THE LAST
EMPRESS OF
FRANCE

CHAPTER ONE

OF BLOOD AND SUN

SPAIN, ONCE THE WORLD'S MOST IMPORTANT POWER, WAS TOTTERING LIKE HUMPTY-Dumpty. At the turn of the nineteenth century, it was under attack by a foreign power and weakened by internal struggles. The South American colonies, Spain's primary source of wealth, were in revolt, greatly reducing the country's revenue. It was an era, historians note, that brought dramatic breaks with the past. It was a time when everything changed for the country.

And there was another threat as well, an even more dangerous one: Mother Nature. In the first decade of the nineteenth century alone, the country was confronted by an almost biblical spate of disasters: droughts followed by floods that killed thousands, earthquakes, famine, harvest failures, even a plague of locusts. There was also a yellow fever epidemic which, according to one visitor from Britain, "left the poor dropping like flies." Panicked rural dwellers fled to cities in hopes of escaping the disease.

In the face of the natural disasters and its geography—rugged mountain ranges, swaths of arid desert, high plains and steep valleys—Spain was nearly powerless. Communication was difficult, and travel almost impossible. Roads were few and ill-maintained; banditry and smuggling flourished. Communities were isolated from their neighbors and left to get by any way they could. Often they found themselves at the mercy of unscrupulous local power brokers and landlords who taxed them and conscripted men into their service. Making the picture worse was the country's move toward a cash economy, a shift that many, including artisans, soldiers and farmers, found difficult to understand after centuries of paying by barter or service. It left many falling ever deeper into debt and poverty.

Spain's absolutist monarchy only added to the problems. The crown rested on the head of King Carlos IV, a man one historian characterized as "good-hearted, but weak and simple-minded." People called him *El Cazador*, the hunter, because hunting was the only thing that interested him.

Through neglect and disinterest, Carlos allowed Spain, one of the world's most prosperous countries in the eighteenth century, to slide into turmoil, debt and dependency. He saw its colonies in South America, which had sustained the Spanish government with shipload after shipload of treasure, slip away as they wrested their independence from Madrid. Ongoing battles further depleted the government's treasury and disgruntled its army. More rapidly than it could understand or respond, Spain was deprived of both income and its status as a world power. In addition, it was struggling to live down its reputation as a repressive, medieval country, something that had dogged it since the fifteenth century and the worst days of the Inquisition. Although its role in the Church had been downgraded, a sense of menace remained.

Then, in a disastrous move, Spain switched sides and allied itself with France, a country at war with Britain. In one of the most famous naval battles ever fought, Spain witnessed its armada, long a source of national pride, go down in defeat at the hands of Lord Nelson and British ships of war in the Battle of Trafalgar in 1805.

At the same time, a family squabble meant trouble at home. King Carlos detested his son, Ferdinand, who returned the favor and plotted to take the throne from his father.

Into what King Amedeo I of Spain would call the "insane asylum of Spanish politics" strode Napoléon Bonaparte, bringing with him his *Grande Armée* and his vast ambitions. Also in his entourage was his older brother, Joseph.

Napoléon saw Spain as fertile ground for empire-building. Its army was weak after years of neglect in favor of the navy, and the underpaid soldiers were desperate to avoid being sent to fight in tropical South America. In hopes of avoiding conscription, many joined militias that answered only to local leaders. Some groups were loyal to Carlos, others to Ferdinand. Some espoused liberal ideas drawn from the eighteenth century Enlightenment; others had a conservative, religious agenda. But most were interested only in their own skins and making a living. Politics was of little concern. As one salesman said, "I support whichever party is most convenient."

When Carlos was finally forced by his son to abdicate, Napoléon allowed Ferdinand to believe he would officially recognize him as king, reigning as Ferdinand VII. Napoléon asked him to come to Bayonne, just across the Spanish border in France, where they could work out the details.

It was a trap. As soon as Ferdinand arrived, Napoléon sent him off into exile in central France. (It was on the same day, April 20, 1808, that his nephew and future husband of Eugénie, Napoléon III, was born.) Napoléon then named a new king of Spain—his brother Joseph.

In the spring of 1808, within two months, Spain had had three different monarchs.

What followed was months of brutal fighting across the Iberian Peninsula. Great Britain sent troops under Arthur Wellesley, the future Duke of Wellington, to help clear the country of the French. With Spain's army disorganized and hamstrung by financial neglect, the British were forced to rely on help wherever they could find it. Most of it came from diverse local groups fighting in the hills and forests. They were called guerillas, their name coming from the Spanish word for war, *guerra*, and which literally meant *little wars*. These warrior bands had sprung up in the wake of the country's chaotic political scene and gave the world a name for a type of fighting that had existed for centuries: *guerilla warfare*.

Guerillas were autonomous, often maverick groups that oper-
ated independently, frequently hiding out in the hills or blending
into the populace. There were many different types, each with
subdivisions ranging from groups of rogue professional soldiers
to tradesmen and farm workers, and from ultraconservative to
staunchly leftist. Loyalties changed often: from Ferdinand to his
father, then to Napoléon, then back again.

Most people in Spain sympathized with Ferdinand, the deposed king. Others were drawn to the Napoleonic cause, seeing
in the French leader the kind of strength and authority necessary
to restore Spanish integrity and security. They were called *afrancesados* and were a small minority, probably no more than twelve
thousand in a population of more than ten million.

Among the afrancesados who fought on one side and then
switched to another was a young artillery commander named
Don Cipriano Palafox y Portocarrero, the man who would later
become Eugénie's father. His reasons for switching support from
Ferdinand to Napoléon are unclear. He may well have decided
that restoring Ferdinand to the throne was a hopeless cause. Cipriano's mother was a famously outspoken liberal, so perhaps her
words were the determining factor. Or was it a family feud? Had
Cipriano become fed up with his older and hotheaded brother
Eugenio who dabbled in conspiracy theories and was constantly
stirring up revolts? Did Cipriano feel changing sides was the only
way he could protect his family after Eugenio was arrested and
imprisoned in November of 1809?

What is clear is that somewhere along the way, he had become
impressed with Napoléon's personality and authority, because in
1810, he forswore his Spanish army rank and joined the army
of King Joseph. It was a fateful decision, one that would ripple
through generations.

Cipriano would follow the Napoleonic star until its final
burnout at Waterloo in 1815, then find himself stranded in Paris.
He was only thirty-one, a dashing war hero with a patch over the
eye he'd lost in an artillery accident, a wounded leg that left him

with a limp and a chest full of medals, some pinned on by Napoléon himself. But he was also on his own, with no job and little income, and as far as Ferdinand—now back on the throne—was concerned, Cipriano was a die-hard liberal no longer welcome in his native country.

But Cipriano was not alone: Paris was teeming with other Spaniards hoping to escape the political turmoil of their country. Among them Françoise Kirkpatrick y Grevignée and her daughters. Cipriano had done business with Françoise's husband, William, who had been US consul in Malaga and also a wine merchant. Cipriano also had warm feelings about Françoise, because she had once tried to help him make peace with his older brother Eugenio when they were battling about income from family property. When he discovered the Kirkpatricks were in Paris, Cipriano hurried to call upon them. He was warmly received.

But he was also surprised—and delighted—to find that their daughters, who were only young girls when he knew them in Spain, were now grown-up and extremely attractive. Especially the oldest daughter, Manuela. At age twenty-one, she was beautiful and vivacious, and people were immediately drawn to her. She combined, according to the American George Ticknor, "Andalusian grace, English genuineness and French facility." Cipriano was smitten.

It was not a match that won favor with Manuela's father, even with the ties of friendship, business and shared political views. Cipriano was, if not penniless, a second son with no prospects and limited resources. His war wounds had left him in uncertain health. Plus, he was considered a traitor by the Spanish monarchy and barred from his own country. William wanted more for his daughter.

Under Ferdinand, Spanish politics, which had seen kings come and go at the speed of light, began to settle down, and William felt his business and role as US consul were once again secure, so he brought his family home. At the same time, the Kirkpatrick family joined a group of Spanish nobles lobbying the king to let afrancesados, including Cipriano, return permanently.

It was good timing. King Ferdinand was eager to reestablish Spain's role on the world stage and, for that, he knew he needed his best-educated and highest-ranked nobles, so he overlooked fluctuating loyalties. He also decided his most prominent citizens should not quibble among themselves, an ironic decision for a man who had spent his entire life battling with his family. He ordered Cipriano back to Spain for a limited time and told him to settle his quarrels with Eugenio.

Cipriano's romance with Manuela that had begun in Paris was rekindled in their native country.

Even though he was a second son and an afrancesado, he also was a grandee of Spain, one of the highest-ranked nobles of the country. Therefore, he needed the king's permission to marry. When Cipriano asked to wed Manuela, Ferdinand demanded a genealogy of the bride's family to determine whether she was good enough for his errant noble.

The genealogy was at hand: the Patent, as it was called, had been prepared in 1791 for a Kirkpatrick family succession question and updated when William, Manuela's father, sought and then obtained Spanish hidalgo status, that is, official ranking as a gentleman. The document showed Kirkpatrick family connections back to Robert the Bruce and early kings of Scotland with baronies and other titles sprinkled in through the generations.

It also told the horrifying story of Manuela's great-grandfather, Robert Kirkpatrick, a supporter of Bonnie Prince Charlie, who was beheaded after the 1745 Jacobite rebellion in Scotland. It was an event that would haunt the family.

Ferdinand was satisfied. "Let the good man [Cipriano] marry the daughter of Fingal," he pronounced. The King was confused: Fingal is in Ireland; the Kirkpatrick family came from Scotland. It is easy, however, to understand Ferdinand's perplexity. Manuela's mother was half-Spanish and half-Belgian. Her father, William Kirkpatrick, was a Scot and, therefore, a citizen of Great Britain, but he was also the consul of the United States in Malaga and had connections in South America and Asia. The Kirkpatrick family was a crazy quilt where languages, cultures and even loyalties were patched together.

It mattered not. On December 15, 1817, the strong-willed Manuela defied her still-disapproving father and married Cipriano in Malaga. Willliam, irritated and disappointed, refused to attend the wedding. The father–daughter relationship would remain strained throughout their lives.

CIPRIANO MAY NOT HAVE BEEN WEALTHY OR HAVE POSSESSED ONE OF THE MOST IMPORtant titles in Spain, but he was entitled to call himself the Count of Teba, and Manuela was now a countess.

The count was a soldier at heart: he was not content to sit at home and ignore political developments. When King Ferdinand repudiated the country's constitution in 1823, Cipriano joined the liberal forces revolting against the king's action. The uprising was quickly put down, and an angry royalist mob turned on Cipriano, calling for his death. Hundreds of Cipriano's fellow liberals were killed by the mob, but he escaped death when Manuela boldly stepped in front of the crowd and begged for her husband's life. Manuela was "dynamite," Prosper Mérimée would say, and her determination to protect her husband, no matter what his weaknesses, would find an echo in Eugénie's own actions.

The king, angered by the revolt, had Cipriano thrown into prison in Santiago de Compostela where he was held for eighteen months before being allowed to join Manuela in the city of Granada in Andalusia. The couple, now exiled again from the royal court in Madrid, lived in a small house. It was here that Manuela, making the best of her husband's house arrest, established a liberal salon.

Andalusia—where Eugénie would be born—was an area so drenched in swashbuckling history that it almost refused to let a newer age seep through its old traditions. In 1829, Washington

Irving wrote about his travels in the area for his book about Granada, *Tales of the Alhambra*. Just being there, Irving observed, "carries the mind back to the chivalric days of Christian and Moslem warfare, and the romantic struggle for the conquest of Granada." It was not "a country cultivated and civilized," he said, but he was thrilled by "the rude mountain scramble; the roving, haphazard, wayfaring; the half wild, yet frank and hospitable manners" which imparted a special character to the people of the area.

Like generations of people before and after him, Irving fell under its spell. "The temperature of a summer midnight in Andalusia is perfectly ethereal," he wrote. "We seem lifted up into a purer atmosphere; we feel a serenity of soul, a buoyancy of spirit, which render mere existence happiness. But when moonlight is added to all this, the effect is like enchantment."

Granada had once been the capital of a Muslim emirate and home to a vibrant Jewish community. It was a metropolis that prided itself on its rich and diverse heritage and cherished the spot high on its hills which was known as the pass of "The Moor's Last Sigh." Legend had it that this was where Boabdil, the last Muslim ruler in Spain, stopped as he left in exile and turned for his final look at what had been his beloved capital city.

Here, too, a nearly destitute Christopher Columbus came to plead with their Most Catholic Majesties, Isabella and Ferdinand, for funds to seek out a new route to India. Only as he was dejectedly leaving the city was he called back and told that his venture would be financed after all.

That was in 1492, the year marking the final conquest of Spain by the Christian rulers and the brutal expulsion of Muslims and Jews.

In departing, they left behind not only the dazzling Alhambra but also a style of life more open and relaxed than nearly any other place in Europe. Granada's mystique would linger and find its voice in song:

The dawn in the sky greets the day with a sigh for Granada.
For she can remember the splendor that once was Granada . . .

A different translation of the lyrics from Spanish makes Granada's spell clear:

Granada . . . of lovely women
of blood and sun.

It was here in 1826, under a sky said to be vibrating with light and where every stone spoke of art and "splendid warfare," that Eugenia de Montijo was born. Her birth came during an earthquake, an "omen," according to local lore, and she would live her life as though another could occur at any moment.

She was the second of two daughters born to Cipriano and Manuela. Her sister Francisca, called Paca by the family, had arrived two years earlier shortly after they had been ordered into exile in Granada.

Manuela seemed meant for Granada and Granada for her: the music, the lifestyle, even the unrelenting sun—she loved it all. One Spaniard could well have had her in mind when he told foreign travelers about Granada: "*Ah Dios, Señores!* What a city you are going to see. Such streets! Such squares! Such palaces! And the women—ah, *Santa Maria Purissima*—what women!"

The "dynamite" Manuela would make her home a magnet for musicians, artists, writers, philosophers and foreign visitors, and her parties with their music and scintillating conversation became legendary. The French writer and preservationist Mérimée would be a regular visitor and become a close friend of the family.

One person, however, was not thrilled by the parties: her husband. Cipriano's years as a soldier and a prisoner made him solitary and nearly ascetic; financial struggles left him extremely frugal. These were characteristics he imposed on his two daughters. He declared that their childhoods should be "serious," devoid of frills and unnecessary things "as befits the life of poverty for which you are destined." They were to wear plain linen dresses throughout the year and were always to walk, leaving the carriage at home for all but the longest trips.

Cipriano had absorbed the liberal ideas his late mother espoused, especially the progressive ones about women's education. His daughters were not to sit idly at home embroidering, he decided. They were to be outside, active and useful. He established an almost military-style regimen for them. He taught them to ride astride rather than sidesaddle, gave them fencing lessons and took them sailing, swimming and hiking. The girls thrived, especially Eugenia, or Eugénie as she would become known. She proved herself to be a natural athlete. She loved sports and excelled at them; she never seemed to tire. She was also something of a daredevil, a tomboy, people said, and she loved taking risks. When it came to swimming, she did so in all weather, even storms. On more than one occasion, she had to be rescued after nearly drowning. Paca may have been gentler and more malleable, but she, too, loved the outdoors and frequently was the initiator of pranks the girls played.

It was Eugenia, however, who earned a reputation as a wild child. She was often late to lunch, no matter how many times she was called, and when she appeared, her plain linen dress might be covered by a used matador's jacket or hide trousers a stable boy had outgrown and that she had pulled on for riding. There might even be a bullfighter's hat perched on her head.

Despite rules and restrictions, it was a free and easy childhood. Eugenia idolized her father and followed him everywhere, begging for more romantic stories of Napoléon, the campaigns, the battles, the triumphs and even the terrible losses.

But all that abruptly ended in 1834 when Cipriano learned that his still-estranged brother Eugenio, Eugenia's namesake and godfather, was dying. It was hardly a surprise: Eugenio's health had been declining for some time, and his mind, too, had been deteriorating. He was known to erupt into horrendous rages. His wild life of conspiracy-mongering and womanizing was paying terrible dividends. When his wife demanded a separation, Eugenio packed her off to a convent. There had been no children, and as a result, Cipriano became heir to the Montijo family fortune and Eugenio's numerous titles.

What happened next is a family legend retold and embellished through the generations. It's clear Cipriano's two sisters disliked the idea of the Montijo family's wealth falling into the hands of Cipriano and his so-called foreign wife, so they arranged or staged a marriage between the ailing Eugenio and a very young woman who was probably the mistress of one of Cipriano's brothers-in-law. Shortly thereafter, the young woman announced she was pregnant with Eugenio's child. Nearly everyone was stunned. There was no way this infirm and crazed man could father a child, they said.

Here, fantasy enters the story. When Manuela got word of the forthcoming "blessed event" of the child's birth, the family legend alleges, she flew into action even though she was still legally confined to Andalusia and prohibited from going to Madrid where the Montijo mansion was located. Calling on friends for help, she got herself invited to a ball the king would be attending in the countryside and then into a quadrille in which the monarch was dancing. Taking advantage of the moments they were together in the dance pattern, she asked him to let her attend the birth of the supposed heir. Ferdinand, taken aback by her beauty and unexpected presence, agreed.

Arriving at the Montijo mansion in the capital city, Manuela was told the birth was imminent. She strode into the birthing chamber and heard a cry. The new mother was panting and sweating when suddenly a baby boy was conjured up. In fact, the newborn heir turned out to be an orphan child who had been smuggled into the house.

Both Manuela and Cipriano were present for the birth, and so the ruse failed. The child would be cared for by the Montijo family and become a colonel in the Spanish army. The putative mother was pensioned off and disappeared into history.

Eugenio died July 16, 1834, and Cipriano—and his "foreign"

wife—duly inherited his numerous titles and wealth. Officially Eugenia's father was now the Eighth Count of Montijo and could move back to Madrid.

EUGENIO'S DEATH CAME AT A TIME OF RENEWED TURBULENCE IN MADRID. CHOLERA WAS killing hundreds of people each day, and there were reports that an army opposed to Ferdinand's rule was approaching the city. The army had the support of the Franciscan friars who were accused of poisoning Madrid's wells.

When shouting erupted outside the Montijo mansion on July 17, 1834, Eugenia opened a window to see what was happening. She was shocked to see one of the friars being stabbed to death, then dragged through the streets and kicked as rioters set a neighboring church on fire. It was an incident that would weigh on her throughout her life.

At least eighty priests were murdered in the riots. Don Cipriano decided Madrid was no longer safe for his family. Not even waiting the few days until his brother's funeral could be held, he immediately sent them away.

On July 18, Manuela, the new Countess of Montijo, and her frightened daughters left for Paris.

THE JOURNEY MEANT LONG HOURS ON BAD ROADS. JULY WAS HOT, AND THE CARRIAGE, pulled by mules, was stifling. The road to Paris, however, was blocked by guerillas worried that travelers from Madrid would bring cholera to the area. While they waited to be given permission to continue through Barcelona, Manuela discovered she had a friend in the city, a famous bullfighter. When he heard what was happening, he announced he would not go into the ring unless the protesters allowed Manuela and her daughters to pass. The guerillas, more upset about missing a performance by one of Spain's greatest bullfighters than about cholera, backed down and allowed the countess and her family through.

For the very first time, Eugenia would set foot on the soil of the country she would one day call her own. She was eight years old.

Manuela was eager to get to Paris as soon as possible. It would be a homecoming for her as her sister, Catherine de Lesseps, was there. Eugenia and Paca would be surrounded by cousins, including one named Ferdinand de Lesseps.

Pleased as she was to be with her family, Manuela quickly found a place of her own where she could entertain and enjoy her new wealth and status. She enrolled her daughters in the most fashionable school in Paris, the Sacré-Cœur convent on the rue de Varenne. The school, now the home of the Musée Rodin, had beautiful stone buildings and a large, attractive garden.

It had been founded shortly after the French Revolution by a nun, Madeleine Sophie Barat. The school was designed for upper-class young ladies who would marry men of equal or better status, become mothers and manage a household. Barat was deeply religious and believed girls needed to be separated from boys to be educated. Boys would go to their own schools and study history, geography, science and politics as well as engage in sports. Girls, under her guidance, would be taught Christian principles, learn to be "pleasant" around others and follow the dictates of society. It was a sure recipe for rebellion.

Long before Eugenia and Paca arrived, some students found the atmosphere stifling and rebelled, notably Amantine Aurore Lucile Dupin de Francueil, who would go on to a life as a novelist under the nom de plume George Sand. She would defy convention by wearing trousers and smoking, becoming the mistress of composer Frédéric Chopin, and calling the education at the convent school "mediocre."

Eugenia and Paca were bored with the school and would frequently sneak off to explore the streets of Paris and spend time with shopkeepers and beggars. Unlike their classmates, the girls had not spent their days at home with their mothers honing their homemaking skills plucked from books like Hester Chapone's

Letters on the Improvement of the Mind. The book had been a best-seller for more than sixty years and translated into several languages, including French, by the time Eugenia and Paca arrived in Paris, and it was one of the major texts that mothers throughout England, America and France used to prepare their girls for marriage and family.

The sisters were accustomed to active days outdoors followed by evenings spent in their mother's salon listening and talking to writers and artists. The Sacré-Cœur school frustrated them with leisurely strolls in the gardens and some gentle horseback rides, always sidesaddle, as their only exercise. They squirmed under the tutelage of nuns who set them endlessly reading the lives of the saints.

Their father shared their low opinion of the school. In 1836 Don Cipriano dropped everything in Spain, stormed into Paris and pulled his daughters out and enrolled them in a gymnastics school run by Colonel Francisco Amoros y Ondaneo, a friend of his from the Spanish army.

Amoros had run several gymnasiums in Spain before his support for Napoléon forced him into exile in France. There he built the largest gymnasium Paris had ever seen and developed exercises specifically to train French soldiers. In the year before Manuela and her daughters arrived in Paris, Amoros had decided to expand his operations and began offering physical training to civilians. As unusual as this was for young girls, it was just what Cipriano wanted for his daughters.

Amoros based his work on Johann Pestalozzi, a Swiss educator who "encouraged harmonious intellectual, moral, and physical development" through an intense "use of activities, excursions, and nature studies." He also ardently believed that teachers should be trained. Until then, there had been no qualifications for becoming a teacher, and the bulk of education was left to nuns and priests.

Gone at last for Eugenia and Paca were the boring lives of saints. Gone, too, were those gentle walks and horseback rides.

In their place came serious study, demanding exercises and sports like fencing to strengthen both their bodies and their minds. In 1838, Amoros reported to Eugenia's parents that "she enjoys physical exercise, and her character is good, generous and firm" but her temperament seemed "sanguine and emotional."

MANUELA WAS IN HER ELEMENT IN PARIS. SHE HAD THE MONEY, TIME, SOCIAL STANDING AND freedom to live the way she wanted. Her husband, meanwhile, had returned to Spain, leaving her to indulge her love of socializing and entertaining without complaints or constraints. She relaunched her salon, clearly delighted to be the center of her guests' attentions. The salon drew Paris's leading literary lights, chief among them a friend she had made in Spain, Prosper Mérimée.

Mérimée, a polyglot and a man of diverse talents, had spent time with their family in Granada and was only too happy to find them now ensconced in Paris. He adored Manuela and the tales she told him. One story in particular caught his attention, about a cigarette girl named Carmen. Mérimée had developed a new literary form, the short novel or novella, and a character like Carmen was perfect for one. He published *Carmen* in 1845. Within a few years Georges Bizet would tailor the story into an opera.

Although Mérimée remained unmarried, he found pleasure in the family setting at Doña Manuela's with her two young daughters. He especially admired Eugenia for her high spirits, calling her "a lioness with a flowing mane." He took her and Paca under his wing and regularly worked with them to perfect their French, often sharing his love and appreciation of the past with them. Eventually, he even brought the girls to a shooting gallery where they learned to use pistols.

He also introduced them to a friend of his, Marie-Henri Beyle, better known by his pen name of Stendhal but always called Monsieur Beyle by Eugenia and her sister. Stendhal, too, was a bachelor, and like Mérimée, he was entranced by the two girls—

and they were entranced with him. He was older than Mérimée by some twenty years and had campaigned with Napoléon, as their father had. Stendhal had served in Bonaparte's government as well and had traveled widely in Europe. His stories made them feel closer to their absent father. "The evenings when M. Beyle comes are special," Eugenia wrote to Cipriano. "He tells us about all the things that happened during the Empire. His stories are so amusing and we get to go to bed later."

The time they spent with Stendhal was not only amusing but eye-opening. He encouraged them to "look upon life as a masked ball." But if they were intrigued with him, he was taken with them and would dedicate a chapter of his masterpiece *The Charterhouse of Parma* to them.

THEIR LIVES, ONCE SO FREE AND EASY, WERE NOW CRAMMED WITH ACTIVITIES. IN ADDITION to sessions at the Amoros gymnasium and study and outings with Mérimée and Stendhal, their mother had also hired a British governess named Miss Cole who would expand their English skills.

Then there were their visits to the dentist. Manuela knew this was good for her daughters' health and well-being, but beautiful smiles also had become imperative for women as they moved through society. Young women, especially, needed lovely white teeth and not a hint of bad breath if they were to attract suitable husbands. French dentistry, once the best in the world, had fallen behind the times, and now everyone who was anyone went to an American dentist.

The most sought-after dentist in Paris was Dr. C. Starr Brewster, whose patient list could have been torn from the social register. His practice was so successful that in 1847 he would hire a young assistant named Dr. Thomas Evans, who would later establish his own practice. Manuela added her name and those of her daughters to Brewster's list of clients and then continued with Evans when he succeeded Brewster.

What began as a fashionable choice would turn out to be the most crucial decision for Eugenia's life.

MANUELA GREW RESTLESS IN PARIS, AND IN 1838, SHE WHISKED EUGENIA AND PACA OFF TO England and sent them to board at Royal York Crescent School in Clifton, a small town near Bristol. Twelve-year-old Eugenia hated it. Her classmates, mostly daughters of the English upper classes, took one look at her red hair, the "flowing mane" that so charmed Mérimée, and began calling her Carrots. Also, they delighted in mocking her accent.

Although she was miserable at the school, Eugenia admitted she was proud of her growing competence in English. "I'll translate for you when you come to visit," she bragged in a letter to her father.

She soon found a friend in another unhappy, homesick student, a Hindu girl from India. Her classmate so fired her imagination with marvelous tales of Indian splendors that Eugenia joined her to plot a getaway from the bullying and misery. They sneaked out and boarded a ship in the nearby Bristol port that was bound for India. A sharp-eyed teacher, however, spotted them hiding on the ship and dragged the two girls back to school.

Although being returned to school dispirited Eugenia, far more upsetting news lay ahead. In March of 1839, Don Cipriano fell ill in Madrid, and Manuela went there as soon as she received news of his illness. Recognizing Eugenia's discontent, she had taken the girls back to Paris by this time, and they remained there with their governess as Manuela made the difficult trip across the Pyrenees in winter. The girls used their time without their mother gleefully, pushing their freedom to the furthest limit, tormenting their governess who finally called in their friend Mérimée for help.

Mérimée knew, as Eugenia and Paca did not, that their father was seriously ill and realized the girls would soon be called to Spain and probably then remain there. In a letter to their mother, he wrote, "I have been so fond of those children that I simply can't get used to the idea of not seeing them again for a long time . . . instead of our two little friends, I am afraid that [when next I see them] I shall meet two prim and haughty young ladies who have quite forgotten me."

Mérimée was correct about their leaving. Within a few days, Manuela sent word to the governess to bring Eugenia and Paca to Madrid immediately. This was not easy. It was still March and a blizzard brought them to a stop and a delay of a week near the French–Spanish border.

When they finally arrived in Madrid, the girls were too late. Told of their father's death, Paca broke down in hysterics. Eugenia went upstairs to her room, closed the door and refused to come out for two days. She was thirteen and had lost the person she loved most in life.

Manuela realized something had to be done—and quickly. Her daughters could not be allowed to languish in their grief. In the years of their absence, politics in Spain had changed once again. On the throne now was Isabella II, the young daughter of Ferdinand. Manuela, Countess of Montijo, and now a grandee of Spain in her own right, saw an opportunity to establish herself at court. She became the queen's most important lady-in-waiting and with that began a new career: finding husbands for her daughters.

CHAPTER TWO

MARRIAGE-GO-ROUND

MADRID WAS ENJOYING A PAUSE BETWEEN BOUTS OF POLITICAL UPHEAVAL AND MILITARY uprisings in 1842 after the widowed queen who had been regent, Maria Christina, fled to Paris. She left her teenage daughter on the throne with a parliamentary president to run the government.

For madrileños, it was a chance to return to their cherished lifestyle—a late breakfast, a lazy lunch followed by siesta until the heat of the day had passed, and then the long, beautiful warm evening of music, dance and conversation.

For Manuela, Countess of Montijo and Grandee of Spain, home from Paris, it was a chance for her to do what she saw as her duty: find wealthy, titled husbands for her two beautiful daughters, Paca, who was eighteen and Eugenia, now sixteen. The role would also let her pursue her own love of entertaining and socializing, with the added advantage of the Montijo mansions and wealth. Although the conditions for inheritance varied in different areas and different communities of the country, nineteenth-century Spanish law allowed women to inherit. In the Basque region, for instance, the heir was to be "the most worthy person." Neither sex nor age was specified.

Manuela knew her appointment to the royal court as a lady-in-waiting to the young queen would also help her quest. She ran through a list of eligible bachelors for her daughters and settled on one for Paca, the Duke of Alba, then twenty-seven. His title was the most distinguished of all; even better, he was Spain's richest man. His lineage, like Manuela's, included Scottish royalty as well as Spanish nobles. No one would have called him handsome, but there was a calmness about him that made Manuela believe he—and his fortune—would be a perfect match for her gentle eldest daughter.

What she didn't know was that her other daughter, the high-spirited Eugenia, believed she had fallen in love with the quiet, timid young duke. Her feelings for Alba reflected what would always be a defining characteristic of Eugenia's personality: her strength and determination attracted those who, like the shy Duke, seemed to need protection or someone to care for them.

When Manuela told Eugenia it was Paca and not her who would marry the duke, Eugenia was staggered. She did not hide her feelings: she said she would kill herself. She argued with her mother and wrote a passionate "farewell letter" to Alba. "Don't try and stop me," she wrote to the duke. "Perhaps you'll say I'm romantic and silly, but I know you're generous enough to forgive a poor girl who has lost all those she loved and who is being treated so cruelly by everyone, even by her mother . . ." She added a postscript: "Don't try to stop me, it's madness. I shall end my life far away from the world and its affections . . . I've made up my mind as my heart is broken." She then made her suicide attempt by drinking a glass of milk in which she had dissolved the heads of phosphorous matches, but only succeeded in making herself ill.

Eugenia, excitable and volatile, was still a teenager at this time, and may have been influenced by Alfred de Musset's *The Confession of a Child of the Century* that hammered home a sense of disenchantment with which Eugenia could identify. She felt she belonged to this "ardent, pale, and neurotic generation" born to celebrate liberty that "made their hearts beat with the memory of a terrible past and the hope of a glorious future." Musset wrote of "a world in ruins . . . Frightful despair stalked over the earth."

Only love could transcend the horrors of daily existence. Love, Eugenia believed, had disappeared from her life.

In her letter to the duke, written as she was smarting from her mother's decision, she begged him to "love your children equally, never hurt their feelings by showing more affection for one than another." Nonetheless, a hint of reality crept into the letter when she said that she knew Paca loved him as well. She quickly recovered from her suicide potion.

Eugenia's behavior, however, prompted Manuela to postpone Paca's wedding and once again take the girls to Paris. It was June of 1843, and buying Paca's trousseau was the stated reason for the trip, although Manuela also hoped the journey would take everyone's mind away from Eugenia's behavior, the family squabbles and the gossip they stirred up.

Manuela called in the dressmakers and lacemakers. She and her daughters would be dressed in the height of fashion, with designs from Paris and a sparkle of accessories from her native Andalusia—especially the fan. The *abanico*, or fan, was the Spanish woman's main tool: it was, one writer said, the equivalent of a man's sword. It kept her cool, it accented her outfit, it could hold a small pencil or a tiny flacon of perfume in one of the sticks, and, according to some, it sent messages. While "the language of the fan" was merely a marketing ploy created twenty years earlier by a British fan maker, young women nonetheless had fun "speaking" fan, hoping if they carried it open in their left hand, a young man would get the message to *come talk to me*. Or by resting it closed on her right cheek, the señor would know the señorita was saying *yes*. The fan had grown in size and importance. The Royal Fan Factory was in Valencia on the Mediterranean coast, where influences from the East still flourished and were absorbed by designers. It turned out masterpieces, including many with paintings on the leaves done by leading artists of the day.

Black was the staple color of the upper-class Spanish woman's wardrobe, reflecting the influence of the Catholic Church but also the state of the country's economy. With the loss of its colonies, the dyes and colorful fabrics that had come from those faraway places nearly vanished from Spain's marketplace; those that remained carried prohibitive price tags. Black, on the other hand, could be made from home-grown products.

Still, because Manuela was Andalusian, she was used to the richer colors and fabrics that continued to arrive via the Mediterranean from eastern countries, and she loved the metallic threads and intricate embroidery of the *trajes de luces*, the traditional "suits of lights" worn by bullfighters. Those suits had originated in Andalusia. Manuela was also used to the vibrant costumes of the Romani who made their home on the trails and byways of the area. She would have made sure those influences distinguished the gowns she chose for herself and her daughters.

When they arrived in Paris, Prosper Mérimée was there to greet them and delighted to see that the children he was "so fond of" had become young ladies, very beautiful ones, and that they had not forgotten him. In between the rounds of shopping, fittings and socializing, they rekindled their friendship with the writer and spent much time together. But Manuela kept her eye on the calendar. It wouldn't look good to stay too long, and winter was no time for travel, so in October, she packed them up again and returned to Madrid and final preparations for Paca's wedding.

Paca married the duke in February 1844, and this brought Eugenia a surprising new freedom. She could now escape from her mother to spend time with her sister at the magnificent Liria Palace, Paca's new home as Duchess of Alba. With her mercurial temperament, Eugenia forgot her previous passion and grew closer than ever to Paca. In the duke she found a friend, one whom she would depend on through the years.

She was still a wild child at heart, however, and sometimes reckless. She enjoyed drawing attention to herself. During one fair, Eugenia took her love of pranks and dressing up to a new level. She and a friend disguised themselves as Romani dancers and fooled some English tourists, stunning them when the two girls began speaking English. Eugenia would keep her penchant for practical jokes all her life.

LIKE THE ATHLETE SHE'D BECOME AT THE AMOROS GYM, EUGENIA TRAINED REGULARLY. SHE continued to fence and, whenever she could, swim and sail. She once drove her little carriage, a phaeton, at such speed that it threw her and her passenger into a ditch, narrowly avoiding serious injury. When the irritated Manuela described the incident to Mérimée, he wrote to say most men would be thrilled to find themselves in a ditch with her beautiful daughter.

Yet Eugenia kept her mind active and busy, as well. In the years spent at home in Spain, she discovered the works of the French socialist Charles Fourier and absorbed his ideas about poverty and class, frequently debating them with her mother's guests, much to Manuela's annoyance.

Eugenia also wrapped herself in the history and culture of Spain. "How sad that the Moors were driven from the country!" she wrote to Paca from Seville after visiting the Alcazar. "Does it not look as if the Christians came merely to destroy?" She wrote about watching the Romani dance and sing, and then dancing herself to the rhythm of castanets. She became, as she said to Paca, an *"aficienda en extremo,"* a fanatic enthusiast of bullfighting, and bragged about meeting one of the most famous bullfighters of the day, the Andalusian José Redondo, known as El Chiclanero.

Manuela had not finished her matchmaking, however. In hopes of attracting the right bachelor for Eugenia—and because she herself craved social life—she opened up the Montijo palaces of Ariza and Carabanchel for Spain's first costume balls, events that became legendary. For Eugenia, it felt almost like a return to her childhood when she enjoyed the challenge of embellishing her plain linen dresses with found bits of clothing. She even wrote Mérimée asking him to send accessories that would make her costumes—shepherdess, Polish woman, Sicilian girl, Romani—

authentic and spectacular. Unfortunately, she did not show any talent for the theater: her only contribution to her mother's musical entertainment, a walk-on part in Bellini's *Norma*, ended in her being laughed off the stage.

Nonetheless, one thing soon became clear: while the men were attracted to Eugenia, she did not return their interest. Not a single suitor tempted her, much to Manuela's displeasure.

To escape the gossip around the failed matchmaking attempts, Manuela chose to vacation in a quiet little French spa in the Pyrenees called Eaux-Bonnes, the "good waters." There, in the summer of 1845, she and Eugenia met a French singer named Eléonore Brault Gordon. Although she was the widow of a British officer, polite society saw her as an "adventuress," someone who had been the mistress of several men.

What caught the attention of the two Spanish women, however, was Gordon's disclosure that she had played an active role in helping Prince Louis-Napoléon Bonaparte try to overthrow the government in 1836. Prince Louis-Napoléon, a nephew of the first Napoléon, hoped to make a name for himself by winning support of the army in Strasbourg where there was a huge military base and use it to overthrow the monarchy of King Louis-Philippe. Gordon described how she "used her charms" to distract the officer in charge long enough to allow the prince to make his move. It failed, as did a second coup attempt in 1840 which landed Louis-Napoléon in prison—where he was still being held as Eugenia and her mother listened to Gordon's story.

What the singer didn't reveal was that she was Louis-Napoléon's mistress. Then again, there was no hiding the fact that he and she were extremely close. "Bonapartism is my religion," Gordon said.

For Eugenia, Gordon's "religion" brought back memories of her much-loved father and rekindled the excitement she found in stories he and Stendhal had told her about Napoléon. "I leave you to imagine my feelings!" Eugenia told a friend. "A conspirator—a prisoner—a prince—a Napoléon!" It sounded to Eugenia like a fairy tale come to life. She said she would like to visit Louis who was imprisoned in Château de Ham, a fortified château in northern France. Carried away by the romance of the imprisoned prince, she said she was ready to lay down her life for him and give him her fortune. Soon, she began regularly wearing violets, symbol of the Bonapartes, in her hair or at her waist.

Meeting Madame Gordon was a revelation for Eugenia and one that changed her mind about the future of Bonapartism. She had largely written it off earlier that year after meeting and dancing with another prince, this one named Napoléon-Jérôme Bonaparte. He called himself Plon-Plon, as did everyone else, since as a child he couldn't pronounce the name Napoléon.

Plon-Plon was Louis-Napoléon's cousin and bore a striking resemblance to Napoléon I. When in Madrid to court another woman, he had spotted Eugenia in her mother's salon and made a play for her. Rumor had it he tried to seduce her, and Eugenia was repulsed. She described him as "unworthy of the famous name he bore" and told him to go away, little realizing she had made a lifelong enemy.

Others, meanwhile, continued trying to win Eugenia's heart. She had already turned down four proposals, one from the Duke of Osuna who once rescued her and Manuela when their boat capsized during an outing on the Queen's Lake, now the public Retiro Park Lake in Madrid. Osuna was part of an old Spanish noble family and was genuinely in love with Eugenia, but she wasn't interested. A cousin, José de Xifré, gambler, drinker and smoker also got a *no* from Eugenia, as did the Frenchman Prince Albert de Broglie. Ferdinand Huddleston, a wealthy British aristocrat, she rejected as well. "I'd rather be hanged from a gibbet than marry an Englishman," Eugenia said.

By the end of 1848, however, Eugenia began to feel loneliness. Paca had become a mother, and the endless social activities Manuela organized had become wearisome. Those circumstances probably contributed to her deciding she was in love again.

This time the object of her affections was the Duke of Sesto who, like Eugenia, spoke several languages and had been tutored by some of the most outstanding educators of Spain. He began flirting with her, then sent passionate letters. She responded eagerly only to discover that the duke was using her to get to the real object of his affections: her married sister Paca. Humiliated and depressed, Eugenia again attempted suicide, this time refusing to take the antidote for the poison she'd swallowed.

After days of watching her daughter decline, Manuela begged Sesto to persuade Eugenia to take the antidote. When the duke arrived at her bedside, he leaned over and whispered in her ear, "Where are my letters?"

Eugenia, in "a blaze of contempt," swallowed the antidote. "You are Achilles's spear that heals the wounds it made!" she hissed to Sesto.

WITH THE MADRID SOCIAL SEASON IN FULL FORCE, MANUELA AGAIN DECIDED TO TAKE HER hot-tempered daughter back to Paris before a scandal erupted over the affair. But Eugenia cared little about gossip or "the heartless world of sensual, frivolous men." She was drawn to the political conflicts and progressive movements swirling around her.

It was a new France that Manuela and Eugenia returned to. After nearly eighteen years, the July Monarchy was dead. "Citizen King" Louis-Philippe and his family had fled as the country went through a bloody revolution in June 1848 to emerge as a republic, one governed by a constitution and elected representatives. It also heralded the return of Prince Louis-Napoléon Bonaparte, who carried a name that still resonated strongly with people in France. As it turned out, his imprisonment in 1840—coinciding with a decision by France to bring back the remains of his exiled uncle, the first Napoléon, from St. Helena—increased his popularity and generated an outpouring of sympathy. His popularity grew even larger thanks to a number of political essays and other articles he wrote during his confinement, which were published by newspapers and magazines around the country.

By 1846, Prince Louis-Napoléon was convinced his time had arrived. After six years of imprisonment, he escaped from Château de Ham by disguising himself as a workman and made his way to England. There, with help from friends and fellow conspirators, the prince worked out plans for returning to France and gaining power.

It took two years, but the machinations and propaganda paid off. In a dramatic move, France elected him as its president. The man who'd been imprisoned by the French government was now chosen to head it. To remind the public of his heritage, Louis-Napoléon called himself the Prince-President and, at the same time, swore to uphold the constitution written by a committee that included Alexis de Tocqueville, the chronicler of the United States, and which limited him to one four-year term as the country's ruler.

Eugenia and her mother made a far less dramatic return to Paris: they went to the dentist. Whether to renew their place in the clientele list of a society dentist or to treat a toothache is unclear, but what is significant is that the American Thomas Evans was on duty when they appeared. When another patient arrived obviously in pain, Eugenia asked Evans to treat him even though she had the next appointment. During her time with the dentist, she expressed concern about Spanish refugees in America and asked if he could help her send financial support to them. Evans, moved by the dignity and kindness of his young Spanish patient, said he would try. The impression Eugenia made on the young dentist would become important in the years ahead.

Amid everything that was happening, however, Eugenia was despondent. The Sesto betrayal still angered her, and she found no pleasure in the activities her mother began organizing: they were purely social. Not even an evening in the salon of a Bonaparte, Princess Mathilde, cousin of the new Prince-President, could improve her mood. She wrote Paca that she didn't know anyone there, and no one talked to her.

But one of the Bonapartes knew about her. The pained patient in Dr. Evans's office happened to be an aide to Louis-Napoléon. He conveyed to the Prince-President how impressed he was with the beautiful young woman who ceded her place to him at the dentist's. Eugenia and her mother found themselves invited to the next ball at the Élysées Palace.

The Prince-President, a well-known womanizer, noticed her immediately. Her hair, no longer carrot-orange but now a burnished auburn, was beautifully styled. She wore her gowns cut to show off the milky white shoulders toned by years of swimming, sailing and fencing. The dress also dipped low enough to reveal a hint of other delights. Her waist was trim and looked as though it needed very little help from her corset to make a man want to measure it with his hands. And her eyes! Some said they were blue, but others claimed they were violet. Plus, there was a wildness about her that boded well for other physical activity. Louis-Napoléon, Prince-President of France, could hardly contain himself.

They danced and they talked. When Eugenia mentioned meeting Madame Gordon and how impressive she was, the Prince-President concluded that Eugenia was aware of his intimate relationship with the singer and began plotting his next move. He invited her and Manuela to another ball, this one at the Château de Saint-Cloud.

They arrived in full evening dress ready for a gala evening but instead were escorted to Combleval, a chalet in the park where they realized they were to have a private dinner with the prince and his secretary—just outside Louis-Napoléon's bedroom. They grew wary.

Louis-Napoléon offered his arm to Eugenia for a stroll in the park while his secretary took Manuela's arm. Eugenia recoiled and stepped aside; she reprimanded him and said proper etiquette dictated he should offer his arm to her mother, not her. Embarrassed, the Prince-President agreed without saying a word. The evening was over. Eugenia and her mother returned to the carriage and promptly departed. Only later did they learn about

Gordon's intimate connection to the prince, and they were aghast to realize that he thought Eugenia shared the singer's easy virtue.

With Eugenia still distressed the following day, Manuela decided to take her on a cruise on the Rhine, hoping that would calm her. It was the beginning of what seemed to Eugenia like endless wandering. They traveled on to Brussels, Seville, Wiesbaden and then London to attend the Great Exhibition at the Crystal Palace in May 1851. The nonstop travel was wearing.

When at last they returned to Madrid, they learned that the man whose behavior had sent them on the road had just engineered another coup d'état. Napoléon, as Prince-President, believed he had the support of the country, and with secrecy and help from his half brother, the Duc de Morny, as well as the army and his closest advisers, Louis-Napoléon overturned the constitution and named himself emperor. He then orchestrated a nationwide election to validate the governmental change. Although the results showing overwhelming support for the coup were questionable, France was once again an empire.

The festivities surrounding his coronation as Napoléon III were a magnet that drew Manuela and Eugenia back to Paris. They arrived in time to witness his return from a triumphal tour of France and were again invited to a ball at Saint-Cloud, this one a celebration. It was clear Eugenia had never been far from the new emperor's mind. As Austria's ambassador to France Count Hübner said in his diary, "It was a very mixed company, the diplomatic corps, wives of the ministers, the Marquise de Contades; the young and beautiful Montijo girl was much singled-out by the President."

From then on, invitations poured in for events at the royal residences in Compiègne, Saint-Cloud and Fontainebleau. The previous rebuff was forgotten, and Louis-Napoléon returned to his hot pursuit. More than once, he dropped hints in Eugenia's ear; each time she refused to share his bed. "What is the way to your heart?" he finally asked. She responded as a properly reared Spanish maiden would: "Through the chapel, Sire."

Not long afterward, during a hunt at Fontainebleau, Eugenia, then twenty-six years old, captured everyone's attention with her riding skills: she was the first one in at the kill. Napoléon was so impressed that the next day he decided to give her the horse she had ridden. It was clear that Napoléon had learned his lesson in the aftermath of the disastrous evening at Combleval. This time every nuance of royal protocol was honored. The gift was sent, as required, by Napoléon's aide to Manuela, rather than directly to Eugenia. It was seen as the start of the official courtship.

On December 2, 1852, Prince-President Louis-Napoléon confirmed his role as Emperor Napoléon III and moved from the Élysée Palace to the royal residence in the Tuileries. He knew, as did his family and everyone else, that he needed a wife to give him an heir to the throne and ensure his dynasty. Speculation about his choice was rife as his entourage went on the hunt for candidates for empress. Napoléon, however, already had made up his mind. He had been given the nickname "the Sphinx" and now proved he deserved it, biding his time, strategizing and saying nothing as the rest of the world chattered about whom he would choose. Several royal princesses were considered, and at least two refusals arrived. Napoléon saw his chance and pounced. He announced that as a result of the rejections—rejections he had anticipated and may have engineered—he now felt free to follow what his heart had been telling him all along.

On January 15, 1853, the minister of the imperial household, Achille Fould, delivered Napoléon's official proposal to Manuela: "Madame la Comtesse, a long time has passed since I fell in love with your daughter, and ever since then I have wanted to make her my wife. So today I have come to ask you for her hand, because no one could make me happier or is more worthy to wear a crown. I beg, however, that should you give your consent, then you will not allow this project to become widely known before we have completed all our arrangements."

By *arrangements* the new emperor meant he needed to quiet

the opposition to his choice of Eugenia and, at the same time, sell her to the French public.

Even before it was formally accepted, opposition to the marriage came from numerous directions. Napoléon's minister of the interior, echoing most members of the government, grumbled, "We didn't make the Empire so the emperor could go and marry some flower-girl." People around the court whispered about how Manuela, tutored by Mérimée, had "played the game," urging Eugenia to hold herself aloof in order to capture Napoléon.

Nearly everyone in the Bonaparte family was against the marriage. Napoléon's uncle, Prince Jérôme, said he knew his nephew would marry "the first skirt who turns his head and then won't sleep with him." Plon-Plon, still smarting from his rejection by Eugenia, reacted with his habitual contemptuousness. "You go to bed with women like Mademoiselle de Montijo, you don't marry them!" he admonished the emperor.

As for the French public, most were disappointed, saying Eugenia was "not good enough" for the throne of France. If they were to have a foreigner as queen, they wanted a royal princess, perhaps one of Queen Victoria's large brood or even one of the czar's daughters.

One of the most stinging rebukes came from Britain's ambassador who warned that "The Emperor has been captured by an adventuress." *The Illustrated London News*, however, noted that "the Emperor's selection of a private individual to share his throne has caused, in the female portion of society, a degree of jealousy . . . it is really difficult to conceive."

Spaniards, on learning the news, were horrified. Eugenia was a grandee of Spain and connected to some of Spain's most powerful families. As far as they were concerned, she was marrying beneath her. They felt the Bonapartes were nothing but upstarts, not really royal at all.

Some Frenchmen, however, were delighted. Among them was Alexandre Dumas *fils*. His novel, *La dame aux camélias*, had been published in 1848 and was now being turned into an opera by Giuseppe Verdi to be called *La Traviata*. "It's the triumph of love over prejudice, of beauty over tradition, of emotions over politics," he wrote about the upcoming marriage. "It's the arrival of liberty, of fantasy itself, over the rigid dogma and rites of monarchy."

Napoléon III himself echoed those sentiments when he addressed his parliament the day before his civil marriage to Eugenia. Although he admitted he was a "parvenu" in the royal ranks, he said he'd had the good fortune to carry "a glorious title bestowed by the votes of a great nation." Now he would marry "a woman whom I love and respect" rather than a foreign princess. Eugenia would be the "ornament of the throne," much as his grandmother, Joséphine de Beauharnais, had been as the first wife of the great Emperor Napoléon I. He also emphasized that Eugenia had spent much of her life in France and had been educated here; she was of noble birth, and "a good Catholic." He presented the Patent tracing her lineage back to early kings of Scotland and listed all the connections to nobility in her mother's family.

Eugenia herself was torn. Since her birth, it had been drilled into her that her fate—the fate of all women—was to marry and have children. And she did love children. Her nieces and nephew, Paca's children, were a delight to her, and she was deeply touched by the poor youth she saw on the streets—she regularly gave money to them as well as to several charities. Marriage, however, had always seemed like something for the future. But now she was twenty-six, and at times she wanted to cover her ears so she would not have to hear her mother's increasingly shrill admonitions to marry.

Plus, she had to admit to herself that the constant progression from one capital city to another, from one spa to another, always to another ball in search of a suitable bachelor, had become boring and tiresome. Soon, she feared, people would begin labeling her an *old maid*, and then there would be no hope, no role for her at all, only contempt.

What more could she want? she asked herself. She was being offered a crown, a throne and a quiet, gentle man who had a lovely voice, wonderful manners and a charm that enraptured everyone. Even though he was not handsome, he was the most eligible bachelor in Europe, and, anyway, good looks were not something she valued most in a man.

And she *was* in love—in love with Bonapartism, the grandeur of the First Empire, its power, its aura of success and glamour despite its unhappy end. She had dreamed of the restoration of the empire since her girlhood when she was bombarded with stories about the glories of Napoléon I, a dream that was recharged when she met Gordon. That is what she saw now when she looked at Napoléon: an empire renewed and restored, with herself as part of it.

What's more, Eugenia knew that she and Napoléon had many things in common. They both loved the outdoors; they loved to ride and enjoyed sports. More importantly, they shared many of the same goals, and she believed together they could accomplish great things. She had read his *L'extinction du paupérisme* which he wrote in 1844 during his imprisonment at Ham to outline the ways he would seek to eliminate poverty. Even though they came from two different generations—Napoléon was nearly two decades older—they shared a deep concern for the working class and its needs. Eugenia's adored father had urged her to live a "useful life," and here was a chance to do so. And perhaps, she reasoned, Napoléon's calm and careful ways would moderate her volatile nature. Perhaps she, in turn, could protect him from people trying to take advantage of him.

She said *yes*. Eugenia would become Napoléon's wife and empress of the French.

The decision, however, did not entirely put her worries to rest. In a letter to her sister Paca in Madrid, Eugenia said "Everyone's fate has a sad side. Two things will save me, I hope, my faith in God and my desire to help the unlucky classes who are deprived of everything, even work."

She also knew that marrying the emperor would allow her to escape what their maid Pepa had said: "Women are born to knit stockings." Eugenia wrote, "I always knew I wasn't born for that, and had a proper role in life . . . yet today I regard with dread the responsibility that will fall on me."

One of her initial concerns was how to present herself to her new subjects, how she would appear to them and how she should behave. Much as she had always enjoyed being the center of attention with the somewhat outrageous antics of her youth, she was in an entirely different position now, and one much more important. Realizing she needed advice and training, Eugenia recalled sitting in the theater and being "inspired" as she watched performances by France's most famous actress, known mononymously as Rachel. It was to Rachel that she now turned for lessons in self-control, how to command an audience and especially how to perfect her curtsy. (Many years later Eugenia would discover that Rachel, like Madame Gordon, was also one of her husband's mistresses.)

As wedding plans went ahead, Eugenia suffered an unexpected blow in her personal life. Three days before the ceremony, her great-aunt Catherine de Lesseps died. Catherine had warmly welcomed Eugenia, Paca and Manuela when they first came to Paris in 1834 fleeing political unrest and the cholera epidemic. She had been almost a second mother to Manuela and a grandmother to the two girls. Her death brought a dark cloud of sadness over what should have been a moment of great happiness.

Eugenia recognized, however, there was no way to delay or alter the plans. She drew on her own resources of strength, as well as the training for appearances before the public she had had from Rachel, to go through with everything the wedding required. Nonetheless, Eugenia was badly shaken when crowds booed her on her way to the Tuileries Palace for the civil ceremony on January 29, 1853. "She was as pale as death and showed a considerable amount of nervousness," wrote Lady Augusta Bruce, a lady-in-waiting to Queen Victoria, who was one of the invited guests. Even the jealous Princess Mathilde, who had once hoped to marry Napoléon herself, felt pity for her. But her brother Plon-Plon, still pouting in his role as rejected suitor, remained spiteful. He bowed to the emperor but ignored Eugenia.

The next day promised to be even more overwhelming when she and Napoléon were to exchange vows in a religious ceremony at Notre-Dame Cathedral. "Nothing could be more splendid than the decorations of the Cathedral," Lady Augusta said in her letter to the Duchess of Kent. "Velvet and ermine—gold and silver—

EUGENIE EMPRESS OF THE FRENCH IN HER BRIDAL COSTUME.

Empress Eugénie in her bridal dress. *Photographer Amanda Barrett, Smithsonian American Art Museum*

flags and hangings of all colors were combined and harmonized with the splendid costumes of the clergy, the uniforms, civil and military, and the magnificent dresses of the ladies."

Church bells throughout the country were set to ring the joyful news, and the cannons at the Invalides were fired in salute, but once again crowds along the royal route to the cathedral were unfriendly . . . that is, until a vision in white velvet, lace and diamonds stepped out of the carriage.

Slowly, Eugenia turned to face the masses assembled in front of the cathedral . . . and dropped into an elegant curtsy. The crowd, immediately charmed and flattered that an empress would curtsy to them when they usually had to curtsy to *her*, went wild and began applauding and cheering. *"Vive l'impératrice!"* ("Long live the empress!") they cried.

With one simple gesture, Eugenia had conquered Paris.

For that day at least.

CHAPTER THREE

DEMANDS OF DYNASTY

IF THERE WERE A JOB DESCRIPTION FOR *EMPRESS*, IT WOULD HAVE ONLY ONE LINE: *produce an heir.*

Eugénie knew that, and so did everyone else. What she hadn't expected, however, was to sit through a banquet with the eyes of everyone else fixed knowingly on her . . . waiting for her to go to the emperor's bed.

Yet there she was after two long exhausting days of festivities and rituals, sitting at a dinner with the entire imperial court watching her and her new husband, absorbing every detail of their behavior. As she sat under those watchful eyes, Eugénie was still fighting against the grief she felt over the death of her aunt just three days earlier. Though she managed to maintain her composure, the empress must have wanted to scream for them all to leave.

They left Paris immediately for their honeymoon after a family luncheon that followed the long wedding ceremony and procession to the Tuileries Palace. Onlookers said the ugly carriages in the procession looked as though they were being driven by men in uniforms from a comic opera.

Napoléon, who had already earned a reputation for keeping things to himself, wanted to surprise Eugénie and had not told her or anyone else where they were going to spend their honeymoon.

He said he wanted to ensure their privacy and asked his cousin, Princess Mathilde, to organize a "bridal apartment" in the small country house of Villeneuve-l'Étang, tucked away on the grounds of the Château de Saint-Cloud.

While Eugénie changed into her red velvet and sable going-away outfit, Mathilde cornered Napoléon and told him she had also organized a stop for them at the château itself on the way to the honeymoon cottage. He did not realize what was in store.

NAPOLÉON AND EUGÉNIE ARRIVED AND WERE SHOCKED TO FIND THE CHÂTEAU LIT UP AND members of the imperial court in formal dress lined up outside, ready to welcome them and celebrate their marriage with a gala dinner. Any hope for a private, peaceful honeymoon vanished.

And so the emperor and his new empress smiled and resigned themselves to a long and boring dinner.

By the end of the two-hour long meal, Napoléon III had grown impatient and restless. Eugénie, nearing collapse herself, already recognized the sign in her husband: he was twisting the end of his waxed mustache, wondering how he could end the evening without offending the court. She leaned over and whispered to him to just stand up and go. "You're the emperor," she reminded him. "You do not need anyone's permission." She would follow.

With the push from his wife, Napoléon strode rapidly to the door. Eugénie rose gracefully after him. When she reached the door, she turned, faced the court and curtsied, much in the same way as she had done before the crowd in front of Notre-Dame Cathedral.

The deep, elegant curtsy became her signature, and people would call it *la révérence Eugénie*.

Once she reached the doorstep, she found an angry emperor. No carriage had been ordered for them, he discovered, so they were forced to wait in the cold January night while he called for one. He apologized to her and said he was furious with Mathilde for sabotaging his plans.

AND THUS BEGAN THEIR HONEYMOON. WHAT HAPPENED NEXT HAS BEEN THE SOURCE OF speculation ever since, although according to what the empress later told a friend, the first night was postponed as the emperor realized his bride was nearly prostrate with fatigue.

Only Eugénie and Napoléon know the full story, but it seems clear that the first night they spent together was not a night of pleasure for either party. Servants reported Napoléon did not look happy leaving the royal bedchamber, and a gardener who saw their coach pass the next morning said they were sitting silently at opposite ends of the seat.

Yet, Eugénie's devoted lady-in-waiting, Aurélie Bouvet-Carette, was to write optimistically some years afterward, "The Emperor and the Empress passed the first days of their married life, happy in their love, solitude and seclusion."

Eugénie herself later would say to her friend Cécile Deles-sert, "Physical love, what a filthy business. Why do men think of nothing else?"

What exactly the empress felt as she faced her first night in Napoléon's bed remains an unanswered question. She was twenty-seven years old and a virgin. At most, she had shared a few furtive kisses with suitors. There is no record of whether her mother ever discussed marital relations with her. More likely what she knew of sex came from Paca, her older, married sister. But it seems safe to assume that Eugénie was totally inexperienced sexually at the beginning of her marriage. She may also have read some of the stories of ghastly wedding nights that were common in the French press in the second half of the nineteenth century. One, in particular, would have sounded foreboding to any woman read-ing it: a writer named Séverine described her marriage to an ex-perienced man, twenty years older than she, and how she faced "a vile action, a defilement . . . a profanation of her whole being, the squashing of the fragility by the force."

Despite Eugénie's standoffishness with men, rumors about her lack of virtue had circulated, including sly whispers from the Bonapartes and others opposed to the marriage. A cruel and anonymous epigram caught on: "If tonight Napoléon found a maidenhead / It means Eugénie had two."

In reality, Eugénie seemed to love the drama and excitement of a romance, but had little or no interest in the sexual aspect of it. Many male historians have labeled her *frigid*. One writer identified her as a woman attracted to power and lumped her in with "those who gratify their ambitions and not their senses," to explain her choice of husband.

It is more likely that Eugénie was asexual or demisexual, someone who could be sexually stimulated only after a strong personal bond was established.

Innuendo about her premarital behavior continued unabated and spread concurrently with those about her supposed frigidity.

"It is very difficult to ascertain anything like the truth about her," Lady Augusta Bruce wrote shortly after the wedding. Eugénie found herself in a situation that has bedeviled women from time immemorial: damned if you do, damned if you don't. Behind the rumors that spread around her were those from people with their own political agendas or with a personal dislike of the empress. Some of those stories grew out of Eugénie's love of sports and the dances of her native Spain. To courtiers used to rigid protocol, seeing a woman ride at breakneck speed or dance a fandango could only mean she was not a real lady. They painted her as an adventuress, a woman of questionable morals.

An upper-class woman at the middle of the nineteenth century—in other words, a *real lady*—should have been the ornament Napoléon III described when he stated his marriage plans before the parliament. She would obey the laws of France, which was the only country in the world at the time that legally defined and limited the role of women. Although a few others had documents that legally regulated governing, none of them were as restrictive for women as the Code Napoléon. The emperor's uncle, Napoléon I, was a misogynist and had circumscribed women's roles in the code half a century earlier. The code still governed the nation. The only roles they were allowed under these laws were marriage and family. Any opinions one possessed were to be those of her father first and then of her husband. The same applied to any money or property she had.

As far as sex was concerned, physical pleasure was not considered part of life for an upper-class woman: that was for men and lower-class women. And voting? Perish the thought! At the time, only Pitcairn Island granted women suffrage. The Kingdom of Hawai'i had allowed women's voting but rescinded it before the territory could be annexed by the United States. French women, upper-class or not, would not have the right to vote until almost a century later, in 1946.

Napoléon III, the new bridegroom, was forty-four years old. He was not merely experienced, he was concupiscent. He had already had a string of mistresses and had fathered three illegitimate sons by two different women. He was quoted several times saying, "Usually, it is man who attacks: as for me, I defend myself, and I often capitulate."

His "official" mistress at the time he became Prince-President of France was an unsuccessful actress named Harriet Howard. Her presence at many state occasions angered and scandalized his family and courtiers. Historians have claimed that the reason Napoléon kept her was that she financed his presidential campaign in 1848 and his coup in 1851. That, however, is not true. Recent research shows that most of the funding came from a powerful monarchist association that backed Napoléon, believing he would be a benign, compliant ruler. Furthermore, Howard's family was far from wealthy—her father was a shoemaker—and none of Howard's previous lovers (one was a well-known jockey) had the financial wherewithal to provide her with the wealth that would in turn have been necessary to pay for his political adventures.

By the time Napoléon returned to France in 1848 after his two failed coup attempts, Howard had already become an embarrassment to him. She was demanding marriage and showing up uninvited at his public appearances, encounters that were widely reported in the European press. Eugénie was known to read French, Spanish, English and, sometimes, Italian newspapers daily, so she likely was aware of the liaison.

Napoléon knew he could not conduct a search for an empress with a mistress hanging onto him, so he bought off the unhappy Howard with an estate, a title—Countess of Beauregard—and a British husband. Also one million francs, which she demanded as part of her settlement.

Finally Napoléon was free to issue his proposal to Eugénie, the woman he had desired for two years with a passion he did not try to hide during the wedding. Lady Augusta wrote the following day that she had been struck by how he showed his emotions: "That he is passionately in love with her no one doubts, and his countenance on late occasions, as well as yesterday, wore a radiant and joyous expression very unusual."

At the same time, Lady Augusta noted Eugénie's contrasting paleness, but said she believed "her beauty and engaging manners will . . . gain for her, for a time at least, a greater amount of popularity than [those] who now blame the marriage expect." Describing the empress's appearance, Lady Augusta said that with her "beautifully chiseled features, her nobly *set-on head*, [sic] her exquisitely proportioned figure and graceful carriage" she was "like a Poet's Vision!" But, Lady Augusta added with a note of pride, Eugénie's "grace and dignity" should be attributed to her Scottish Kirkpatrick blood. Lady Augusta's family, the Bruces, were prominent Scots.

The only account that exists of Eugénie saying she was in love with Napoléon was in a letter she wrote to her sister Paca shortly after becoming engaged to the emperor: "I love him. His heart is noble and devoted. When one knows him in his personal life, one appreciates him."

Augustin Filon, who would become tutor to the imperial couple's son and then secretary to the empress, believed what she felt for Napoléon "was probably less passionate affection, but [rather] deeper friendship." However, in her memoirs, the loyal lady-in-waiting Madame Carette was to claim that the empress loved the emperor "passionately."

That supposed passion did not, however, translate to the bedroom, and apparently Napoléon, with his "habit of promiscuity" and preference for experienced women who "attacked" him, bungled when it came to his intimate relations with Eugénie.

As long as an heir was necessary, however, the imperial bedroom could not be abandoned, and the empress soon became pregnant. Three months later Eugénie lost the baby in a frightening miscarriage which put her through seventeen hours of pain and suffering. Rumors circulated about the causes of the miscarriage, and Eugénie herself speculated about them in her letters to Paca. The empress, who had been criticized for her reckless riding, admitted she fell from a horse a few days before the incident but did not sense anything wrong at the time. She felt the first symptoms while taking a warm bath two or three days later, but what truly brought on the miscarriage is unclear. Her personal physician, Dr. Darralde, told her she might have suffered a placenta rupture, a common cause of miscarriage.

Eugénie was bedridden after the miscarriage and depressed. The Austrian ambassador wrote that he was shocked by the lack of kindness and compassion that the court showed to the empress in the aftermath. She wrote to Paca that she felt "desperate," after all she had gone through was for nothing. Her dream of having a "pretty baby" like her sister's had been shattered. It was probably at this time Napoléon ended his attempt to be faithful and returned to his *petites distractions.*"

Madame Carette wrote that the first miscarriage had made the empress "delicate," which explained Eugénie's drastic mood swings, with outbursts of incredible energy followed by times of near-total collapse. Soon there were rumors of another pregnancy and miscarriage. Mérimée, however, wrote to Manuela that Eugénie's headache during a ball was not a sign of what everyone hoped and that none of the people "more versed in the subject," such as Eugénie's personal physician, saw any sign of a pregnancy.

In 1855, Eugénie did become pregnant again, and she was determined to carry this child to term. She retreated to the quiet spa at Eaux-Bonnes where she had spent time with her mother a few years earlier. The warm waters there had long been considered curative, and doctors recommended bathing in them and drinking a glass of the water three times a day. Napoléon came frequently to visit her.

Feeling stronger and more confident after taking the waters as it was called, Eugénie returned to Paris and the Tuileries Palace to await the birth. The pregnancy was then official, triggering an ancient tradition of the monarchy. Eugénie was no longer seated across from Napoléon during meals, but now sat to his right, close beside him, a position where the ruler was seen as protecting his consort and the future heir.

She would need all the protection and strength possible as she faced still another long-standing royal tradition: giving birth in public to prevent any switching of babies. She knew her aunts had tried to fob off an orphan child as the heir to her uncle's fortune, and she was aware her predecessor Queen Marie-Antoinette had had to give birth with more than two hundred people crowded around her to watch her deliver. In Eugénie's case, only members of the Bonaparte family were invited to witness this event in order to confirm the child as the rightful heir.

Eugénie went into labor near midnight on Friday, March 14, 1856. The court physicians arrived. At the same time the Bonapartes gathered and stood at the door of the empress's bedroom. Hour after hour on Friday and Saturday, the empress struggled until the pain became so great her screams could be heard throughout the palace. At times attendants helped her to stand

and let her recover her breath between spasms. She pleaded with Dr. Darralde for help.

The physician took the emperor aside and told Napoléon the only possibility would be to use forceps, but that, if he did so, he could not guarantee both mother and child would survive. There was a risk of crushing the baby's cranium or breaking the mother's pelvis. Whom should he save in case of emergency? he asked the emperor. Napoléon's answer left no doubt about his love for Eugénie. "Save the empress," said the distraught emperor.

Eugénie continued in agony through her contractions, pushing off the bedcovers. Napoléon's cousin Plon-Plon, who would lose his place as heir to the throne if a boy was born, watched and carped, "How can you call a woman pretty with legs like that!"

Doctors stood by, nervously conferring and clearly panicked the empress would die while under their care. They had good reason to worry. Nearly a quarter of pregnant women died in childbirth at that time, a rate so high that hospitals were known to bury them two to a coffin to disguise the death rate.

Napoléon Eugène Louis Jean Joseph Bonaparte, the *Prince Impérial*, was born March 16, 1856, at three in the morning. His father's joy was boundless; he kissed everyone he saw. Church bells rang throughout the country; cannons at the Invalides fired a 101-gun salute.

The prince's mother, however, was in no condition to celebrate. She was debilitated and physically damaged by the torturous delivery. An early visitor to the royal cradle remarked at how large the baby was. The little prince's size may have contributed to the difficulty of the birth; one of the attending physicians said he had never seen suffering during labor such as the empress had gone through. She was bedridden for days, unable to stand or walk unassisted until the end of May. When she first tried to get up, she faltered and fell back. Servants caught her before she hit the floor and urgently called for the royal physicians.

Their diagnosis was startling: the empress had suffered a broken pelvis during the delivery. She was incapacitated for months after the diagnosis, and doctors warned her that her life would be endangered if she ever had another child. Everyone agreed Eugénie "paid the penalty with her health" to give an heir to the Fourth French Dynasty.

Queen Victoria sent one of her medical advisers to see Eugénie in May 1856. "The poor empress is not ill in health," the queen wrote in her diary after hearing his report, "but has not yet recovered from the results of her severe confinement . . ." She worried that Eugénie "will get into low spirits if she cannot go about with the emperor . . ."

Although Napoléon would never again share Eugénie's bed, his concern for her was sincere. In August 1856, nearly half a year after the prince impérial's birth, the emperor was to write that he was still deeply worried by the poor health of his wife who "requires constant medical attention."

EUGÉNIE'S FRAGILITY DID NOT STOP THE ROUTINES OF THE IMPERIAL COURT, ALTHOUGH IT did delay one important one. A royal baptism had to be organized and celebrated, although it was not scheduled until the empress had regained her health. Pope Pius IX was named godfather to the princeling, and the pontiff responded by sending Cardinal Patrizzi from Rome with the Golden Rose—a gold vase filled with twenty-three roses, also made of gold—for the mother. It was considered the highest tribute the pope could pay to a woman, and Eugénie treasured it and kept it close throughout her life. (After the prince impérial's death, she gave the Golden Rose to the abbey which she herself had established to look after the imperial tombs. It was later stolen and has not been recovered.) The cardinal remained to stand in for the pope at the baptism and officiate at the ceremony.

Chosen as the prince impérial's godmother was the queen of Sweden and Norway, a choice that reflected the wishes and interests of both the emperor and the empress. Queen Josephine was, like Napoléon III, the grandchild of Josephine de Beauharnais, first wife of Napoléon I. She was also a politically active woman who was the main adviser to her husband Oscar I, then king of the two Scandinavian countries that were then united. The queen's role as more than a mere consort was a factor that would have appealed to Eugénie.

On June 14, the infant boy was taken by imperial carriage to Notre-Dame Cathedral for his baptism in front of six thousand guests. Austrian Ambassador Hübner said he'd never seen a more beautiful service, but the British representative, Lord Cowley, scoffed that it was "more theatrical than religious." He also noted that he didn't think the crowd outside the cathedral was very enthusiastic. He may have been looking at it through the prejudiced eye of a representative of a country that had long been at odds with France, because others recorded a radically different picture—that the crowd was enthusiastic, filling the streets with cries of *"Vive l'empereur! Vive l'impératrice! Vive le prince impérial!"* as the imperial family arrived.

Although the new mother was said to be radiant in her blue court coat with a 136-karat diamond tiara sparkling atop her auburn hair, Eugénie admitted she felt nervous carrying the baby prince impérial in front of the crowds outside the cathedral. Maybe, as Mérimée wrote to Doña Manuela, because "those who know about such things find the boy enormous for his age" and noticed that the nurse "who was carrying him, clearly found this hard going." Napoléon III took the baby in his arms and held his son up to the crowd. A huge cheer erupted. "The baptism has done more for us than a coronation," the proud father whispered to his exhausted, but still radiant wife.

Loulou, as his family came to call the prince, would not have noticed: he was asleep. After the service, he was carried home to the Tuileries Palace to be put to bed in a spectacular cradle designed for him by architect Victor Baltard, who would become famous designing Les Halles market and the church of Saint-Augustin in Paris. The cradle had been given to the emperor and empress by the city of Paris and was designed in the shape of a

Cradle of the prince impérial. *Musée d'Orsay, Dist. GrandPalaisRMN / Alexis Brandt*

ship like the one on the city's coat of arms. It was crafted from rosewood, gilded bronze, vermeil, silver and enamels.

The cradle was appropriate for the *Fils de France*, the designation given to all previous heirs to the throne, and Napoléon wanted his son to carry the title as well.

Waiting to tuck the royal baby into his magnificent bed was his new English nurse, Miss Jane Shaw, who was, in a way, another gift. She had been chosen by Queen Victoria and sent to the imperial family. Miss Shaw would watch over the prince throughout his life.

As Loulou was given into Miss Shaw's care, his parents, their families and all the assembled guests sat down to a magnificent banquet in his honor: crayfish bisque, truffled young turkey, Provençal-style beef fillet, carp and asparagus.

The wines were magnificent. They had been chosen by a man from Bordeaux who was a connoisseur of vintages from that region, and who had recently been appointed *préfet* of the Seine department—one Georges-Eugène Haussmann. Thanks to Loulou's father, Haussmann would soon make a mark on Paris that would turn the city into a place as dazzling as the baby prince's cradle.

EUGÉNIE WAS ENTHRALLED BY HER SON AND SPENT EVERY MINUTE SHE COULD WITH HIM. She was too attentive, thought Dr. Ernest Barthez, the baby's doctor. She worried about everything: the wind, the cold, the sun, not enough air. Whenever the prince was sick, she refused to leave his bedside. Eugénie, always impatient, thought her four-month-old baby should be as "alert and responsive as a ten-month-old baby," the doctor wrote his daughter. The empress was like every new parent, he said: she thought she knew everything, but she was, in fact, interfering, getting in the way. He advised the nurses and the prince's nanny, Miss Shaw, to ignore the empress's recommendations.

Loulou was, from the moment of his birth, in school to become emperor. At six months, he was strapped to the saddle of his pony; at nine months, he was enrolled in the Grenadiers of the Guard and was posed standing for a picture, grasping a piece of furniture and wearing a miniature version of its uniform. By the time he was three, he was attending military reviews at his father's side. His parents wanted it made clear that their son was "under the protection of the army by making his relationship with it visible to every eye." The emperor said he "wished to cultivate in the child the taste for military affairs."

Eugénie was in agreement, as was Augustin Filon, their son's tutor. Loulou's parents were both outstanding riders, Filon noted, so it was to be expected he would ride regularly and have military interests. He was, after all, the grandnephew of Napoléon I.

Nonetheless, they all recognized that the prince needed a formal education as well, and as the boy grew, Filon implemented a program of literature, history, mathematics, philosophy, military arts and languages.

It was not enough, Eugénie said. She wanted "an education of character and will . . . to awake a spirit of initiative in one who in time would have to 'will' for millions of human beings."

Filon was impressed and found her views on education "very sensible, very broad, and for the time very novel." He was also impressed with his young charge, "a charming boy," he said, with "delicate skin and a grace in his movements that might have been envied by a girl." The comments and the prince's "feminine slenderness" brought out the mischievousness of his mother who loved dressing up or masquerading. She dressed Loulou as an eighteenth-century noblewoman and took the photo of the disguised prince to his tutor who said he didn't know the child. Eugénie was delighted with the success of her joke.

But "the feminine cast in the prince's beauty was of very short duration," Filon wrote later, for Loulou was just "a regular boy" with the same rebellious tendencies. After one hard ride when he was about seven, the prince described his horse's canter with a slang word. His mother castigated him, but he replied, "Mother, your French is outstanding. But you are a foreigner and sometimes you don't understand the subtleties of the French language."

Loulou inherited his mother's restlessness and daredevil personality. He could be reckless and courted "danger willingly and deliberately"; he had a taste for "the most perilous games." One day, Filon saw him "walking above the void outside the balustrade of the second-floor balcony, going from one window to the other along the narrow ledge." The terrified tutor pulled back silently to avoid surprising his pupil and precipitating a fall.

The Little Prince, as the palace staff and press referred to him, also had his mother's tender heart and would empty his pockets of any change he had whenever a beggar approached him, much as Eugénie had done as a girl. She worried, however, that he did not grasp the meaning of wretchedness or poverty. She wanted to take him with her on her visits to the poorest of the poor, but those in charge of the boy's safety vetoed the idea.

From his father, the prince impérial inherited the "dreamy sweetness" in his eyes, as well as his appreciation of all things military.

Loulou spent hours with both his parents every day, and they made nearly all official trips together as a family. Filon was impressed by the "close and relaxed intimacy [that] bound the child to his father and his mother." Napoléon indulged him, however, and it was left to Eugénie to administer discipline. When she found him playing in the emperor's office, Eugénie wanted to send him to his room. "Let him be," Napoléon said. "He'll have enough discipline later."

CHAPTER FOUR

TO BUILD A DREAM

ALMOST FROM THE MOMENT IT WAS FOUNDED, THERE WAS SOMETHING ABOUT PARIS, SOME-thing intangible, and, as one historian noted, "a true mystique . . . an aura of desirability." Henri IV felt its draw when he agreed to convert from Protestantism to Catholicism to become king of France in 1589. "Paris is worth a mass," he reportedly said. Paris. Not France, not even the crown. But *Paris*.

Perhaps what inspired him was hearing a mass in Notre-Dame Cathedral, as colored light danced across his doublet when the sun illuminated the rose windows. Perhaps the city's riverside location tempted him; Paris looked like a giant *chou à la crème*, or cream puff, cut in half by the Seine, the river that carried away yesterday's sins and brought in today's hopes. And there on an island in the center of it was that beautiful Gothic cathedral.

By the time he converted, the cathedral was already four centuries old, and Henri IV immediately went to work to make the rest of the city match the splendors of Notre-Dame. His goal, he said, was to make Paris not only the true center of government and capital of the country but also "the capital of the universe." In his short reign—little more than a decade—he created public projects and gardens that would make Paris the most modern and gracious city in Europe of the time. His plans for wide boulevards and expansive green spaces would serve as a blueprint for much of what was to come.

In the centuries that followed, every monarch wanted to put his own stamp on Paris.

However, Louis XIV, the Sun King, grew tired of the city and its problems and instead governed from his beloved château in Versailles, neglecting the capital city.

The French Revolution of 1789 also took its toll. Paris had become decrepit. Napoléon Bonaparte had arrived on the scene with his longing for grandeur and his desire to make Paris the "most beautiful city that ever was"—but Waterloo scuppered his plans.

By 1848 when his nephew, Napoléon III, managed to return to the city where he had been born, Paris had become a tired old lady whose once-glamorous gowns were showing wear and dirt.

That old lady was the city Eugénie de Montijo embraced fervently when she first saw it as a child. It was filthy, overcrowded, stinking—and endlessly fascinating. Its aura still lingered. Paris was totally different from the rugged countryside of Andalusia where Eugénie spent her early years, but she loved the city, so delighted to explore it that she and her sister often played hooky from school to investigate its nooks and crannies. Paris, she discovered street by street, had character, excitement and creativity.

Her husband agreed. Paris was not only his birthplace but also, he believed, his birthright. After Waterloo he and his family had been banned from France, and Napoléon spent his life moving from one country to another—Switzerland, Germany, Great Britain—never settling and fiercely clinging to his conviction that his real home was always Paris.

Eugénie, after a similar childhood with her family in exile, also experienced years of rootlessness as her mother led her from one European capital or spa to another in search of a husband. The perpetual movement had begun to feel oppressive, and Eugénie must have thought of Ovid's plaintive words in *Tristia*: "I'm weary lying among distant peoples, [distant] places . . . now thoughts come to me, of what is not here." What was "not here" was her own hearth, her own home.

In Paris, she and Napoléon at last found the place where they could make their home, a city where they would create their dynasty and their destiny. They would pour their hearts and souls into it. Paris and their dreams for the city would draw them together despite their vast differences in age and personality.

Napoléon was prepared. He had been influenced by the ideas of Saint-Simonianism, a political philosophy that combined socialism and technocratic pragmatism. One writer described it as "a grand alliance of industry, science and the arts," but it also had a strong element of feminism that would resonate with his wife over the course of her reign. Even before he became emperor, Napoléon had marked up a map of Paris with colored lines showing where he wanted streets to better link monuments, parks and buildings, at the time reached only by filthy, narrow streets and separated from main thoroughfares.

Eugénie must have been excited to see his ideas mapped out.

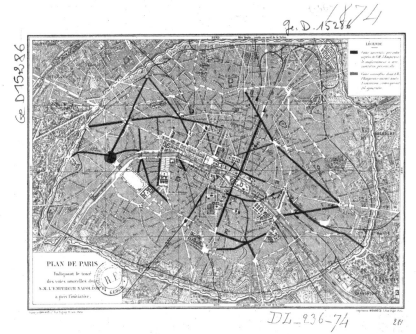

Napoléon III drew colored lines to redesign Paris's geography. *Gallica.fr. BNF, Graveur Erhard Frères*

In between his colored lines, she could begin to imagine what she could do as well. She visualized sites where she could develop her own ideas for improving the lives of women, children and the poor. Visions grew in her mind of schools and hospitals that were spacious, modern and beautiful.

And best of all, she had the seed money—the 600,000 francs ($288 million) which the city of Paris had given her to buy a diamond necklace as a wedding gift. Now she would put it to use.

Like Napoléon, Eugénie was prepared for the job, at least in her heart. All her life she had sympathized with the poor, with the barefoot children she had seen running in the streets of Granada, with the sick and battered women who begged on roadsides. Her pocket money went to them, her shawls were given to them. She would go home late, ragged and broke, after stopping to comfort them and spend time with anyone whom she had seen suffering.

Impoverished girls were the ones most at risk, Eugénie knew, the ones whose lives were in jeopardy and were most likely to be taken advantage of, abused and then left to suffer the consequences alone. These girls were her first thought when she considered the jewelry money from the city. She would use those funds to buy them a future.

Eugénie's plans came together quickly: an oasis, an idyllic spot for girls who had nothing. It would be a boarding school with a "real" curriculum, good religious education and a chapel, of course. Good teachers, too. There would be physical education and sports, and classes where girls could learn skills that would enable them to earn a living. Each girl would have her own bed, her own physical space, and there would be gardens for food and play as well as fresh water and good sanitation.

Central to her vision was her own involvement. She included an office for herself so she could visit, select new students and provide whatever was necessary to help the girls.

Eugénie was ready to go to work.

Only one thing, or rather, one person, stood in the way: Georges-Eugène Haussmann, the man Napoléon had put in charge of renovating Paris and making it a clean and modern city. Haussmann would have Napoléon's map as his guide when he began clearing neighborhoods and building the wide avenues that would give the city its enduring distinction and beauty.

His mission was to make Paris fit the new industrial and up-to-date France Napoléon III imagined. The préfet destroyed medieval parts of the city and in their place created broad boulevards, new apartment buildings and an underground sewage system, then added street furniture—the lampposts, newspaper kiosks and railings that still define Paris's character.

Haussmann had been hired because of his faults, according to the minister of the interior, Victor de Persigny. Persigny had interviewed Haussmann and recommended him to Napoléon as the man who could get the job done. "It was a strange thing," Persigny wrote, "but it was less his talents and his remarkable intelligence that appealed to me, but the defects in his character. I had in front of me one of the most extraordinary men of our time; big, strong, vigorous, energetic, and at the same time clever and devious . . . Whereas a gentleman of the most elevated spirit . . . and noble character, would inevitably fail, this vigorous athlete . . . full of audacity and skill, capable of opposing expedients with better expedients, traps with more clever traps, would certainly succeed." It was as though Persigny chose a fullback to do a job that ordinarily would have gone to a ballet dancer.

Haussmann did succeed, but not before he came face-to-face with another vigorous, skillful and audacious figure: the empress herself. The baron went out of his way to ignore her. In his opinion, she was imperious and out of her league, a woman who should mind her own business and let men like himself manage things.

As far as Eugénie was concerned, Haussmann was a misogynist and typical bureaucrat, one of the interchangeable pieces that kept the machinery of government running. She had met him years earlier at a ball in Bordeaux and found him obsequious, an inveterate social climber who was always quick to point out that he, like the emperor, was a godson of Prince Eugène Napoléon (which was a lie). Although she was fond of Haussmann's wife, she wanted nothing to do with the baron and did her best to avoid him.

Eugénie began her campaign to create a school for poor girls by poaching one of Haussmann's key architects, Jakob Ignaz Hittorff. He was an obvious choice. Hittorff had a reputation as an outstanding architect for both secular and religious buildings. Perhaps more importantly, he had also worked closely with Eugénie's lifelong friend and architectural adviser, Prosper Mérimée, now the inspector of public monuments. Hittorff had been the architect for the redesign of the Place de la Concorde and Paris's Church of Saint-Vincent-de-Paul, built for the Sisters of Charity, an order of nuns known for their work with abandoned children. Eugénie had earmarked the order to run her new school.

Although Hittorff was the architect, it was abundantly clear that the empress was the one in charge and controlled all aspects of the project. To stay within the budget—Eugénie's 600,000 francs—Hittorff proposed using part of an existing building for the school and the proposed sixty students. Eugénie vetoed it and told the architect she wanted her school to be able to welcome three hundred girls, not just sixty. A larger enrollment would help more people and make a bigger impact, she said.

Startled by the sudden change, and now even more worried about the budget, Hittorff suggested a site on the far western edge of Paris. Land was cheaper there, he told the empress, and you would pass the school on your way from the Tuileries to the Château de Saint-Cloud, making it easy for you to visit.

No, she responded. The school must be in the city, in an area accessible to those in need but, yes, definitely in a spot she could reach easily because she intended to be involved with all aspects of it. Hittorff argued that there was not enough space in the city to stay within the budget, but the empress was not swayed; this was her first major act as empress. It had to be exactly as she wanted it: it had to be perfect.

Haussmann must have cringed as he heard about the project. She'd already commandeered one of his best architects, and what Eugénie wanted now could take land he needed for *his* renovations. It would play havoc with his promise to the emperor that the work would be done in time for the 1855 Universal Exposition. Haussmann knew full well her 600,000 francs would never begin to cover the costs of her expanded project. Financing for his own work was already strained, and there was no way public funds and taxation could cover the totality of the Paris renovation, especially if Eugénie's school was included.

To raise the necessary money, he and Napoléon came up with several plans, including one used by Henri IV to finance the Pont Neuf in the sixteenth century: grant private developers rights to land and buildings the government had appropriated in exchange for monetary backing. This was a system similar to modern sponsorship, and it succeeded. The bridge was built and still stands.

Nonetheless, Haussmann was determined to hold onto every centime they raised and not let any of it escape to Eugénie's projects. He knew he would need all of it to complete his other work—the near-total renovation of a city, the largest project of its kind ever attempted—before the Universal Exposition opened. (It was later shown that Haussmann conveniently managed to hold onto enough money to line his own pockets.)

The empress was not about to let her project be lost in the whirlwind of changes Haussmann was orchestrating. Although she fully supported Paris's renovation, she was keenly aware of the despair among residents as homes were demolished, businesses were torn down and wide swaths of the city were reduced to rubble. As buildings and entire neighborhoods were appropriated, thousands of people were left homeless, priced out of the market and shunted off to the suburbs. Eugénie was angry and accused Haussmann of constantly thwarting programs aimed at helping the underprivileged.

Finally, however, the empress finagled a plot of state-owned land on the rue Faubourg Saint-Antoine, in the run-down twelfth arrondissement of the city. The baron was probably relieved: the site already belonged to the state, so he wouldn't have to use money from his budget to buy it. Plus, it was in a working-class area that had little love for the monarchy. Haussmann had scant interest in the working class and its problems, especially those who didn't support the Second Empire. Let the empress do what she wanted with that awkward piece of property, he thought.

Hittorff, Eugénie's architect, was less than pleased. He proposed a site on the Île des Cygnes, and then a backup location at the coal market on the Quai Mazas. No, and no, she said. Eugénie was determined to hold tight to the plot in the twelfth arrondissement. Finally, Hittorff admitted defeat and accepted the empress's Faubourg Saint-Antoine plot. He acknowledged that Eugénie was right about one thing: the site could be reached easily from both the Tuileries and Saint-Cloud. He retreated to his drawing board and went to work.

Napoléon, like Eugénie, had prioritized improvements in the lives of the working class and was happy with his wife's choice. Putting her school in the center of neighborhood of workers who largely had voted against the empire in the 1852 election would clearly show how important social concerns were to the Second Empire and hopefully go a long way toward discouraging future protests and uprisings in the area.

It was left to Hittorff to come up with a design for the oddly shaped plot—an octagon with two elongated sides. Streets on each of the long sides and houses around the other sides made the design even more challenging. He also had to deal with the empress's exacting demands for the newest and best technology available: central heating, fresh water, a sewage system, laundry facilities with mechanical washing machines, an individual washstand for each of the three hundred girls and water filters on the main pipes. Buildings on the property had to include dormitories, classrooms and a chapel. Gardens had to be planned, as well as a play area for exercise. His budget was stretched, then stretched again.

It was ironic, but appropriate, that his inspiration for the design of Eugénie's project finally came from jewelry—also the very source of its funds. The shape of the plot of land reminded him of a pendant necklace, and Hittorff plowed through archives of jewelers to build on his idea, finally coming up with a design Eugénie approved. Unlike the one the city of Paris had proposed for her as a wedding gift, this was a "necklace" the empress was happy to accept.

"*La Maison du Collier*, The Necklace House," Haussmann scoffed when he saw the plans. As far as the chauvinistic préfet was concerned, all the empress was doing was making more work for his office and interfering in his plans. At least the city and the imperial government had agreed to foot most of the bill. A good thing, he felt, as the cost for the necklace house had more than tripled, and just as he feared, he was being asked to come up with some of the budget overrun. As much as possible, Haussmann ignored the project, not even bothering to visit the site when the emperor and empress were there. That suited Eugénie perfectly, whose barely concealed contempt for the baron was no secret. She wanted nothing to do with his bulldozing, high-handed ways.

Hittorff, meanwhile, was struggling. He probably wanted to hide whenever he learned the empress was coming on one of her frequent visits. Each one seemed to bring more demands: better ventilation in the infirmary, improved heating in the chapel, porcelain washbasins—not zinc—for the girls.

Eugénie had begun planning for the school shortly after her wedding in 1853, but haggling over the site and design kept work from beginning until late in 1854. It would go on for nearly five years, but even skeptics had to admit Hittorff's final plan was a beautiful, modern campus with a creative design solution. It was also a durable solution: the Fondation and its buildings exist today. But Haussmann was right, too: this brick-and-mortar necklace cost more than three times the amount the city had provided for an actual diamond necklace. The final total shot up to a staggering 1,607,000 francs, nearly $775 million in today's dollars.

By 1856, enough had been completed that Eugénie could officially open the school. She had given birth to the prince impérial a few months earlier, and dedicating the school was one of her first official outings after her difficult labor. She decided to make clear how dear to her heart the school was by naming it in honor of her beloved son: the Maison Prince Eugène Napoléon. It would later be renamed the Fondation Eugène Napoléon and, up to today, still trains underprivileged young people in Faubourg Saint-Antoine.

Eugénie devoted much of her personal funds to its maintenance and administration. In addition, she provided 300 francs every year for each student. She also made sure that each girl who finished her education there left with a paying professional job that would let her be independent. And Eugénie made it clear she would work to make sure more jobs and more careers would be open to them.

ALTHOUGH SHE WAS DETERMINED TO NOT CUT CORNERS WITH THE SCHOOL, THE EMPRESS was quickly learning the political art of compromise. While she saw herself as a serious, working empress, as "the inheritor of a tradition of female benefactors," she was acutely aware that getting something important done was sometimes more important than waiting for perfection.

Eugénie had only been married for a few months and had already begun work on the Maison Eugène Napoléon when she attended the annual Salon de peinture et de sculpture in 1853. She was staggered, nearly struck dumb when she saw a large painting by Isidore Pils, *The Prayer in the Hospice*, showing two nuns praying with children suffering from scurvy. The painting, she felt, was speaking directly to her, telling her what she must do. She promptly bought it.

Within days, she was informing the redoubtable Haussmann that a new children's hospital was essential and needed immediately. Children's health could not be postponed. When he tried to put her off by proposing a run-down old hospital she could try to convert, it further confirmed her opinion that Haussmann was nothing but a "graceless" functionary who looked down on women and only paid attention if the emperor involved himself. With an I'll-show-you attitude, she surprised Haussmann and accepted what he proposed and then went to work.

The Hôpital Sainte-Marguerite had been founded more than a century earlier by another Spanish noblewoman, Marie-Thérèse, first wife of the Sun King, Louis XIV. The queen had created it as a residence for foundling children. Another sign, Eugénie thought, like the painting. It was a validation, almost a blessing, of her plans: another Spanish consort acting on her own because of her concern and love for children. Although the decrepit hospital more recently had been used for women, it was happily near the home for girls she was building. They were in the same neighborhood, so she'd have access to both, and the entire area would be a testament to the Second Empire's commitment to bettering the lives of the working class.

Although she was still overseeing every aspect of the Maison Eugène Napoléon's construction, Eugénie threw herself into the new project, organizing the remodeling of the building, bringing in beds for children and calling once again on the Sisters of Charity of Saint-Vincent-de-Paul to take on the caring duties.

In less than a year, the hospital was open and 425 children were being treated there. The Pils painting which had inspired Eugénie was hung prominently in the hospital's chapel.

With its renovations, a schoolroom, workroom and gymnasium were added for the patients, and Eugénie renamed it the Hôpital Sainte-Eugénie. Over the next five years, more than three thousand children would be cared for there. In the years ahead, Eugénie would also add a hospice for convalescent children to the hospital in Berck-sur-Mer on the northwest coast of France. The "marine cure" developed there had helped many, she learned, and as a swimmer and lover of the sea herself, she saw it as the ideal way for children to recover full health.

She was also drawn there by the story of a woman who helped with the care of sick children, Marianne Brillard, known as Marianne-Toute-Seule, that is, Marianne-All-Alone. Madame Brillard had lost her husband and four of her six children in a cholera epidemic and had been living on her own in an isolated cabin, surviving by caring for the children of fishermen. Eugénie tapped Marianne-Toute-Seule to care for the children sent from Paris, and she herself would dedicate the hospice and the growing medical center as the Hôpital Napoléon, a facility that remains in operation today. As many as eight hundred children at a time would be sent there for hydrotherapy treatments and the fresh air of the sea.

EVEN AS EUGÉNIE WORKED FOR THE WELL-BEING OF CHILDREN, SHE AND NAPOLÉON WERE engaged in yet another and even larger project: the greening of France.

Like his wife, Napoléon was a lover of the outdoors, and he'd had his eye on the Bois de Boulogne ever since he'd returned to France. Paris needed public parks like those he'd enjoyed in London, and in Napoléon's mind the old royal hunting grounds, now overgrown and neglected, were the ideal spot to begin creating them. He set Haussmann and his team of architects and engineers to work, but he also knew that he could count on the empress, with her love of sports and nature, to be a fervent supporter and an active partner.

They would use the 2,000 acres of royal woods on the western edge of Paris as the catalyst for the largest environmental rejuvenation of a city ever done. In just seventeen years, Eugénie and Napoléon would add numerous parks, squares and green spaces to Paris and plant more than 600,000 trees in the city, an accomplishment never since matched.

The Bois de Boulogne was transformed into a country paradise with thousands of trees and flowers, streams, meandering paths, lakes and fields for sports. There was also a concert hall, a brasserie, an aquarium and a theater. The old hunting grounds, once limited to kings and their guests, would become a model for city parks around the world and bring outdoor pleasures to all.

It was only natural that Eugénie, who insisted on green spaces around her own projects, would also take a key role on the board responsible for the Jardin d'Acclimatation at one end of the park. The Jardin was designed as a location for exotic plants and animals brought in from the colonies to acclimate themselves to the French climate. The empress, an animal lover since her youth, brought her son to introduce him to the variety of beasts housed there, and she was delighted when the emperor ceded the park to the city so that it was open to everyone, aristocrats and workers alike.

The writer Maxime Du Camp was infatuated with the park's new glass houses—built in Eugénie's favorite cast iron and glass construction materials—for their "shadows of mystery where sand whispered beneath the feet." Du Camp was not alone: all Paris, it seemed, came to walk its flower-lined paths, admire its rare animals and then buy specialty items from its gardens and eggs and feathers from the fancy fowl on view.

Even plummeting temperatures did not discourage the public. One winter day, the crowds were surprised to see a young American woman, Lillie Moulton, skating beautifully on one of the frozen lakes. Moulton was already a well-known singer who had trained in London with Jenny Lind, now married to an American banker in Paris.

"The coldest day that Paris has ever known, since goodness knows when, has suddenly burst upon us," Lillie wrote to her mother in January of 1863. "I had just received the skates you sent me for my Christmas present," she said, "and I was wild to try them." She was surprised she had the lake almost to herself, but "skating is just dawning on the Parisians." Among the crowds that watched her from the lake's banks, Lillie recognized the emperor and empress. "As we saw the emperor, who was on skates, coming toward us, I felt dreadfully frightened, for it [was] the first time I had ever spoken to a sovereign."

And he was struggling, Lillie recalled. "His Majesty held in his hand a short stick with an iron point, such as are used in climbing the Alps, and managed to propel himself forward by little right-legged shunts, his left leg not daring to do anything but slide, and stopped like an engine nearing a station, puffing and out of breath." The emperor was intrigued by Lillie. "Dare I ask such a perfect skater as you," he said, "to skate with so humble a skater as myself?"

"He was a humble skater indeed!" Lillie told her mother. "I wished that someone would relieve me of this responsibility. Suppose his Majesty should fall! The emperor skated on silently, intent on balancing himself. He stumbled at every stroke; but as I was on his left side—the weak one—we got along very nicely."

The emperor then took Lillie to meet the empress and skate with her. Now the American singer was impressed. "The empress was dressed in a more suitable style than the other ladies . . . though crinolined and high-heeled, [she] had a short skirt. But I forgot everything, gazing at the empress, who appeared as a vision of beauty, with a bright color in her cheeks, her eyes sparkling with animation. We sped on our way . . ."

Lillie Moulton so dazzled the imperial couple that they asked her to teach the prince impérial, then six, to ice-skate.

"He is very sweet, and talks very intelligently for his age," Lillie wrote. Eugénie, too, was eager to practice the new sport. Once while skating together, she and Lillie took a fall when a man, skating backward, knocked against them. "That same evening there was a ball at the Tuileries," Lillie wrote, "and when the empress came to speak to me she said: 'How are you? I can hardly stand up.' I answered, 'I am worse off, your Majesty; I can stand up, but I cannot sit down.'"

THE BEAUTY, OPENNESS AND FRESH AIR OF THE PARKS WERE IN MARKED CONTRAST TO THE Paris Haussmann faced as he began his city renovation. Paris, one pessimistic reformer wrote, was "an immense workshop of putrefaction, where misery, pestilence and sickness work in concert, where sunlight and air rarely penetrate." The complaints did not stop Haussmann who knew he had the emperor's backing as he created verdant parks, wide streets and dressed-stone buildings where there previously had been clusters of houses overhanging cobbled passages and warrens of alleys. No area was more indicative of that than Les Halles, Paris's derelict central market. Napoléon demanded that it be overhauled and cleaned up quickly. The unsightly mess had to be gone before the world arrived for the 1855 Universal Exposition which Napoléon had scheduled in a competitive response to London's Great Exposition with its Crystal Palace in 1851.

The project did not start well: its first building was a disaster. The emperor called in the architect, Victor Baltard, and, in his usual soft, gentle voice, expressed how much he hated the building. Napoléon insisted on fresh air and beauty for the market: "giant umbrellas and nothing else." Hearing the displeasure in that quiet tone, Baltard surely feared for his job.

At that point, it was Eugénie who's said to have stepped up and suggested how it could be done. It was hardly surprising that she'd be involved. She was, as one historian wrote, "a leading proponent of civil engineering, city planning and building projects." Eugénie and Napoléon had been impressed with the new techniques used for the Crystal Palace at the Great Exhibition in London in 1851, and she put forth her idea to use the cast iron and glass construction to make "permanent umbrellas" or pavilions. Eugénie believed a structure like the Crystal Palace would solve many of the problems of Les Halles—bad ventilation, poor lighting, inadequate sanitation and haphazard storage conditions—and that it would cost less than an enclosed building of brick and mortar.

It would also be vastly more attractive than the ramshackle buildings that marked the old market. Napoléon concurred, especially after he heard Baltard sing the praises of the steel-and-glass architecture of the new train stations.

It was left to Haussmann, however, to make room for the so-called umbrellas. He responded by razing a huge swath of Paris that once again left residents outraged and on the verge of revolt as they were forced from their homes and places of work. "Only the rats remained," one displaced resident said. Most people ended up far from where they had lived and worked, in places that soon became sites of rebellion and political agitation against not only the Second Empire but nearly every government of France since that time.

But the new Les Halles was a revelation. It was four times the size of the old market. Each of the ten new pavilions, or umbrellas, that Baltard designed housed a specialty: one for fruits, another for fish, and so on, but most importantly, none of them would hold an abattoir. For health and hygiene reasons—and the fact that the smell was unbearable—Napoléon had banished slaughterhouses to the edge of the city. Almost overnight, sanitation and air quality in the market area improved, and Les Halles became a tourist destination as well as a flourishing market. Unfortunately, the outer suburbs housing the slaughterhouses now also housed many of the forcibly uprooted and discontented residents.

UNDER THE IMPERIAL COUPLE, PARIS WAS BLOSSOMING AND BECOMING A PLACE EVERYONE wanted to visit. They had made that not only possible but easy and comfortable. Railroads ran to every corner of the Hexagon, as France was nicknamed because of the country's shape. Trains welcomed travelers at their enormous, attractive stations, or *gares*, such as the Gare du Nord in Paris—which, like Les Halles, featured Eugénie's beloved glass-and-steel construction to accommodate both passengers and trains. Streets were clean and easy to stroll, and shops and restaurants drew the crowds in to sample their wares.

All of France felt the wave of modernization. Eugénie and Napoléon seemed to be everywhere, opening new medical centers, museums and manufacturing plants, greeting ships that crowded into the new ports and boats that jammed the modern canals. Communication, too, became easier and faster with telegraph poles and lines sprouting like weeds and an expanded postal service. The country's banking system had been overhauled as well so that the ordinary French could obtain credit for personal and professional projects, resulting in new businesses and factories popping up everywhere.

France was on its way to becoming a leading industrial power, a fact that became clear when the Universal Exposition opened in 1855. Here was an event where the country could display its bourgeoning advances and achievements, as well as Paris's new look. Even Queen Victoria came to see it. Her visit marked the first time a British sovereign had set foot on French soil since the Hundred Years' War, and she was hardly alone. Five million other people came, paid their entrance fee (the first time one had been charged for a fair) and passed through a new invention: the turnstile. The world got a first look at Foucault's pendulum, the hydrostatic percolator that produced fifty thousand cups of coffee each day, and another new invention, the baby bottle. They also saw for the first time a system that would become the cornerstone of the French wine industry and which was a pet project of the emperor's: the classification of Bordeaux wines based on their quality and price. Locals, however, grumbled about the crowds and costs. "Rents for shops in the more elegant quarters of Paris have reached insane amounts," groused one resident. "Everyone is upset about the influx of provincials and foreigners who are saturating the market and forcing prices up."

Watching over it all and welcoming visitors to the exhibition was the empress—or at least an enormous portrait of her. *The Empress Eugénie Surrounded by Her Ladies-in-Waiting* was painted by Franz Xaver Winterhalter, who had also done portraits of Queen Victoria and other royal figures. The paint was barely dry when the work was hung in the central pavilion, where it dominated the space.

For most visitors, that was the most they would see of the empress, because during that summer she would realize she was pregnant and retreat to the spas at Eaux-Bonnes, doing everything she could to protect this baby, the future of the Bonaparte dynasty, the future of France.

CHAPTER FIVE

STICKS AND STONES, BRICKS AND MORTAR

FROM THE DAY OF HER MARRIAGE, EUGÉNIE WORRIED ABOUT CLINGING TO SOMETHING OF herself. "I who used to be so obsessed with my liberty am in chains for the rest of my life," she wrote her sister Paca on the eve of the ceremony, "never by myself, never free, amid all that court etiquette, of which I'm going to be the principal victim."

She was determined to be not only the empress of the French, but also Eugénie de Montijo and hold on to her own culture, her own family, her own interests. She wanted someplace to escape the stifling protocol of the palace and keep those things alive.

In 1855, two years after her wedding and coronation, Eugénie's confidence in her role as empress had grown. But so, too, had the pressures of court life and with it her need for privacy.

Eugénie found her hideaway in the *hôtel particulier*, or town house, on the Champs-Élysées that had belonged to Marshal Jacques Lauriston. She bought it and set about turning it into a home for her family when they visited from Spain. It was to be more than a private hotel: it was to be a place where she could literally let down her hair and be a sister, a daughter, an aunt—not an empress. There she could relive the past when she had sat up late arguing politics with her mother and giggling with her sister. It was her sister and closest friend, Paca, who was foremost in her mind, and Eugénie renamed the town house in her honor: l'Hôtel d'Albe (Alba House) after Paca's title as Duchess of Alba. She hired Hector-Martin Lefuel, known for designing a theater for the Château de Fontainebleau and a new wing of the Louvre, to renovate it.

In the process, she discovered a new pleasure: interior design. With a house of her own for the first time in her life, she could make choices to please herself alone. No one, not the state or the public, not even her husband or mother, was peering over her shoulder.

She began accumulating furniture and artworks she loved, gravitating especially toward work by female artists. Among them was Marie Octavie Sturel Paigné, whose work the empress had first seen two years earlier at the Salon of 1853 where Sturel Paigné won the Gold Medal, the top prize. Eugénie was so excited by the young woman's vigorous use of color that she immediately purchased a painting and asked her to do more for her own rooms at the Château de Compiègne and then commissioned designs for tapestries. The bright colors of Sturel Paigné's flowers were an ode to Spain and meant home to Eugénie.

So, too, did the Orientalist style paintings by Henriette Browne which the empress bought. Henriette Browne was the pseudonym of Sofie de Saux, wife of a French diplomat whose assignments had included Turkey and North Africa. These were intimate works that appealed to the empress's fondness for paintings, as well as her love of the colorful and exotic that recalled the multicultural mix of the Granada of her youth.

Dance in a Posada by Eugène Giraud brought Granada even closer. Its portrayal of uninhibited dancers conveyed what Eugénie was seeking: freedom, joy and the past when she had thrown herself into gypsy dances and festivals.

In 1865 she found another property on avenue Gabriel which she saw as perfect for a guesthouse for visiting friends. It was not far from her primary residence at the Tuileries Palace and offered enough space for a garden her guests could enjoy. As with Alba House, she turned to the Péreire Bank for a loan and hired the same architect.

The new house became known as l'Hôtel de l'Impératrice, the Empress's Hotel. By the time it was completed in 1866, Eugénie was forty years old, and promoting France, its might and influence, its arts and products, had become second nature to her. Even though, as with Alba House, she could choose whatever she wanted for the interiors, Eugénie de Montijo had been woven into the empress of the French. When she wanted a new painting for the Hôtel de l'Impératrice, it was as empress that she made the decision: she picked *Interior of a Silk Store* by Florent Willems. Eugénie had a strong affinity for silk. Visitors had only to glance from the painting to the silk-covered walls, drapes, upholstery and her own gowns to grasp that she was making clear the importance of the silk industry to France.

The empress had also discovered she could use decor to promote France's international status, and she embraced the idea. She and Napoléon had welcomed the first Japanese delegation in 1862 as a prelude to full trade relations with the country. Soon after, Asian influences began appearing in Eugénie's interiors. She painted some rooms of the Empress's House red with black trim and displayed pieces she had been given by Asian governments, as well as others Napoléon bought for her when he saw that her enthusiasm for the style was more than a political cause. When his half brother, the Duc de Morny, died, Napoléon bought his large collection of porcelains for her. She put some on display in the Empress's House but held back some of the most important pieces for what she would call the Chinese Museum. In their newness and novelty to Europeans, the arts and crafts of Asia became lumped together as *Chinese* no matter their country of origin.

Her initial inspiration for the museum had come in 1861 when, after five years of negotiations, she and Napoléon formally received a delegation from Siam, today's Thailand. The meeting restored relations that had been severed in 1686 and produced a spectacle never before seen in the ballroom of the Château de Fontainebleau. King Rama IV, who was seeking to modernize his country and who would become famous as the inspiration for *The King and I*, sent three ambassadors to France with their entourages and forty-eight crates of gifts—no, make that forty-seven because one broke open when their ship docked in Toulon and was revealed to hold preserved peppers packed for the ambassadors' personal snacks. The crates had been sent ahead to Fontainebleau to be opened and displayed to the court.

The court was awed as the crates disgorged gold and silver fabrics, gold cups, a belt of gold and precious stones, palanquins and jewels. There was also a suit for the emperor with a brocade jacket on which the buttons were diamonds, and breeches in red and gold with enamel flowers on the bottom. The suit made Eugénie's friend Prosper Mérimée laugh. He had been invited to the ceremony and wrote to Eugénie's mother that the emperor would have a "very scratchy bottom" if he sat down wearing it.

When the Siamese ambassadors themselves arrived at the entrance of the Fontainebleau ballroom, they dropped to their elbows and knees and, holding gifts high with their hands, began crawling toward the emperor and empress. Napoléon and Eugénie watched from their thrones with faces they held determinedly impassive to camouflage how startled they were.

Mérimée said he was impressed with the ease Eugénie displayed throughout. He was especially impressed when she got up from her throne to kiss the cheek of the twelve-year-old son of the second ambassador, who was the personal representative of King Rama IV. The ambassador himself was thrilled. He patted his son on the head and said, "My son, [from now on] your days will always be happy."

The emperor also stepped down from his throne and raised the first ambassador to thank him. The delegation prostrated itself again to crawl backward out of the ballroom at the end of the ceremony.

The Fontainebleau ceremony was only the second time Eugénie had been included in a diplomatic presentation, and her presence was seen as a reflection of her growing influence and the increasing confidence Napoléon had in her ability to handle governmental affairs.

The empress's participation was particularly notable because it came at a time when the emperor was working to cement France's role as a major world power with colonies and trading rights that enriched the home country. Asia's carvings, silks, paintings and dishes accomplished that. So did the appearance of cloisonné, lacquer and porcelain which were unknown in Europe at the time and which were unfailingly tempting.

As was the opium.

For years, more and more Western traders had slipped through the cracks of the controlled ports of the East and hauled out shiploads of goods, finally forcing the reluctant governments of Asia to open to trade, albeit on the unequal terms dictated by the "foreign devils."

Eugénie had fallen in love with these exported products at first sight, and her love affair with Asian art became the physical manifestation of Second Empire foreign policy.

The policy had taken shape during the Second Opium War when France was drawn into the conflict on the side of the British who were trying to force their way into the city of Canton. In 1856, a French missionary was executed as riots broke out in that city following the Chinese government's attempt to end the opium trade. In the wake of the victory won by the better-armed European powers, China capitulated, legalizing the opium trade, granting trade advantages and access to the interior of the country. Troops of the victors went unrestrained, running rampant, looting the Summer Palace and occupying the Forbidden City. The result was a plethora of Chinese arts and crafts snatched, packed and sent to Europe.

Spoils of war, but also symbols of France's power. Eugénie felt French people should be proud of them and organized a public exhibit in the Marsan Pavilion of the Tuileries Palace to show them off. There were jades, turquoises, cloisonné enamel vases, a few deadly weapons and even the body armor of the Qianlong emperor.

As she worked on the exhibit and nurtured her idea for a museum, much like museum curators today, Eugénie worried, bothered by stories about how much of the treasure and artwork had been stolen by troops sacking Chinese imperial sites. When a French commander presented her with a Chinese ceremonial necklace that he had had made into a rosary for her, she rejected it, troubled by the transformation of the artifact and fearing she was accepting stolen goods.

The political acumen she showed by refusing the gift was further reflected when, after seeing the court's reaction to the treasures in the crates, she announced the display of Siamese gifts would be opened to the public so it could appreciate France's international importance. She also stepped up her planning for what would be known as the Chinese Museum, that she designed to exhibit France's influence and power to important visitors at the Château de Fontainebleau.

As always, Eugénie was in a rush to complete the new project. She nagged the designers and workers nonstop and devoted hours to its preparation, choosing fabrics, wallcoverings and furniture.

When the imperial family arrived at Fontainebleau on June 2, 1863, for its annual stay, the rooms of the museum were filled with crates. Eugénie was exhilarated and charged in, ripping open crates, one after another, putting a vase here, a bowl there, hollering at footmen about placement of display cases and furniture. A sofa over there, chairs here, the palanquin in the center—no, on the side. No orchestra conductor ever directed as untiringly as she did.

By June 14, just twelve days after she had arrived, Eugénie was ready to stage a private inauguration of the Chinese Museum. Just one more thing: she hung Winterhalter's large canvas *The Empress Eugénie Surrounded by Her Ladies-in-Waiting* in the vestibule. She may not have sought personal publicity, but she wanted to leave no doubt about who was responsible for the museum. Then she prepared to personally greet the guests. Her librarian remembered the scene as almost a work of art itself. She was on a large sofa with "her back to the door opening to the lake and the garden surmounted by the dark sky sparkling with stars."

It was more than a pretty setting, however. Eugénie's message had come through. "The museum declared Eugénie's active role in France's international relations," one historian wrote.

The Eugénie who dedicated the Chinese Museum was a far different person from the one who had built Alba House eight years earlier. She was no longer the enthusiastic young woman who had tried to reproduce her childhood haunts and hold on to her past.

Instead her background became a tool, something she used to draw others to her. Nowhere was that more apparent than in Biarritz, the fishing and smuggling village on the southwest coast of France, in the heart of the Basque country.

It would be there where Eugénie de Montijo reigned as empress of the French. There, her memories and stories would come bubbling out to attract and enchant. There she would find her home.

IN 1854, NOT LONG AFTER THEIR WEDDING, EUGÉNIE TOOK NAPOLÉON TO BIARRITZ. AS THEY walked along the rugged Atlantic coast, Eugénie stopped at an outcropping and said with pride, "Here's where I nearly drowned one time and had to be pulled out of the ocean."

Napoléon watched the beautiful white-capped waves thunder onto the shore. The turbulent ocean was just like Eugénie. Her tempestuous, unrestrained personality had attracted him from the first time he saw her.

"I will build you a house here," Napoléon said. He bought a large parcel of land on the edge of the sea and, using his own money, not government funds, began the construction.

Within two years, Villa Eugénie had risen and become its namesake's favorite retreat. It was everything she longed for: proximity to Spain and her family, and a place she could swim, hike, ride and sail. Court life and its structured etiquette were far away.

Plus, she loved the Basques for their strength and independence. They were people of the border, people who lived with their hearts divided yet entwined in two different cultures to become a unique group of their own—neither French nor Spanish but Basque, the descendants of isolated farmers and herders who thrived in the Pyrenees mountains on the frontier between the two countries. It was something Eugénie could understand because her heart was also divided between France and Spain.

She found comfort in the Basque country and sought it out at the most difficult times. Her mother had taken her to the nearby spa of Eaux-Bonnes to nurse a youthful broken heart. When she suffered a painful and depressing miscarriage, she returned to heal both body and spirit in its warm, curative waters and the warmth of the Basque people.

On each of her visits, the Basque people welcomed her back as a kindred soul who understood and delighted in their culture and traditions. They remembered her as the little girl who came there on vacation and talked to everyone, who played in the fishermen's boats and was such a daredevil that she would swim even in storms. When she became empress, they wrote to her saying they thought of her as "our blonde fairy" and hoped she would bring her magic back to them.

The villa Napoléon built for her was in the shape of an *E* to honor its chatelaine, and like Biarritz itself, it seemed to grow of its own volition. Prosper Mérimée was a frequent visitor and wrote that each time he arrived it looked as though twenty new houses had been built. Soon there was also a new harbor, a casino, hotels and more and more stores to cater to the growing population and number of visitors.

Villa Eugénie was designed as an escape from court life for

six weeks or longer beginning in August; space was included for friends and family to join the empress. Among them were her sister Paca, her husband and their three children, who brought nurses, governesses, secretaries, maids and other staff. And then fellow royals, like the queen of Spain, the king of Belgium, the Prince of Wales and the king and queen of Portugal came to call. Each new visitor meant added space to accommodate them and their entourages.

Napoléon now, like his wife, was thoroughly caught in the spell of the Basque country. He continued adding more land to the domain until there were nearly 60 acres of trees, vineyards, meadows and even a lake, all edged by the long Plage de l'Impératrice, the Empress's Beach. This was no idle, flattering name for, just as when she'd been a child, the empress swam nearly every day no matter the weather—the stormier, the better. "Some days the water is so cold it takes great determination to jump in," she wrote in a letter once, "but I haven't missed a day yet."

With the birth of the prince impérial, Villa Eugénie continued its growth. The prince had his own little "court": his nurse, his tutor and the physician Dr. Ernest Barthez.

Although Eugénie kept the interiors light and elegant, Spain was near and never far from her heart. She hung a magnificent series of seven Gobelins tapestries telling the story of the knight errant Don Quixote, a reminder of her Spanish childhood and her own wandering life.

Here, for the first time, Eugénie also gave full range to what became known as Louis XVI-Impératrice style. She ordered furniture that recalled the straight lines of Marie-Antoinette's rooms but had the pieces, especially chairs, made larger and more comfortable with extra cushioning. Because the villa was a vacation house, she wanted an intimate and relaxed approach in its interiors, one suited to private and personal time with her family and friends. Barthez, the physician, remembered the comfort, particularly of his bed, and the wonders of his modern bathroom. In his memoirs, Barthez sounded like the writer of the Goldilocks fairy

tale as he described the rooms as "not too large, not too small."
They were just right.

Biarritz was a door for Eugénie that swung open not only to
her past and her youth but also to a French joie de vivre she could
share and encourage. With court strictures left in Paris, she organized dinners and balls that welcomed people from all walks of
life, titled or not. Both the emperor and the empress were eager
to recreate and promote "*les arts de la table*" which had been part
of the legacy of Empress Josephine, and which Napoléon remembered from his childhood when he spent time at Malmaison. As a
result, he and Eugénie entertained frequently and with flair.

Even Queen Victoria, who had then been on the throne for
nearly twenty years and who had probably been at more glamorous events than anyone else, was impressed. At a *souper* given in
her honor, Victoria, who was thirty-six, noticed Eugénie's attention to detail and was dazzled by the lighting and garlands of
flowers that were hung throughout the room. "It was one of the
most beautiful and majestic events we have ever attended," she
wrote in her diary.

The copious lunches and dinners were prepared by the loyal
Jules Gouffé who introduced Napoléon and Eugénie to dishes
made famous by the *mères lyonnaises*, the Lyonnais Mothers, who
used their culinary skills to perfect a wide variety of dishes that
would become staples of French cuisine, using local products,
such as truffles and eels, in a skilled and refined manner. Although
many courses were served at each meal, Gouffé paid careful attention to the size of the portions, knowing the emperor, who was
plagued with stomach problems, would only pick at his food. The
wines, one regular guest wrote, were always superb, but at a time
when fermentation had yet to be fully controlled, they could also
produce some nasty surprises—bottles that would explode, wines
that were acidic and pétillant.

The meals were "not solemn," Barthez wrote. The emperor
willingly joined in the conversation and "gave it a certain tone,
behaving more like a husband than an emperor." The empress was

"more vivacious and lively, talked a lot and had a full-throated laugh, but the emperor, though calmer, would laugh, too, when there was a good reason." Barthez expressed regret that he had not recorded what the emperor said because it was frequently "right on target, instructive and sometimes even spiritual." After the meal, Napoléon frequently stayed with his guests, smoking and talking, while the empress took people to her favorite spots in the area.

The sea and the mountains were her natural habitat, and she loved and delighted in sharing them. Often, however, her guests were less enthusiastic. She led visitors on long hikes into the Pyrenees, inducing friends to climb the Rhune mountain with her. They would begin on donkeyback, and the empress had her own donkey, whom she named Cendrillon, the French equivalent of Cinderella, because, as in the fairy tale, the little animal did all the work. When the path became too steep for Cendrillon and her fellows, Eugénie led the way on foot. No one could keep up with her, however, and complaints flew like leaves in the storms she loved: our shoes are being ruined and our feet hurt, said the women; we're so out of breath we can't even help the women, said the men. Eugénie only laughed and egged them on to the summit where they could see both Spain and France spread below, two countries at their feet.

After a sailing expedition of hers left many of her guests seasick, the frustrated empress grumbled to Napoléon, "My ladies are always ill, by land or by sea."

When she tried to introduce her visitors to bullfighting, they were more than ill, they were repulsed. Her friend Mérimée likewise spurned the idea of the corrida, which he labeled a "cruel game"—but Eugénie's husband, always eager to please her, admitted he enjoyed the pageantry and the enthusiasm of the crowds.

It seemed strange that with her pleasure in bullfighting, Eugénie could still be horrified when she encountered a man leading a sheep to the slaughter to feed his family. "It's awful to kill an animal," she said as she petted his sheep. "I don't want that to happen." So she bought the animal herself and took it back to the Villa Eugénie.

Barthez was dismayed. How could a woman who loved all living creatures so much that she'd carry insects outside "to a better place for them" rather than killing them—still countenance bullfighting and "enthusiastically cheer a good *estocada* [sword thrust]"? There seemed to be no real answer. But Eugénie had been attending the corrida since her childhood and knew many of the most famous and skillful matadors. She admired their grace and courage, she said, but her appreciation of their skills did not translate into equal appreciation on the part of her French friends, and her attempts to promote the corrida in France met with little success.

Her attitude toward animals was not the only contradiction in Eugénie's personality, Barthez realized. When she was out walking in Biarritz, he said, she would spot children who were injured or who did not look well and would bring them back to the villa for him to treat. But when the idea of a village hospital was proposed for children with scrufola—a form of tuberculosis that manifested in enlarged lymph glands like tumors on the sufferers' necks—she snapped back that Biarritz was a vacation spot for visitors to come see titled people, and their pleasure should not be ruined by having disfigured children in the neighborhood.

"She had a selfishness about pleasure," Barthez wrote, "and a horror of pain."

Eugénie sought to entertain and amuse her guests with organized games and outings. When she learned about a scene in the Meyerbeer opera *Le prophète* that included roller-skating, she couldn't resist trying the new sport. Meyerbeer had used roller skates in a winter tableau to give the impression the performers were ice-skating. Roller skating became all the rage with rinks everywhere, it seemed, many with live orchestras. There were roller-skating gyms and even schools that taught roller-skating in cities like Bordeaux.

Eugénie, however, had no difficulty finding a place to skate.

She had her own rinks in the halls of royal residences and soon began outfitting her friends and ladies-in-waiting to join her. Their skates resembled today's inline models but lacked the ability to turn or stop. Rumors said Eugénie solved the problem by discreetly positioning footmen to catch them if they fell or crashed into a wall. That's what happened to John Joseph Merlin, the Frenchman who invented roller skates. Merlin plowed into an expensive mirror and shattered it along with the violin he was playing when he tried to demonstrate his creation to a crowd at a ball in 1760. His accident put the brakes on roller-skating's popularity, and it took several years before interest in trying the "wheeled shoes" reignited. Another century would pass before an American named James Leonard Plimpton devised the four-wheel models that let skaters pivot.

But if courtiers and Second Empire ministers were stunned to see the elegant empress flying down the elaborately decorated halls to greet them, they held their tongues. She was the empress, after all.

Her "selfishness about pleasure" was expressed in myriad ways. On one occasion in Biarritz, Eugénie decided to take a group of visitors on a hike to the ancient town of Sare on the border with Spain. They were intrigued by the isolated village itself, which was known for its plethora of fifteenth-century houses, but getting there required a strenuous climb. Sare, they discovered, was nestled against the Pyrenees and included a warren of caves that, for generations, had been home and storehouse to smugglers who crossed the mountains clandestinely from France to Spain and back again with contraband. The smugglers also were famously Bonapartists, because the first Napoléon had relied on their skills to get weapons into Spain for his war.

It was probably no surprise then that waiting for Eugénie and her party in one of the caves was Michel, the most famous smuggler of the day. Eugénie had known him as a child, and now he welcomed her and her entourage with a magnificent feast of products whose origin, he assured them, was "local." Then he and his friends began to play music, and the tempo increased as the light faded. "The empress simply could not stop herself," wrote Dr. Barthez, who was among the hikers. "Throwing off her hat and cloak, she started to dance a particularly graceful fandango. She was completely unaffected and altogether enchanting, the look on her face being one of pure delight."

Eugénie's natural exuberance took over in Biarritz. She eagerly joined in games of hide-and-seek and leapfrog after dinners. Once, seeing a wheelbarrow beside the road, she hopped in and, giggling like a naughty child, had her companion push her down the path. Her uninhibited behavior must be because she is Spanish, the doctor decided.

But it was more than that: it was an appreciation of the country which she saw as a key in French and Spanish relations. It was here in the Basque country at Saint-Jean-de-Luz where Louis XIV had married the Infanta Maria-Theresa to end the Franco–Spanish War; it was here where French and Spanish diplomats had negotiated numerous times. Napoléon I had spent time here, as had Napoléon III's mother.

Those events resonated with her personally, and she wanted to commemorate them, finally finding a way to do so in her garden. Like her predecessors, Empress Josephine and Queen Marie-Antoinette, she found making a garden gave her a chance to express her own personality in a private and personal endeavor, yet bring together the strands of French history and knit them into a whole. She planted flowers, flowers and more flowers in all colors. The riot of colors may have expressed her own Spanish heritage, but the violets were pure Bonaparte, and the lilies a reminder of Louis XIV's Bourbon dynasty which had ruled France in some of its most glorious moments and to which the Bonapartes felt themselves connected. There were roses, too, the favorite flower of Empress Josephine, Napoléon's beloved grandmother. She had made them the stars of her magnificent garden at Malmaison, one Eugénie grew to know well when she showcased it at the 1867 Universal Exposition.

Eugénie also drew inspiration from another garden she would showcase at the Exposition: Marie-Antoinette's at the Trianon. The empress had become fascinated with the ill-starred queen when she herself became the wife of a French ruler. She had even asked the emperor to take her to visit the Trianon on their honeymoon. Living in the spaces Marie-Antoinette had inhabited and assuming responsibility for the queen's Maternal Societies further intensified Eugénie's preoccupation and association with her predecessor. Not only did she emulate the queen's gardening passion but she also began collecting objects and furniture that had belonged to her.

Empress Eugénie costumed in eighteenth-century style. *Metropolitan Museum of Art*

In doing that, Eugénie joined the fad at the time: interest in Marie-Antoinette. It had been initiated by the publication of the memoirs of Napoléon I's finance minister, who wrote romantically of her as the "most sacred hostage" whose "execution constitutes something worse than regicide." A group of young writers and artists in the 1850s glommed onto the theme, idolizing and idealizing the beautiful, elegant woman with a tragic fate.

Among the group were the Goncourt brothers, Jules and Edmond, who were "self-styled esthetes, art critics, diarists, and prolific historians of eighteenth-century art," and who also wrote a best-selling biography of the queen. They also gave their name to France's most important literary prize.

By the time it appeared in 1858, Eugénie was already pursuing her own interest in Marie-Antoinette's life, particularly in her gardens which, for her, were the tangible remains of the queen, a place she could feel her presence as she walked through the grounds and stood beneath the trees Marie-Antoinette had planted. Eugénie set out to bring the gardens back to life and, in the process, realized the queen knew what she was doing: "she was an enlightened gardener cognizant of contemporary trends in science and garden theories."

That appealed to Eugénie's own love of science, and in her gardens, she sought to show the progress French horticulture had made in widening the range of plants that could be grown. In emulating and expanding on the queen's work, Eugénie also created a farm, but hers was no play farm like Marie-Antoinette's at the Petit Trianon. Rather, the ever-practical empress built a small working farm that produced both food and revenue—as well as a home for Cendrillon and the rescued sheep.

During one stay in Biarritz, she learned of an agricultural project for women run by a priest in the nearby Basque village of Anglet which immediately intrigued her. Father Cestac showed her and Napoléon the school he had created twenty years earlier for girls abandoned by their families and women who had been prostitutes. When he told the empress that education for girls was the best remedy for poverty and prostitution, he discovered he had a kindred spirit. He hoped to go further, he said, and establish a horticultural and agricultural school for girls, a school to be managed by the Sisters of Marie. The empress immediately offered her support and, in 1867, with her own money bought 150 hectares (371 acres) of land in Amotz, near Biarritz, for the school. The project was never to be completed, an unfortunate casualty of the Franco–Prussian War. But Eugénie's garden in Biarritz, as well as those she established and restored elsewhere, would become, according to one historian, a "living patrimony, inscribing the gardens from the past into a legacy for the future."

With the open and welcoming atmosphere she created in Biarritz, the gardens were a testament to Eugénie's transformation from the tempestuous young Mademoiselle de Montijo to the empress of the French, a leader who had mastered herself and her country.

CHAPTER SIX

THE EMPRESS'S NEW CLOTHES

SEVEN YEARS. IT HAD BEEN NEARLY SEVEN YEARS SINCE EUGÉNIE MARRIED NAPOLÉON. Seven years since she had stood in a sparkling gown before the altar of Notre-Dame. Seven years since she had faced down the curious, almost prurient, crowd and curtsied like the empress she'd just become. And what had she accomplished in that time? Only one thing that meant anything to her: she had a son, a beautiful boy whose every antic delighted her. And yet, shouldn't she have done more? Something that made the world a better place?

She knew from childhood she didn't fit the role her maid saw for women—knitting stockings. And she certainly was not going to be a slave to any man, as her husband's uncle, Napoléon Bonaparte, would have cast her. No, she knew she had "a proper role," and it was time to take it on. In May of 1859, Napoléon announced he was leaving France temporarily to lead his army in the campaign in Italy for control of the Papal States, and he proclaimed Eugénie would govern in his absence. For the first time, a woman would govern France on her own.

The news was not widely welcomed. Plon-Plon, the emperor's jealous cousin, reacted snidely when he learned that Napoléon had named the empress as regent. "What stupidity to entrust the government to a fashion plate, for the Empress is nothing else," Plon-Plon had said.

Fashion plate? Eugénie dismissed that criticism with a tart "He's a fool," and she was determined but also nervous as she took on the regency. (Napoléon had wisely cleared Plon-Plon out of Eugénie's way by sending him to an obscure post managing an occupying army corps in Tuscany, then pacifying him by arranging a marriage with Princess Clothilde, daughter of Piedmont's King Victor-Emmanuel II.)

Eugénie approached her regency "with sober humility," Augustin Filon, her son's tutor later wrote. Attending the weekly ministerial meetings and reading reports on internal and external affairs, she quickly gained confidence and decided to address the Senate and the Corps Législatif, much like addressing Congress in the United States. She got a standing ovation. "The Empress Regent . . . displays the same grace and intelligence in her new position that she has hitherto shown in all," *The Illustrated London News* reported after her speech. The reporter was astonished that she did not curtail her charity work when she took on her new responsibilities. "This is what women do," the empress said.

Eugénie threw herself into governing and found she quite enjoyed it. She feared she would be bored once the emperor returned from Italy and her regency ended, but Napoléon was impressed by what she had done, and once he arrived back in France he asked her to continue attending ministerial meetings.

Nonetheless, she was still seething about Plon-Plon's scornful *fashion plate* remark and searching for a way to respond. She had begun to grasp how appearance could be used to political advantage, thanks to her husband's guidance. In announcing their engagement, for instance, Napoléon had presented her as a devout and caring woman who would be "the ornament of the throne." And through portraits of her, he set about making sure she matched the image he had described, the image of the ideal Frenchwoman of the day.

He hired an ambitious artist named Édouard Dubufe to do her official portrait. Dubufe had hopes of being named court painter, but his depiction of the empress satisfied no one when it was shown at the Salon of 1853. Eugénie was portrayed with auburn hair and the olive complexion of a Spaniard—and of a woman who spent hours outdoors. She wore a dark dress trimmed with gold lace and was laden with strands of pearls. Dubufe portrayed her, in the words of historian Alison McQueen, as "an active, independent, and, most important, a Spanish woman, despite her social life in France and her extensive international travel."

Contemporary critics were more direct. "Awful," they said. "She looks too Spanish." Redheads were rare enough in France to be considered alien in their own right. People were wary of them and the supposed powers they might have. Only a few generations earlier, redheads had been executed as witches, and prejudice against them still ran strong.

Even Eugénie's friend Prosper Mérimée was disappointed by the Dubufe portrait. He wrote to Eugénie's mother that it would be "painful" for her to see the painting because the empress appeared to be bored and her arms looked like "two white blood sausages."

Dubufe claimed it was all the result of poor placement and poor lighting at the Salon, and he tried again, turning out a new portrait that subtly but significantly altered the appearance of the empress. Now she wore a white ball gown, her face had narrowed, and her skin was porcelain. Gone was any hint of red in her hair. He painted it nearly black. He also replaced her heavy jewelry with flowers. There was no official reaction to the second painting, but after paying for it, Napoléon hung it in an out-of-the-way spot and never again hired Dubufe, although years later, Eugénie did.

In his place came Franz Xaver Winterhalter, who already had done several portraits of royal figures, including many of Queen Victoria and her family. Winterhalter knew a dose of flattery mixed into his paint would keep him employed into old age.

He was also well aware of the standards of the time, that "a rosy hue, a delicate pallor and a fresh complexion . . . were the key to flawless beauty." No red hair. Winterhalter's paintings of Eugénie "conformed to gendered perceptions of her public role," according to a contemporary writer. Over the next several years he produced some of the most famous and most glamorous portraits of her, including the group portrait with her ladies-in-waiting. It was widely copied and the popularity of this painting established that this was the desired image of the empress.

By then, however, the strong-willed empress probably was already chafing at the image of her being presented to the public. Yes, it made her seem like the ideal "ornament of the throne," but it missed the essence of her personality, her strength, her determination and the role she was carving out for herself.

Ironically, inspiration on how she could display those attributes was to come from fashion, a dress she saw at a ball at the Tuileries Palace just a few months after Plon-Plon's disparaging

Empress Eugénie and her ladies-in-waiting by Franz Xaver Winterhalter. *Château de Compiègne, Franz Xaver Winterhalter, GrandPalaisRMN (Domaine de Compiègne) / Daniel Arnaudet*

remark. It was during the 1859–1860 Christmas season when Eugénie spotted Princess Pauline von Metternich of Austria in a gown that was completely different in style from those other women were wearing. "May I ask you, Madam, who made you that dress, so marvelously elegant and simple?" she asked the princess. Pauline responded, "An Englishman, Madam. A star who has arisen in the firmament of fashion."

"Well," the empress replied, "please ask him to come and see me at ten o'clock tomorrow morning."

The star summoned to the Tuileries Palace was Charles Frederick Worth.

WORTH WAS BORN INTO A POVERTY-STRICKEN FAMILY ON THE EDGE OF THE FENS IN ENgland's East Midlands. At age twelve he was apprenticed to a London department store where he got his first exposure to luxury fabrics. He often slipped away from his job to visit the National Gallery where the beauty of the fabrics in portraits fascinated him.

By the time he was twenty-one years old, he had managed to save five pounds, and with that and his ambition—but not a single word of French in his vocabulary—he set off for Paris where he somehow talked himself into a job at the famous dry goods emporium of Gagelin et Opigez. There he met the saleswoman Marie Vernet, who would become his wife, his muse and his model, as well as his biggest promoter. Within a few years, and with the help of a Swedish colleague, Otto Gustave Bobergh, they opened their own shop at number 7 on the fashionable rue de la Paix.

Madame Worth was convinced that her husband's brilliant, original designs deserved a wide audience. When she happened to spot the young and distinguished-looking Princess Pauline von Metternich alighting from a carriage at the Tuileries Palace, she knew she had found the woman who could make Worth's name. Pauline already had a reputation as a fashion-addict and trendsetter at the imperial court in her native Austria.

Mrs. Worth armed herself with an album of her husband's

sketches and, a few days later, went to the Metternich residence where she requested an audience with the princess. "I opened the album," Pauline wrote in her memoirs, "and what was my surprise to find on the front page a charming dress, on the second page a perfectly ravishing dress! Immediately I sensed an artist." She summoned Madame Worth, who had been waiting nervously outside. Marie Worth explained that her husband had just opened his own shop and was so eager to have the princess as one of his clients that he would let her name her own price for a gown. Pauline could not resist. She ordered two dresses, one for day wear and one for evening, but, she stipulated, she would pay no more than 300 francs for either, considerably less than what she paid for other gowns.

It was hardly a surprise when her new 300 francs evening gown caught the attention of the sharp-eyed empress.

As a youth, Eugénie dressed in a devil-may-care manner, throwing on bits and pieces of other clothes she found to dress up the plain linen dresses her father insisted on. Even as empress, in private she wore whatever caught her fancy and would be manageable in the sports and outdoor activities she loved. Often they were clothes she bought ready-made; her only dressing gown was purchased at a market for her by one of her ladies-in-waiting. The first time Princess Pauline met Eugénie was at her villa in Biarritz, and the empress was wearing a red flannel shirt tucked into a shortened black skirt with a wide leather belt. She said it was her "summer outfit."

It must, therefore, have been exhilarating for Eugénie when she met Charles Frederick Worth, because he told her he could design and make clothes for her that reflected the "real" Eugénie, not the idealized one. He also understood her desire to use her position to help others. Making clothes, he pointed out to her, was a way of creating jobs, especially jobs for women such as seamstress or embroiderer. That was a cause that resonated strongly with the empress, and she began to pay attention to what he was recommending.

Eugénie was not personally extravagant. She retained the frugal habits she had acquired as a child, but her husband believed spending lavishly was necessary to create an image of imperial majesty and glamour. As well as creating jobs, Napoléon told Eugénie, beautiful clothes made France look strong and important, and he encouraged her to dress in a regal fashion "on behalf of the nation."

Nonetheless, sometime later, when Worth brought her a beige gown of heavy silk woven with a design he had copied from a Chinese shawl, Eugénie rejected it. "It would make me look like a curtain," she declared. Worth responded, "But, Your Majesty, this will make the silk-weavers of Lyon very happy." She was adamant, however. The weavers had not been supporters of the empire, she said, and they had a history of revolting against government, so why should she support them?

Worth explained that there were dozens of women in his salon waiting to find out what the empress had ordered. Those women, all of them "leaders of fashion," he said, would beg to have gowns like the empress, so the looms of Lyon would work nonstop.

By bringing up the *canuts*, as the silk workers were known, Worth had touched a sensitive spot. Napoléon III and Eugénie were only too aware of "the bipolarity between Paris and Lyon." Napoléon's uncle and namesake Napoléon I had imposed the use of Lyon silk on the courts of the countries he conquered, but the silk weavers had, as Eugénie pointed out, revolted in 1831 and again in 1834 demanding higher pay and better working conditions. Memory of those insurrections and the growing unemployment in the city during the 1850s made the emperor nervous. Lyon now had a population of nearly 300,000 with more than 90,000—nearly a third of the city—employed in the silk industry. Any misstep by the emperor and empress could ignite another revolution. It was, the government declared, "à city to be watched." Eugénie bought the dress.

The reaction to the empress's new dress was immediate. Statistics from Worth's archives showed that the dress caused orders to snowball with hundreds of women clamoring for dresses of silk brocade. Within the next few months the number of Lyon looms in operation more than doubled from 57,500 to 120,000.

The effect on Eugénie herself was nearly as dramatic. She realized her new gown changed her image entirely. No longer did she appear as a light-hearted young woman in a frilly dress. This gown gave her the look she wanted to project: that of a serious woman, a woman in charge. And as a bonus, she had given the French economy a boost.

Encouraged by her success in helping to stimulate business in Lyon, she decided to take matters further. While serving as regent, she had read police reports that emphasized the silk workers' continued hostility to the regime. The empress saw those reports almost as a provocation, a dare, and she decided she would take it. She announced she would tour Lyon's silk factories during a stop on the imperial couple's trip to Switzerland in 1860. She dismissed pleas from government officials that she avoid what could be a dangerous situation.

The city of Lyon, aware of the government's opinion of it, was determined to convince Eugénie and Napoléon III that the fears were baseless, that Lyon was now a city as modern as Paris. The town turned itself into a stage set with draperies, tapestries and thousands of flowers to make everything the couple saw majestic. A photographer was hired to capture the ephemeral decor, and the city's librarian was commissioned to write a history of the visit.

In the midst of all the pomp and ceremony of an imperial visit, the strong-willed empress did not allow herself to be distracted from what she had come to do. She was going to make clear to the troublesome silk workers that the Second Empire understood their concerns and cared about them. Wielding all her charm, she toured one silk factory after another. She received polite if not enthusiastic receptions.

But she wasn't finished. To everyone's surprise, in one factory on her tour, Eugénie sat down at a shuttle loom—and began expertly operating it. The silk workers erupted in wild cheers which echoed throughout the factory. The city librarian, writing his report of the visit, gushed over the "so gracious and so beautiful Empress."

The empress had won their approval.

Or had they won hers? From then on, it was remarked that Eugénie regularly wore gowns of silk brocade woven in Lyon. She had gained an appreciation of the fabric, how it was made and how she could make it work for her.

She also had developed a fondness for Lyon. Perhaps the rebellious spirit of the canuts appealed to her independent nature. Perhaps she also felt gratitude for the impressive elegance that the luxurious fabric bestowed on her, because when there was another downturn in demand for silk brocade a few years later, she made a very public return to Lyon to attend a luncheon organized by wives of the leading silk manufacturers. They presented her with twelve gowns. The empress said she "was struck by the beauty of these tastefully chosen dresses" and promised to work to bring silk brocade gowns back into fashion.

BY COMMISSIONING GOWNS FROM WORTH AND WORKING WITH THE SILK INDUSTRY, EUGÉNIE had not only made a significant step in altering her own image, she had also fostered an entirely new segment of the economy in France: haute couture and luxury. It would become one of France's greatest and most durable economic factors and a treasured piece of its national identity.

Although haute couture translates literally as *high sewing*, through the years it become a catch-all term for *expensive fashion*, encompassing most aspects of the industry. At the time of Eugénie's reign, however, it was rigorously applied to clothes a designer created specifically for one woman. No one else would have the same; it would have been a serious faux pas—social suicide—for a society woman to appear in a dress like another woman's and would have cost a designer their career.

One of Worth's iconic dresses. *Victoria and Albert Museum, London, Dist. GrandPalaisRMN / Image Victoria and Albert Museum*

As the industry expanded, however, Worth grew increasingly concerned about maintaining the identity, quality and exclusivity of haute couture. Inspired by medieval guilds, he pushed to establish a governing body that would ensure its excellence. The result was the Haute Couture Federation, which today continues to enforce quality criteria. It annually reviews fashion houses to determine whether they meet its stringent regulations for membership. These regulations include the number of employees, the size of the workshop and the number of garments designed and produced. Usually, fewer than twenty are awarded the exacting and prestigious title that allows them to label themselves *haute cou-*

ture. The federation also sets dates for Fashion Weeks and monitors industry standards.

During the Second Empire, under Eugénie's influence, that industry grew rapidly and became the major employer in Paris and a key element in the French economy as it continues to be today. It burgeoned to include lace-making, pattern-cutting, embroidering, perfume-making, sewing, weaving, fan and glove-making and hundreds of other related crafts. It put thousands of people to work: Worth alone would employ 1,200 people in his workshops.

And in 1856, a new creation added even greater numbers of jobs to the industry when the craft of metal-working became part of high fashion.

The crinoline, or hoopskirt as it was sometimes called, had arrived, and with its metal bands it would define the silhouette, the look, of much of the Second Empire.

EVERY MORNING AT THE TUILERIES PALACE, A LUMBERING ELEVATOR MUCH LIKE A DUMB-waiter would descend from the wardrobes above the empress's private quarters, bearing four dress dummies clothed in the different outfits she would wear during the course of the day. Rumor said the clothes dropped directly onto her so that she was dressed "automatically."

The reality was more complicated and time-consuming. It began with undergarments. First, pantaloons, which were slit to make answering a call of nature more convenient. Then a slip, followed by a tightly laced corset, stockings and garters. After those items came the crinoline which Eugénie called her "cage." It was a contraption of concentric circles of steel and whalebone that did indeed look like a large birdcage. It slipped over the hips and fastened at the waist. Wearing one turned the voluminous skirts of the day into cotton-candy-like clouds of fabric.

There were problems, however. Crinolines seemed to grow wider with each season. Some held the skirts out so far that women could not slide their hands into the crooked arms of their male escorts, or even reach down to hold the hands of their children without tipping the cage onto its side. Even learning to sit in them required hours of practice. Despite the difficulties, crinolines became the must-have item in every woman's wardrobe. They dispensed with the need for multitudes of stiffened petticoats under the billowing skirts, and women wearing them seemed to be gliding like swans on water, all the necessary activity of movement hidden beneath the elegance above. In hot weather a nice cooling breeze might drift up underneath.

Men liked the cages, too. There was a seductive sway to a woman's movement in a crinoline, they said, and always a chance of someone bending over too far and providing a glimpse of things usually hidden. That was something the novelist Gyp, nom de plume of Sibylle Aimée Marie-Antoinette Gabrielle de Riquetti de Mirabeau, discovered when her uncle took her to the horse races at Longchamp in Paris. She was twelve at the time. "That day the Empress, whom I had never before seen close to, struck me as superbly beautiful," Gyp wrote. But even more fascinating were others at the racetrack. "All the women jumped onto their chairs. There was an ocean of cages balanced just above me, showing legs which all seemed to me to be short and heavy," the novelist said. Apparently, the only slender and attractive legs belonged to Princess Pauline von Metternich, who was wearing pink stockings with black garters under her yellow gown.

"When the race was nearing a finish all the women suddenly leaned forward, and the pressure of the cages against the backs of the chairs made them shoot up behind like a lot of fans," Gyp remembered. "And then I could see everyone's underwear right up to the waist."

Crinolines could be uncomfortable, and wearers frequently found themselves badly bruised. They presented serious danger, too, especially from fire. The dresses over them were particularly combustible because they were made of highly flammable fabric like bobbinet, cotton muslin, gauze and tarlatan. All were open-weave fabrics that created light, floating gowns which could easily burn. In 1860 alone nearly three thousand women died after their gowns caught fire. The following year Fanny Longfellow, wife of the poet Henry Wadsworth Longfellow, tried to preserve a curl from her daughter's hair by sealing it in an envelope. She did not notice when wax she was melting for the seal dropped onto her gown. It set the dress afire. Her husband tried desperately to extinguish the blaze and remove her crinoline, but in the process he suffered serious burns. Fanny was gravely burned as well and died soon after. Likewise in 1867, the Austrian Archduchess Matilda, aged eighteen and engaged to the future king of Italy, hid her cigarette behind her when she heard her father approaching. It ignited her gauze dress, and before she could be freed from the crinoline, she was severely burned. Like Fanny Longfellow, she died a short time later.

Despite the dangers, Eugénie said she liked her cage because it gave her "her legs." She could stride down hallways as quickly as she wanted; she could even roller skate or ice-skate.

But after her first term as regent, she was ready for a change, and so was Worth. He had grown bored with the endless gauzy fabrics and the crinoline and had new designs he wanted to try. Apparently he also had a share in the Lyon silk industry so that he could be assured of having the fabrics he wanted and increase his income at the same time. The brocade gown he presented to Eugénie was the result, and she began to see the sense of it: a sober gown for a serious role.

By then, she already had mastered what she termed her "political wardrobe" and had displayed it during the official visit she and Napoléon III made to Great Britain in 1855. On their arrival, Eugénie wore a silk gown in a tartan plaid pattern. It delighted Queen Victoria who had done much to make tartan popular after her purchase of Balmoral Castle in the Scottish Highlands. But the gown also served as a reminder of Eugénie's own links to Scotland. Her grandfather was a Kirkpatrick, a Scot from a family with extensive Scottish holdings and financial interests around the globe. It was, in addition, a hint that France was eager for sustained friendship with the United Kingdom as well as improved trade relations.

The empress, however, was nearly stymied by what to wear for the royal dinner at Windsor Castle that evening. The boat carrying the rest of her wardrobe—as well as her jewels and hairdresser—had been caught in a storm in the English Channel and had not arrived. The scene in her private quarters was frantic, but Eugénie remembered well her childhood days in plain linen dresses. She borrowed the simplest, plainest blue silk dress of one of her ladies, sent a maid to the gardens for flowers and asked her to do what she could with her hair. With a nosegay at her waist, flowers in her hair and all the elegant presence she had learned in lessons she'd had in her early days as empress with the actress Rachel, Eugénie was ready for dinner with Queen Victoria and Prince Albert. They were "charmed by her simplicity," the queen was to write in her diary, and the royal children were clearly in love with her. "I wish you were my mother," Princess Vicky, the Queen's eldest daughter, said to Eugénie.

Eugénie's political wardrobe was on display again when she and Napoléon returned to Paris. She was once more attired in a silk tartan dress to remind the French that the imperial trip had been conceived to emphasize cross-channel friendship and trade. The effects began to show up almost immediately: within five years, France would be sending nearly fifty percent of its export silk across the channel to markets in the United Kingdom.

Much of that trade was due to Eugénie's effect on fashion. She was, as one writer said, the "trendsetting fashionista of her day." Her gowns were described regularly in American publications such as *Godey's Lady's Book*, as well as in the French and British fashion press. Reporting about French fashion had steadily increased in the middle of the nineteenth century with the inclusion of hand-colored fashion plates in magazines, and women around the world clamored to see the latest from Paris.

When Eugénie wore a characteristically low-cut emerald

green evening gown to the opera in Paris in 1863 (she was vain about her beautiful shoulders), the press, at first, reacted with horror. How could she? journalists asked. Emerald green, they pointed out, was a color made by mixing copper with white arsenic, the highly toxic arsenic trioxide. For years the news had been reporting on deaths caused by the use of artificial pigments like the empress's green.

Eugénie, however, knew what she was doing. By 1859 a non-toxic alternative had been developed, and the safe pigment was gradually making its way into dressmaking fabrics. It was called *nouveau vert*, the new green or viridian green, and the empress, always interested in emerging technology, said she wanted to "celebrate the innovation" and promote its use. Fashion journals took note, and viridian green gowns suddenly began appearing in the fashion plates.

Thanks to the improved transportation of the time, there was also a growing availability of French products in the United States. American department stores, as well as specialty shops like Tiffany & Co. sent buyers—both male and female—to Paris, and some opened offices in the city. The empress's portrait was on display in shop windows throughout the United States and Europe as though she were a patron of the store. Styles and colors were named after her. The Eugénie Hat won fans when she was first seen in the almost Robin Hood style. Unsurprisingly, it was a hat she began wearing for riding because it was small and compact. Feathers attached to it floated gracefully behind as she rode. It was easier to manage than the large bonnets or wide-brimmed hats that perched on top of the head, and it could be packed without ordering a large hatbox.

There was the Empress Dress for daytime wear and the Imperatrice Dress for evening, and even a Eugénie Blue. Eugénie Blue previously had been called Nattier Blue, named after an eighteenth-century artist who used it often. It was a favorite color of Marie-Antoinette's, and now of the blue-eyed Eugénie who was trying to rehabilitate the Austrian queen's reputation.

One American was especially impressed when he saw the empress wear the color: John B. Young, who had come to Paris to buy for the store he and his partner Charles Lewis Tiffany had opened a few years earlier. Young carried a memory of it home with him and shared it with Tiffany, a master of marketing. The idea for the Tiffany blue box took root. (The date the blue box was adopted definitively by Tiffany is lost in history.)

The fashion press found a receptive audience for articles about Eugénie's wardrobe in upper-class women but also beyond them. Thanks to the advent of sewing machines and paper patterns in the 1850s, middle-class women could now create for themselves copies of gowns the empress wore.

Royalty, especially French royalty, had been seen as leaders of fashion ever since the time of Louis XIV, and royal warrants—that is, being granted use of a sovereign's name on a product—were the standard method of merchandising in the nineteenth century and a precursor to modern celebrity marketing. That exploded in importance when Eugénie came on the scene. Anything that could be associated with the empress was almost guaranteed commercial success. When one of her former dressmakers moved to London and set up shop, she advertised that she had been "seamstress to Empress Eugénie," and promptly became one of the most in-demand dressmakers in the English capital.

Even Worth, whose fame had become international by 1860 and who was the first to put labels in clothes, made sure to include *Dressmaker to the Empress* and her coat of arms next to his own name.

ANOTHER MARKETING TOOL THROUGHOUT THE NINETEENTH CENTURY WAS THE UNIVERSAL Exposition, or world's fair, such as the 1855 one in Paris. The fairs were seen as the best way to showcase a country's achievements and stimulate international trade. The city of Prague staged the first one in 1791 to celebrate the coronation of Leopold II as king of Bohemia. But it was Britain's Prince Albert who devised the template for the rash of fairs that followed when he organized the "Great Exhibition of the Works of Industry of All Nations" at the Crystal Palace in Hyde Park in London in 1851. It was the first world's fair to feature manufactured products as the major attraction.

Napoléon III was quick to follow suit. With his innate sense of salesmanship, he understood that the fairs were "massive, global productions that served the nationalistic interest of the contributing countries," and he scheduled the Exposition Universelle of 1855 in Paris. Although the stated goal was to highlight recent French triumphs in science, the emperor recognized the fashion industry had become a symbol of the brilliance of France and the beauties of Paris. Fashion would both attract crowds and bring in income for France's economy, so he encouraged its participation. The fashion industry responded in force with stands of jewelers, perfumers, couturiers, glove-makers—everything one could think of for the Exposition.

People of all classes poured into the fair, brought there on the expanded railroad network Napoléon III had championed as well as the faster steamships now crossing the Atlantic. It was when, as one writer said, Paris "was discovered by the middle classes . . . and from this time onwards, they came in increasing numbers."

It was the perfect confluence of time and beauty. Jacques Offenbach with his lively operettas was writing the background music for the gaiety of the city and its Exposition, and Empress Eugénie clearly was its star. She drove down the Champs-Élysées in her open carriage as the "ultimate expression of happiness, beauty and success." Every woman, it seemed, wanted to copy her style, her manner, her jewelry and her clothes—even Americans like the young Mary Sterling Rossiter from Maryland, who was presented to the imperial court that year. She wore a dress that was the exact style of one of Eugénie's. According to Emily Bach, curator of the Maryland Center for History and Culture, it was "a court dress that was a two-piece white taffeta gown with beautiful lace trimming and pink velvet geometric designs." The bodice was trimmed with strips of taffeta and edged with lace. Pink grosgrain ribbon bows were attached to off-the-shoulder sleeves and the skirt had three flounces, each trimmed with velvet. The dress is one of the few from the era to survive intact and is now in the Maryland museum.

Mary Sterling Rossiter's attire provides a hint of what one special dress, one Eugénie inspired for the Exposition Universelle, may have looked like. In the months prior to the 1855 world's fair, she had organized a lace-making competition to encourage and spotlight the labor-intensive craft. It took up to fifteen hours to make one square centimeter (about two-fifths of an inch) of *point d'Alençon* lace, making it easy to understand why point d'Alençon had long been considered France's "queen of lace." It was the most expensive lace in the world.

Eugénie said the lace competition would be for creation of accessories such as head scarves and shawls of lace. Twenty-five companies submitted proposals. One, Videcocq & Co., was chosen to make a headscarf in point d'Alençon. Two others were selected to make shawls of Chantilly lace, a black lace. But when the hand-crafted pieces arrived at the exhibition, organizers were stunned to discover that instead of a head scarf, Videcocq & Co. had submitted a dress completely made of point d'Alençon lace. The examining committee from the Ministry of Agriculture, Commerce and Public Works announced that the dress had "achieved an unprecedented level of perfection." It was worth at least 71,000 francs, the committee said. That would be $355,000 today.

The empress bought it, using her own private funds. What happened to the gown afterward is unknown. Although the original seems to have been lost, a pale shadow of what it must have been can still be seen in the Rossiter gown.

Lace-making, however, was not the only craft that drew Eugénie herself to shop at the Exposition Universelle before she secluded herself at Eaux-Bonnes to await the birth of her son. Lucky fairgoers would have seen her at one of the most dazzling exhibits, that of Mellerio dits Meller, a jewelry company which became a Second Empire favorite, thanks in part to the friendship between the empress and Jean-François Mellerio. The two had met when Eugénie and her mother first came to Paris in 1840 and found themselves enchanted by his work with beautiful jewels and his outstanding craftsmanship.

It was Chaumet who made Eugénie's most treasured piece of jewelry, a shamrock of emeralds studded with diamonds. The brooch was the first gift Napoléon had given her. It commemorated a romantic walk the two of them had taken during their courtship when Eugénie pointed out the beauty of clover sparkling with dew. She wore the pin nearly every day.

Empress Eugénie wearing the shamrock brooch on her dress for her first official portrait. *Edouard Louis Dubufe, GrandPalaisRMN (Domaine de Compiègne) / Image GrandPalaisRMN*

With the crown jewels now at her disposal, Eugénie frequently turned to Mellerio to have them reset in the more modern, naturalistic style she favored. She purchased small pieces of jewelry from him that she could give as gifts on her travels. She also bought more important pieces, which she saw as investments. She loved emeralds, diamonds and pearls and had a particular fondness for the black pearls from Mexico. She had a magnificent necklace made from them, which brought them into fashion for the first time.

Napoléon also went shopping at the 1855 Exposition Universelle. He bought Eugénie what was considered the most beautiful fan Mellerio had ever created. The leaves were the famous point d'Alençon lace and the frame was ivory, set with 783 brilliants and 251 rose-cut diamonds. Jewelry was his favorite gift to his empress, and he regularly purchased necklaces, brooches, earrings, bracelets and other items for her birthday and for Christmas. It was said that his wife's neckline displayed the affluence of the empire.

Fashionable women tried to emulate the empress, buying as many as twenty or thirty jewels every month to match their continuously changing wardrobe. Because court etiquette dictated that no one wear the same dress twice at an imperial function, regular visits to jewelers, glove-makers, as well as dressmakers were part of every society woman's routine. The boutiques and salons became social hubs and news sources of the latest scandals and affairs.

As these affluent women shopped and gossiped, they were enveloped in wonderful scents. The emperor's cousin, Prince Napoléon, had done a study after the 1855 Universal Exposition which, he said, revealed that "good smells are linked to better hygiene in the masses." Nice smells, said another writer, were part of "olfactive respect," or politeness. Dresses frequently included strips of cloth that had been marinated in perfume. Women made sure to daub a drop or two on their hands when they went out to be prepared for the *baisemain* as no one wanted to present a bad-smelling hand to be kissed. A few more drops went into the hair, so cheeks turned to receive a kiss also demonstrated proper "olfactive respect." Men were not forgotten in the Second Empire's pursuit of "olfactive respect" either. At least one house, Maison Tamisier, added an Eau Napoléon for its male clientele.

One particular scent wafted through the Second Empire: violet. Parma violets were the symbol of the Bonapartes, and the smell featured strongly in the most popular perfumes of the day. One supplier, Pierre-François-Pascal Guerlain, created a special perfume for the empress called Parfum Impératrice, which he decanted into a bottle covered with sixty-four golden bees, another Napoleonic symbol.

Eugénie made Guerlain the official perfume supplier to the court, but at least two other companies paid perfume homage to the empress as well: Rance 1795 and Creed. Jasmin Imperatrice Eugénie, the seductive floral and spicey scent Creed created for Eugénie, so impressed her that she convinced the house to leave London and relocate to Paris so it would be available to the court at all times. Creed said the mix of bergamot, rich vanilla and amber made a sensual fragrance of warmth and strength, much like the woman for whom it was named. Now, more than 150 years later, the company's flagship operation remains in Paris, and Eugénie's fragrance is still sold there.

THE SUCCESS OF EUGÉNIE'S NEW CLOTHES ENCOURAGED BOTH THE EMPRESS AND HER DEsigner. With his increasing success and confidence, Worth began developing a new silhouette that would be cut closer to the body with fabric gathered behind in a bustle.

Although Eugénie was pleased to see a new style develop, she said there was something else she wanted more urgently: shorter skirts. Long skirts got in the way of her outdoor activities, like climbing the Rhune mountain near her Biarritz villa. They slowed her down.

Eugénie organized what one historian called "a palace revolution" to change fashion. The empress encouraged her ladies-in-waiting to talk about the new style with friends and to order what they called walking costumes of their own. There was resistance; many in the court disapproved, but plans went ahead. Just make the dresses "sufficiently attractive to give wearers confidence and charm onlookers," the empress told Worth.

"Those happy changes in fashions," remembered Madame Carette, were not "a caprice of our elegant sovereign lady, but in truth it was a protest . . ."

Worth's response was proof he was a diplomat as well as a designer. He created a short crinoline that would please the traditionalists in court circles, and draped a tartan-patterned dress, now six inches off the ground, with a plain overskirt. It was a rather minor change and a graceful combination, but it was greeted with howls about the "growing immorality of the times."

Eugénie was not cowed. She and Napoléon had scheduled a trip in 1860 to the Savoy region, where they were to climb the northern slope of Mont Blanc in the Alps and view the Mer de Glace, the Sea of Ice. As they approached the largest glacier in France, the empress pushed aside the blanket that was covering her legs on the mule she'd been riding, hopped off, grabbed a walking stick and began to stride across the ice. Her ankles were showing.

IT WAS 1862 AND EUGÉNIE HAD DECIDED: IT WAS TIME FOR A NEW PORTRAIT. UNTIL NOW, HER portraits had been canvases from which Napoléon and the French public could see their own visions mirrored back at them. Now the empress was going to change that. When people looked at the new portrait, they would see what she wanted them to see: Eugénie, the real Eugénie, not a painted version of the idealized Frenchwoman.

Once again, Franz Xaver Winterhalter was called in, but this time the call came from Eugénie herself, not from Napoléon, not from the government. She would make all the decisions about this portrait.

She may have thought back nearly a decade to when the first

Dubufe portrait was painted. While it was being done, she wrote to her mother that she thought it would be a good one, but the public had a different reaction—she was too Spanish.

Now, after proving herself as the French empress and a successful, effective regent, she felt confident and ready to issue a challenge. She would remind people of who she was and what she had brought to France. People could make of it what they wanted. She worked closely with Winterhalter, overseeing every aspect of the life-size portrait she had hired him to paint.

Portrait of Eugénie that she commissioned to show herself as a reigning monarch and a woman in charge of her own destiny. By Winterhalter in 1862. *Casa de Liria, Wikimedia Commons*

She selected an ornate chair, one that resembled a throne, but on it was the coat of arms of the Alba family, the family of her sister and the most powerful family in Spain. Perhaps she was feeling defiant for, as in the repudiated Dubufe portrait, she chose a black gown and wore pearls. There was no question that her hair was red—no longer "carrots," but now a deep, rich auburn. She is captured in an unusual moment of stillness: contemplative, relaxed and secure in her role. She is bathed in light and gazing into the distance, toward the future. She clearly knows who she is and is comfortable with herself.

And Eugénie wanted no one to forget that she was an empress, so she added a deep royal blue robe with ermine trim. On her head is a simple but heavy diadem said to be in the Greek style, its only ornamentation an enormous diamond placed in the center.

In a final flourish, she handed Winterhalter an inscription to be painted with the date in Latin in the upper left-hand corner of the painting: *Maria Eugenia Guzman/Comitissa Tebae/Gallorum/Imperatrix/MDCCCLXII.*

A Spanish woman, a Spanish grandee, but empress of the French.

CHAPTER SEVEN

READIN', WRITIN' AND REIGNIN'

IT WAS A DAILY RITUAL. EVERY MORNING, THE EMPRESS ROSE EARLY TO BEGIN WORKING HER way through a stack of newspapers—most of them in French, some in Spanish, others in English and a few in Italian.

But on June 11, 1865, she was jolted awake when she picked up *L'Opinion nationale* and read the following words: "Our civilization now recognizes that women have a soul," the paper said. "The signature at the bottom of the following decree also shows they're intelligent, even when they're sitting on a throne."

Eugénie probably laughed out loud. So, she thought, now that I've signed a decree that says Rosa Bonheur gets to be the first civilian woman to wear the five-armed Maltese cross of the Légion d'honneur, the press has decided we women have soul and intelligence. Eugénie knew the artist Bonheur had plenty of both, and so did she, and she'd been fighting her entire life to prove it. She knew, however, that the strength and competence of women needed to be demonstrated repeatedly to make the male-dominated world accept it.

There'd been times when Eugénie felt her entire life was dictated by the words *should not*. What she should not do, what she should not wear, should not aspire to, should not attempt, should

not say, should not ask. Should not think. As empress, she was determined to banish *should not* from the lives of women and ensure
they had the same opportunities as men, opportunities most men
took for granted. The place to start, she believed, was education.

Unfortunately, women in the Second Empire of Napoléon III
were still living under a cloud that had hung over them since the
French Revolution when their behavior had shocked and frightened their male counterparts. Fearing starvation when the price
of bread, the staple of their families' diets, skyrocketed, women
staged a march on Versailles that successfully forced King Louis
XVI and his family back to Paris to address their complaints.
Their protest on October 5, 1789, became a catalyst for the events
and battles that would soon topple the monarchy.

Four years later, men were jolted again when Charlotte Corday fatally stabbed the radical journalist and politician Jean-Paul
Marat in his bathtub. Even the respected historian Jules Michelet
wrote that he believed women were to blame for many of the
problems of the time and were responsible for France's inability
to create a republic.

Women must be brought under control, declared nervous
Frenchmen from all levels of society. Our mothers, our sisters,
our wives, our daughters should not be engaged in politics.

No one believed that more strongly than a young Corsican
general who was coming to prominence as the first consul in the
post-Revolution French government: Napoléon Bonaparte. He
was convinced France needed a set of laws that would outline—
and curtail—the role of women. Those laws, embodied in the
Code Napoléon, denied women full citizenship. They were not
allowed to vote, own property or have money of their own. They
were banned from most jobs and subject to male control—first by
their fathers and then by their husbands. Divorce was outlawed
in 1816. Women were forbidden to wear trousers. Schooling, too,
was denied. Whatever they learned came from their mothers who
taught them how to prepare to be wives.

Women, then, were essentially servants with no say in their

lives . . . nothing more than chattel, but *valuable* chattel because of the amount of money in the form of a dowry they could bring to a man. As one feminist of the time put it, men, when referring to their wives, did not say they married a woman but rather, they "married a dowry" of such-and-such an amount.

With the Napoleonic Code, France, which had been a leader for women's rights through the eighteenth century, became, in the nineteenth century, the only country in the world to legally define and limit the role of women.

Napoléon III, nephew of the Napoléon who had created the repressive body of laws, had a more liberal outlook, but he was too busy building a modern country with a strong economy to get involved with women's issues. Eugénie, however, didn't hesitate to plunge ahead, embracing a cause that would absorb and galvanize her for the rest of her life.

In 1861, she learned about a woman named Julie-Victoire Daubié who had been refused permission to sit for the baccalaureate, the equivalent of an advanced high school degree. Although Daubié came from a poor family, her brother had managed to become a priest and recognized his sister's brilliance and yearning for an education. He was determined to help her. Under his guidance, Daubié quickly mastered Latin, Greek and German. She also learned history and geography and went on to study zoology at the National Museum of Natural History in Paris while supporting herself as a governess.

Daubié had first caught Eugénie's eye two years earlier when she'd gained national attention for her paper on women's poverty. Her well-thought-out and researched paper won a competition organized by the Imperial Academy of Science and Fine Letters of Lyon and was recognized by the academy as a "serious treatise on political economy." For the times, it was also a decidedly feminist document which laid bare facts showing that children as young as eight were laboring in dangerous conditions, that women were paid wages so low they barely escaped starvation, and that they received no education.

By the time she was awarded the prize, Daubié had already earned a *brevet supérieur de capacité*, a teacher's certificate, but as a layperson she was unable to find a real position because most schools were controlled and staffed by religious orders. She then applied for admission to university. French universities said *no*. A *bac*, the common nickname for the baccalaureate—was (and still is) a requirement for university admission, and she did not have one. Without a bac she could not earn a university degree, and without a university degree she could not qualify for a teaching position. It was a vicious circle that, in practical terms, condemned her to a life of penury and prevented her from advancing beyond her employment as a governess.

When Eugénie asked why Daubié had been denied permission to sit the bac exam, she was told Daubié did not have the ministerial permission required of all candidates for the bac. The empress was furious, but as her anger subsided, she recognized an opportunity. In Daubié, she had an ideal person for advancing women's rights.

Eugénie demanded permission to address the council of the ministry of education. Gustave Rouland, the minister of education and religious affairs, had been tiptoeing around the empress but realized he could not refuse a direct request from her.

Eugénie's impassioned appeal before the all-male council was successful. Like Rouland, council members realized they could not refuse the empress and granted Daubié permission to take the bac exam. But, they quickly added, she would have to do so like all other candidates. There would be no exceptions. That meant Daubié, who was thirty-seven, would have to join a group of seventeen-year-old boys in Lyon who were just finishing their high school studies.

It was a surreal moment as the slim, dark-haired, modestly dressed woman entered the examination room. The boys present were nervous, knowing their careers, their entire futures, rested on whether they passed the exam. Daubié's presence unnerved them further. Some sniggered as she walked in; others looked away. They had never before seen a girl in a classroom, let alone a woman old enough to be their mother.

Daubié seemed calm as she accepted the exam papers; they were the same as the ones the boys received and covered math, geography and history, French and philosophy. Can a woman do this? the boys wondered. More puzzling, why did she *want* to do it? Shouldn't she be married and have children? She'd never been to a lycée as they had, never taken the courses they had. And she was so old! Surely it wasn't possible she could pass, was it?

Results, or grades, were awarded as balls representing each of the four subjects. The jury could give candidates a white ball or a black ball or no ball at all for a subject. A single black ball would mean total failure—the student was blackballed from university admission and from most worthwhile employment. A white ball meant the jury was impressed with the work, a sort of A+ grade for the candidate. They had to be given at least one white ball— only one—to be awarded the coveted bac.

For the boys, the wait for results was excruciating. Daubié, however, was used to waiting and used to rejection. She went back to work.

Then, after days of anxious expectation while examination papers were reviewed and graded, came the announcement: Julie-Victoire Daubié had been awarded four white balls. It was an unheard-of accomplishment, a perfect result. For the first time, a woman had not only earned a bac but had earned it with flying colors.

Empress Eugénie rejoiced. She may have been more thrilled by the result even than Daubié, for she had put her own reputation on the line and that of the emperor as well.

But it was more than a victory. It was a gift to all French women, for all time. No longer would they have to stand aside and watch as men gathered all the acclaim and best jobs. They, too, could go to university and earn degrees. They, too, could now finally choose the futures they wanted.

ONE WOMAN. ONE BAC. EUGÉNIE KNEW IT WAS NOT ENOUGH. THERE WERE HUNDREDS OF thousands of other women who had almost no education available to them.

The women of midnineteenth-century France—women Eugénie knew and had grown up with—were nearly illiterate. Of those who were married, almost half could not even sign their names. Of the nearly 50,000 public schools in France, less than a quarter were for girls. None prepared their students for the bac but instead concentrated on giving girls a moral and religious education under the tutelage of nuns.

Middle- and upper-class girls entered these boarding schools or convent schools when they were eight years old and usually remained five years to learn "sobriety, patience, love of work, resignation, moderation in desires, simplicity in tastes," as one manual described the curriculum. The *"arts d'agrément"* or artistic accomplishments such as sewing, music and drawing, were paramount. For lower-class girls, the few schools available emphasized skills, especially sewing.

The arts d'agrément was the kind of education Eugénie herself experienced in her brief time at the Convent of the Sacred Heart in Paris. She hated it: it was useless and boring. She resolved to make a change.

The opportunity arose in 1863 when Napoléon III suffered a setback in general elections and several opposition figures won seats in parliament. Facing the new political reality but also ready to seize the moment as an opportunity to embrace a more liberal program, Napoléon shuffled his cabinet and named Victor Duruy minister of education. Duruy accepted on the condition that the post be limited to education and not coupled with religious affairs as was traditional. Napoléon agreed, even though good relations with the Catholic Church were a political necessity.

The Church, which controlled and staffed nearly all schools, was understandably upset and jittery about Duruy's anticlerical views. Napoléon, however, expressed full confidence in his new education minister, especially after Duruy, a renowned scholar, had assisted him in writing a book about Julius Caesar.

Eugénie was impressed with Duruy's credentials as well and convinced his appointment was a godsend. She and Napoléon had both had loose educations, with him admitting he'd been indifferent as a student and much preferring physical activities, like riding, to classroom work—but teaching himself what he needed to know to be emperor (he always claimed that the six years he spent studying, reading and writing while imprisoned in Ham were his university years). Eugénie, too, was more interested in outdoor, athletic pursuits, and she was also largely self-taught, learning politics and current affairs by listening and arguing at her mother's soirées. Their haphazard schooling made the imperial couple eager to establish an improved educational system that combined the intellectual with physical activity yet also recognized the needs of an increasingly modernized and industrialized France.

In Duruy, they believed they had the person who was essential in bringing that about.

Although French education had been a topic of discussion— and contention—for generations, there'd been little debate about what should be taught or to whom. Education was for boys; girls would learn to be wives and mothers and taught at home by their mothers.

Then, shortly after he became Prince-President in 1850, Napoléon had managed to carve out a small opening for girls. His minister of education then, Alfred de Falloux, ordered all communities with populations of more than 800 to establish elementary schools for both girls and boys. Even still, those for girls were run by religious orders and taught by nuns whose only qualification for teaching was a "letter of obedience" and assurances that they would provide "moral guidance." It was hardly surprising that many, if not most students, paid little attention to their instructors, preferring to gossip in the classroom or sneak out whenever possible.

Empress Eugénie could relate to that remembering how she and Paca had often played hooky. She knew that Victor Duruy, the new minister of education, had ambitious plans to reorganize secondary education and expand primary education, but it was a letter he sent her that grabbed her attention. "Young girls," he wrote, "must exercise and fortify their intelligence through the same instruction of their brothers in high school; they have the same rights as them and are capable to understand the teachings." She asked Duruy to come see her.

Duruy outlined his plans. He wanted to develop a certified teachers' training program so teachers would be, as he said, "soldiers of peace" to fight the "black horsemen of ignorance." He sought to expand the curriculum by bringing back philosophy, which had been dropped in 1852, and adding new classes. Chief among them would be modern languages which, he pointed out, would be far more useful to students than Latin and ancient Greek.

Schools were also to be reorganized to become more attuned to economic realities. Agricultural schools, for example, were told their pupils no longer had to study Latin. And then, with a final flourish that played straight to the empress's own agenda, he added that physical education should be part of schooling programs as well.

Eugénie was thrilled with what she was hearing, but Duruy wasn't finished. In what was considered a radical move, he said he would hire male teachers for the girls, men who had been educated at the Sorbonne—not just nuns. The expanded course of study would run at least six months a year for three or four years, and girls who successfully completed the program would be awarded a diploma. In another move that pleased Eugénie— for she was a devout Catholic—Duruy kept religion as part of the syllabus. Religion, he explained, was good for people; it just shouldn't be in control of education.

But as everything was moving swiftly ahead, Duruy's plans hit a wall. Because money was tight and constructing new schools would be expensive, he proposed that classes for girls could be taught in existing public buildings such as city halls. "What?" decried the bishop of Orléans, Félix Dupanloup. "You would send our young women into public buildings? Buildings that are frequented by all manner of men, and where there might be 'evil-living women'?" Other members of the clergy rallied to the bishop's cry and used their influence to intimidate families to keep their daughters home and out of school.

The matter escalated until it was brought to the council of the ministry of education. Church leaders were confident the council would back them and block Duruy's plan. After all, the Second Empire needed Church support, and the bishop of Orléans, their leader, had a reputation as a liberal who generally supported women's education. They also believed they had an ally in the empress, who attended mass daily. On top of all that, bishop Dupanloup was practically a member of Eugénie's family. He was the illegitimate son of the Italian Prince Borghese who had married Pauline Bonaparte, Napoléon III's aunt.

Therefore, everyone was dumbfounded when Eugénie threw her support behind Duruy.

The bishop, she said, is only interested in upper-class and aristocratic women, those who can afford private schools in private buildings. Even the ideas the bishop has for upper-class women are inadequate, Eugénie argued. He sees them only as "fitting partners" to their husbands, not as individuals in their own right. He completely ignores the needs of girls from lower-class families. They are the ones who would benefit most from the schools in Duruy's plans, she said.

But the empress was not done. In a further rebuff to the bishop, she announced she would send her nieces, her sister's daughters, to study with male professors from the Sorbonne. There, they could study sciences and other topics which would allow them to pursue professional careers if they wished rather than be merely "fitting partners."

With Eugénie's backing, the schools Duruy proposed were approved. They were a long way from the free universal schooling she and the minister of education had hoped for and they still did not prepare girls for the bac, but for the first time, they offered girls secondary courses that would make a difference in their lives.

The direction was clear: girls and women would be educated.

Eugénie had succeeded in removing one major *should not* from the lives of French girls and women.

EUGÉNIE UNDERSTOOD INSTINCTIVELY THAT POVERTY WAS THE RESULT OF MULTIPLE FAC-tors, not a question of character. Her father had told her she was destined for a life of poverty, and she knew he had been wrong about that. No one, she thought, should be destined for such a life. Her religion taught her people were not mere creatures of fate; everyone could play a role in their own lives.

She had seen for herself that most of the poor were women and children. Although upper-class women were expected to be charitable, Eugénie recognized that token approach did not begin to deal with the reality of poverty. Growing up in a family of traders and businessmen, she had seen how her maternal grandfather and uncles built an international company, how they ran factories and mines. For poverty to be eradicated, a structure, a plan was needed.

On becoming empress, she put her ideas into action and organized her personal office to support her actions. She poured money into it from her privy purse, her allowance as empress. To make sure it was managed correctly, the ever-pragmatic empress installed a widow named Madame Pellot, who had come with her from Spain. Pepa, as everyone called her, struggled with French but had no problem with numbers, surprising for the woman who had once told Eugénie that women were only meant to knit stockings. Everyone complained that Pepa was bad-tempered—she could even get angry with Eugénie—but Pepa ran the office with efficiency.

Delegating financial management to others, however, did not mean that Eugénie stepped back from charity work. In Paris, in 1865, a cholera epidemic was sweeping that city. Once, despite Eugénie being in a weak and pale state after suffering from a bad cold, she went from hospital to hospital, reassuring patients that everything possible was being done and that they would soon recover. The next year, when she learned of a cholera outbreak in Amiens, a city 95 miles north of Paris, she did not wait. She ordered her train, composed of seven cars, including a richly decorated family car where she, the emperor and their son shared the space when together. Accompanied only by Marshal Jean-Baptiste Vaillant, the former minister of war who was now the emperor's chief of staff, she went straight from the station to the city's main hospital. When she discovered two children orphaned by the cholera outbreak, she immediately made arrangements for their adoption by other families. She also set up interviews with people unable to work because of the epidemic and provided funding for them.

At a time when nobody knew how the disease spread, Eugénie took personal risks to her health to comfort the dying patients: she leaned over their beds, took their hands in hers and listened to them. Marshal Vaillant was shocked. "You're the empress," he said. "You shouldn't be doing that. You should take care of your own health." Eugénie turned to the old soldier and snapped, "This is what we women do when we're under fire!"

Even her fiercest critics had to admit that her actions had calmed the panic as news of the epidemic spread. Napoléon's staff saw the actions as a political boon and quickly took advantage of the empress's work to cast the Second Empire in a flattering and charitable light, distributing paintings and engravings of her visiting hospitals and notifying journalists so articles about her visits appeared in the press.

EUGÉNIE MADE SURE TO KEEP TRACK OF THOSE SHE MET, OFTEN FINDING JOBS OR HOMES for them and, on at least one occasion, bringing a young girl she'd met into the palace as one of her readers when she learned her family had become impoverished.

There were times when it seemed as though Eugénie must be living at a different pace than other people. Her days were non-stop, her plans and projects numerous, her willingness to face difficult situations unlimited. But people who knew or worked with her realized that her bursts of activity were frequently followed by times of near collapse and depression.

"Very highly strung, her good looks were easily affected by ill health or exhaustion," one historian noted. This was especially so after the birth of the prince impérial. Her temper, never placid, could switch from joy to anger faster than anyone could expect. And then switch back again.

She worked at full tilt to increase job opportunities and salaries for women, especially when her husband announced an expansion of the country's postal system. "Make sure the new jobs are earmarked for women," she told him. He complied.

When she and Napoléon visited Algeria, she learned that male physicians were not allowed to treat women—and there were no female physicians. As soon as she was back in Paris, she launched a medical school for women with female professors. Although Algerian Muslim women would be forced to wait until 1904 to be certified themselves for midwifery and medical care, Eugénie's breakthroughs and her attention to the matter during her reign helped pave the way.

Through all of this, Eugénie still faced constant criticism from men who denigrated women in general and the empress in particular. "To be a decorative sovereign unfaded by the passing years still gave her pleasure whenever she looked in the mirror," wrote one contemporary, "but it did not flatter her self-importance enough. She had to show the world she had more serious gifts, those of a politician."

BUT EUGÉNIE HAD AN ALLY IN NAPOLÉON III. HE HAD GROWN UP WITH AN INDEPENDENT-minded mother, Queen Hortense, and, perhaps that was the reason he had been attracted to Eugénie's vibrant and strong personality as well as to her beauty. He listened to her and trusted her judgment. If government ministers or others whispered about her headstrong ways or complained about her determination to improve women's lives, they were met with the cold stare and frozen silence of the emperor.

There was no question that he also supported the empress's social justice efforts and that his sympathies for the lower class matched Eugénie's. On one occasion he was heard to grumble to the empress, "I am frequently laughed at for wasting so much time trying to make myself popular with the working classes." Eugénie's response was quick and clear: "I don't think it's a waste of either time or effort." She paused, then, knowing her husband had great respect and affection for the British queen, added, "and I'm sure Queen Victoria would agree with me."

Eugénie was, wrote one historian, "a natural feminist." At a time in history when, as another writer noted, "women were practically invisible, except in the home, and not taken seriously as professionals," Eugénie was sending shock waves through the nation. She knew women needed to work, not only for money so they could lead decent lives but also for their own self-esteem.

But even with all Eugénie's concern for women and children, still she found ways to impress the hearts of men with her kindness. The sailors of the French navy, for example, would take steps to enshrine the memory of her kindness and practicality. In 1858, the imperial couple traveled to Brest on the tip of Brittany's Finistère peninsula to inaugurate a new bridge, the Pont Impérial, at the port. As the men of the fleet snapped to attention with the approach of the emperor and empress, one of the sailors hit his head on an iron beam on the gangway. The wound began to gush blood. Eugénie whipped out her white handkerchief and pressed it to his head to stop the bleeding. The handkerchief soon became red—and the idea of the red pom-pom on the *bâchi*, or sailor's cap, was born, an enduring tribute to her caring personality and love of everything about the sea.

CHAPTER EIGHT

MINISTRY OF CHARITY

NEARLY EVERY MORNING, AN UNMARKED CARRIAGE WOULD SLIP OUT OF A SIDE DOOR OF THE Tuileries Palace. In it was a veiled woman dressed in plain clothes and nearly buried under baskets of food, clothing and blankets. It was the Empress Eugénie heading to a hospital, an orphanage or a home for the impoverished.

Poverty had distressed her since her childhood. Her father's advice still rang in her ears: *Live a serious, useful life.* As a young girl, she would irritate her mother by arriving home late. She had been talking with poor people she saw on the streets, trying to find ways to help them.

Even as she readied herself for her wedding, surrounded by the trappings of wealth and royalty, Eugénie's emotions were weighted with thoughts of the poor. On the eve of the marriage ceremony, she wrote to her sister Paca that she was worried about how she would deal with the demands of her new role. "If the hand of Providence has given me such a high place, then it must be so that I can bring together the sufferers and those who could aid them."

Most of the poor, she knew, were women and children—women on their own struggling to support children, women who were ill, women escaping from brutal relationships, women left to suffer the consequences of rape or illicit affairs alone. As a young, single, attractive woman, Eugénie had fought off enough advances from men to have an understanding of the dangers faced by girls who did not have the protection of social status, family and wealth that she had.

Eugénie's solution to try to eradicate poverty was as modern as today's news: a microlending program. In 1862, she established an association that would loan small sums of money to young people to set up businesses or purchase the tools necessary for a trade. It was a radical idea that Eugénie made even more radical with an ecumenical move. She drew in both Grand Rabbi Uhlmann of the Central Council of Israelites and Cardinal Morlot, then-archbishop of Paris, as the organizers of the association.

Perhaps Eugénie was enjoying the opportunity to flex her social muscles and use the opportunity to taunt some old adversaries. In any case, she also brought in her frequent rival, Napoléon's cousin Princess Mathilde, and Princess Clotilde, wife of her nemesis Plon-Plon, and made them vice-presidents of her new association with her as president. The princesses may have squirmed, but there was no way they could refuse an appointment by the empress.

Then, in a perplexing move, Eugénie selected Octavie Haussmann, wife of Baron Haussmann, the man who was redesigning Paris, as treasurer. Perhaps it was a peace offering to her old foe, or maybe this was a bit of a jab at the baron who bristled if he had to dip into his budget for Eugénie's projects. Although she was scornful of Haussmann, she was fond of his wife and often invited her to Compiègne and Fontainebleau.

Eugénie went about her work with a missionary zeal, but she preferred to deflect the spotlight from herself, to spend her time and energy in work and not seek personal glory. This may well have been another aspect of her choice of well-known individuals for leadership roles, although part of her reticence came from her deep sense of duty and faith, of putting God above all. Yet her work would become so well-known that many saw her presence and visibility as vital. Images of her as a charitable figure were created and distributed widely. She became, as one historian wrote, "an instrumental force of social reform."

Unfortunately, nearly all of them focused on her as a beautiful, caring royal who dropped in to hand out charity, not as a hardworking woman dealing with problems and fiscal administration firsthand. Often, pictures of her charity visits, including sketches and cartoons in newspapers or reproductions of paintings, portrayed her at the side of the emperor—even though he had not been present.

Nevertheless, the significance of Eugénie's work struck a chord in the right places. Monseigneur Darboy, the archbishop of Paris who succeeded Morlot in 1863, wrote to the empress that she had "created a Charitable Ministry . . . an honor and a force for the government." He saw it as equal to the political ministries. It was, in many ways, a precursor to modern health and welfare departments.

Her staff for these endeavors consisted of a network of women she selected to direct her toward needy or sick families. In addition to using money from her privy purse Eugénie also bought a life insurance policy of approximately 2.5 million francs designed to ensure that her "Ministry of Charity" would continue even in the event of her death.

Beyond the model she set for health departments, Eugénie's organizational skills also created a template that charitable groups would copy and follow through the years down to modern times. She employed well-known personalities—titled figures were the celebrities and rock stars of the nineteenth century—to both attract the attention of volunteers and contributors and to reach out to diverse sectors of the population.

Eugénie's business acumen and clever personnel moves paid off as wealthy society women clamored to join in and contribute funds of their own. The empress made it clear, however, that those contributions were not what her association was about. She wanted investors from across society, especially children and young people. By making it easy for *everyone* to invest, the organization's capital would grow and its lending capabilities would increase. Just 10 centimes a week made you a shareholder, but those who put in 100 francs became *founders*.

What's more, in another move that presaged modern marketing, these founders received certificates featuring a cameo picture
of the empress. They also had their names published in a national
newspaper, which stroked their egos and inspired others to join.

The empress's program was an enormous success with offices in cities throughout the country. More than two thousand
people—most of whom had no other access to credit—applied
for loans in the first nine months of the program alone, and new
businesses sprouted in their wake: florists, shoemakers, mechan-
ics, hairdressers and more.

Through all of this, however, Eugénie never lost sight of problems on the ground. Although it was by legal decree that she took
over a role created by Queen Marie-Antoinette as head of the
Maternal Societies, it was Eugénie's personal commitment that
made all the difference. The Maternal Societies were designed to
aid poor, married women through their delivery and first year of
motherhood, but they had received little more than token attention in the years following the collapse of the First Empire. That
changed abruptly when Eugénie arrived on the scene.

Motherhood, Eugénie recognized, was both expensive and
dangerous. When she took over the Maternal Societies, nearly
30 percent of all newborns in France would not see their fifth
birthday. Nor would mothers live to see their babies safely into
adulthood. If they did not die in childbirth or its aftermath, as 8
percent of them did, they would struggle to feed their children,
face abuse and/or live with the certainty of poor sanitation and
nutrition. Many women could not afford to pay for a midwife or
hospital care for their labor, let alone the costs of providing the
food and clothes a baby required. Fathers usually were of little or
no help. The story was told of a farmer who was more upset about
the death of his cow than the death of his wife. "It costs money to
buy another cow," he said, "but I can get another wife for free."

Babies, even legitimate ones, were frequently abandoned at
the *tours* or "circulars" of *enfants-trouvés*, the foundling hospitals.
Tours were revolving boxes in which a mother placed her baby,

rang the bell to call a nun and then vanished into the night. The nun on duty then pulled the box with the baby around through the opening and into the care of the state. The *tours* were abolished as one of Napoléon III's early acts.

Now, under Eugénie, Maternal Societies stepped into the breach and supplied a year's worth of the child's needs and help to the mother, who, in turn, had to agree to breastfeed the baby for its first year and have the child vaccinated against smallpox.

Eugénie demonstrated her adroitness in political affairs and public relations when she took on the Maternal Societies. The Societies technically fell under the ministry of the interior which provided a subsidy for their work. To ensure continued government support, Eugénie appointed Countess Walewska, wife of an illegitimate son of Napoléon I who was the minister of state, and the Duchess of Trévise, spouse of the emperor's chamberlain, as vice-presidents. Both women were wealthy (the duchess was heiress of an entrepreneur whose interests included vast wine properties), which was a guarantee of fund-raising success. Eugénie further exploited that with the addition of other rich and prominent women whom she named *Dames protectrices*. The empress herself was a major contributor, but she also used her influence and that of her board members to win bigger subsidies from the government.

Knowing full well the problems facing pregnant women were not limited to Paris, Eugénie pushed to expand operations throughout the country in cities like Lille and Bordeaux. She followed the model she had established in Paris and chose prominent citizens as presidents for regional societies, reviewing their reports and meeting with them regularly. Within the first three years of her presidency, the number of women helped by Maternal Societies expanded nearly fivefold, from 561 in 1862 to 2,656 in 1865.

But it was a double-edged sword, she soon discovered. As numbers increased, so did the cost of health care, which meant a greater financial strain on the very families Maternal Societies were designed to help.

As a mother herself and one who had undergone a painful miscarriage and an excruciating delivery, Eugénie was extremely sensitive to the bond between mother and child. The fact that a child was born illegitimately only increased her concern. As a youngster, she had followed Romani bands and wandered the streets of Granada and then Paris. Those experiences showed her the harrowing circumstances that could force an unwed mother to give up her baby. With her deep love for her own son, she could well imagine the anguish of a woman placing her child in a revolving box in the door of a foundling hospital, ringing the bell, then hiding to watch as a nun carried the baby away from her forever.

That sparked another initiative, one aimed at reuniting abandoned children with their mothers. Unfortunately, Eugénie's work in this field was largely ignored or even hidden. Most reformers thought that abandoning an illegitimate child was the best way to prevent abortion and infanticide, and they could not accept that the best prevention was to provide an unwed mother with a way to deliver her child safely and then help her gain access to work to care for herself and her child. As a result, Eugénie's efforts to help unwed mothers and to bring mothers and children together again was done away from the press and palace circles. Because of that, what success she had—if any—remains unclear.

Despite Eugénie's efforts and improvements in nutrition, the low status of women and their poor economic condition meant mortality rates remained stubbornly high. She was far from discouraged, however, and merely redoubled her efforts. In one week alone, while she was also running the country as regent, she created two day-care centers, or *crèches*, for children under age two whose parents worked outside the home. Then in one single month she organized five more crèches and appointed women to run them. She chaired the committee to reform *salles d'asile*, preschools for children aged two to six years, replacing the four- to five-hour classes with outdoor recreation time and classes more appropriate for children so young. Nearly 1,000 new preschools were created under the empress's direction, with the number of pupils increasing by almost 150,000.

Soon after the birth of her son, the prince impérial, Eugénie created an orphanage system for boys who'd lost both parents and were homeless. She put the emphasis on adoption into a "loving environment" where boys could learn a specific trade. In the first months of its operation, the *orphelinat* saw a hundred and forty boys adopted, no small achievement in a country where adoptions were almost nonexistent. The system drew much of its support from a public subscription in honor of the empress and the baby prince, whom Eugénie made titular head of the orphelinat. She asked that donations be limited to between 5 and 25 francs to insure "equality among donors." There would be no large gifts from those seeking influence. More than 600,000 people responded. When the empress was asked by the directors of the orphanage what they should do to honor her for her work, her response was simple: give me a list of those who supported the program so I can thank them. Her orphanage and adoption system was soon recognized and copied internationally.

If her efforts for children weren't enough, she also took on the Hospital for the Blind, adding a program for outpatients, increasing pensions for many at the same time. She did the same for France's war veterans and provided help for their widows and families. As head of the Central Society for the Rescue of Shipwrecks, she insisted on installing coastal nautical signals that became essential lifesaving tools.

Eugénie's work, especially her successes, did not go unnoticed. In 1865 Napoléon III legally placed all charitable institutions previously under the minister of the interior in the empress's hands, including those for the deaf, the blind, the mute and people suffering mental health conditions.

Convalescent homes (*asiles impériaux*) were also in her portfolio. For the male patients, she introduced a lecture series for those recovering from work-related injuries. It drew notable speakers from both the arts and the sciences, many of whom later published

their speeches as papers. For the women's *asiles*, Eugénie established a library and nursery where they could spend time with
their children while they were recovering. But no lecture series.
Was it because of the prevailing attitude that said women's brains
were less developed? Or was it because the male speakers refused
to "bother with women?"

Unsurprisingly, the criticism still came for Eugénie. At times
the papers even used pornographic cartoons to express their in-
dignation. She's acting more like a man, others said, in grudging
respect.

Eugénie, however, was also a master of persuasion and clever
enough to find ways to compromise. And she could change her
mind when faced with facts.

Such was the case when an opposition politician named Émile
Ollivier began agitating for prison reform. Eugénie first tried to
woo him with charm and dinners at the royal residence. Unsuccessful, she began to question why he was so committed to the
reforms and, taking Charles de La Vallette the interior minister
along, made a surprise visit to the infamous La Roquette prison
for young offenders in Paris. She was horrified.

The Roquette, built in 1836, was a panopticon, a semicircular
building designed so that one person standing in a surveillance
tower could theoretically have visual access to all prisoners at
once. The prisoners were to work in groups during the day then
be in solitary confinement and silence during the night. However, by the time Eugénie visited, all five hundred boys imprisoned there were locked in solitary day and night. The suicides,
premature deaths, and the number of prisoners with mental illness at La Roquette had generated denunciation by physicians and
patrons which caught Ollivier's attention.

Eugénie visited every cell in the forty-year-old prison and spent
time talking to the boys, who were between six and sixteen years
old. Some booed and insulted her, but others were subdued and
despondent. Eugénie was "overwhelmed with pity" and shaken by
the visit. In an immediate about-face, she threw herself behind Ol-

livier's reforms. The following day, La Vallette asked her to head a commission of twelve prominent people (the empress was the only woman) to inspect every prison for young offenders. Ollivier was also put on the committee with men from the medical and legal professions as well as the Paris préfet of police, the archbishop of Paris, and Baron Haussmann, the préfet of the Seine.

The empress called a meeting for the next day and outlined a program of work for prisoners, citing a law authorizing training in agriculture for young offenders which had been on the books since 1850 and which would allow implementation of the work program.

Baron Haussmann was violently opposed. Anything that had the potential to upset "the public order" or interfere with his work renovating Paris was anathema to him. Perhaps he had spent too long as a civil servant, Ollivier suggested in his memoirs, and that had hardened him to charitable causes, or at least blinded him to the problems. When the empress brought up the 1850 law for discussion, Haussmann shocked commission members, especially Eugénie, by ridiculing it and throwing it back in her face. He railed against the "softness" of people in power and "greed" of the lower class. Eugénie held her ground and gained the support of the commission's members to move the boys from La Roquette to farms (*colonies agricoles*) specifically designed to train young prisoners in agriculture.

The two most famous training farms were Saint-Bernard, near Loos in northern France, and another at the château of Guermanez. Eugénie visited both colonies in August 1867. She was satisfied by the good care of the children at Saint-Bernard and the management of its agricultural colony, but Guermanez dismayed her. She found the children were undernourished, poorly cared for and poorly dressed. They were unhappy, and the building where they lived was dilapidated. She ordered the immediate closing of Guermanez and dispatched the children to other farm schools, including the neighboring Saint-Bernard.

Knowing Eugénie had the emperor's support, the commission's work went ahead with the empress now determined to check the state of other prisons. She zeroed in on those for young women such as the Saint-Lazare Women's Penitentiary. Don't go there, begged the préfet of the Paris police. Was he worried about her safety? Or concerned she would be offended by what she saw and heard? Eugénie didn't hesitate. With the préfet and de la Vallette in tow, she arrived at the penitentiary unannounced. She *was* appalled by what she heard and saw; it was a situation as bad as any she had previously seen. Rather than being offended, she went on the offensive. She went from the kitchen to the infirmary and to each and every cell, all the while talking to the girls imprisoned there. She promptly ordered better health care for those incarcerated and general improvements throughout the prison.

Around the time that Eugénie was managing all of this, Napoléon had fallen ill, exhausted by his recurrent bladder stone attacks. He was forced to recuperate at the thermal baths in Plombières and left Eugénie to preside over ministerial meetings. But rather than back down from her prison reform projects, she took advantage of the situation by doing something no one, certainly not Haussmann, expected: Eugénie called up the ancient tradition of French rulers freeing prisoners on the king's birthday. When August 15, the birthday of the first Napoléon arrived, Eugénie ordered several boys from La Roquette freed.

Years later, in describing his work with the empress, Ollivier said, "I was struck by her ability to understand and discuss everything, by an intelligence that always saw the point." Although Ollivier was, at that time, an opponent of the Second Empire, his respect and admiration for Eugénie was clear.

He was, in fact, one of the few who even noticed her work on behalf of female prisoners. The press, which lavished coverage on her visits to prisons for men and boys, completely ignored Eugénie's visit to Saint-Lazare.

Those prisoners were just women, after all.

CHAPTER NINE

EMPRESSING

THERE WAS GOOD REASON NAPOLÉON HAD BEEN NICKNAMED "THE SPHINX." HE WAS HARD to read and rarely confided in anyone, but he was honest with himself. He realized he was in a precarious position. He was nearly twenty years older than his wife, he was beset with stomach problems and gout, and he was a heavy smoker. His son, his heir, was little more than a baby.

There was only one person to whom he could entrust the future of his dynasty and the future of France: Eugénie.

During the first three years of their marriage, Napoléon had begun to realize what an asset his wife was to his regime and to understand she was far more than the beautiful woman he had lusted after. Although she did not have the experience of a skilled diplomat—her face could reflect every thought, every emotion— she *did* possess the kind of charm and openness that made diplomats and other politicians eager to meet and talk to her. She was the perfect complement to his reserved character. She was also loyal, energetic and committed to the same values he was.

After years of traipsing around Europe with her politics-mad mother and, later, at Napoléon's side, Eugénie had developed a fascination for international politics and gained a special understanding of the figures who dominated it.

At the same time, Napoléon recognized that Eugénie, on becoming the mother of the heir to the throne, had won the regard and affection of the public. Because of her health, he knew sharing her bedroom was out of the question; sex was something he could find almost anywhere, though.

But a woman who could help bring his dreams to reality, who could run the country? She was no mere "ornament"; she was the rare jewel the emperor and France needed.

Napoléon announced Eugénie would be their son's legal tutor, or guardian, in the event of his death, and that she would be regent, the person governing France, whenever he was absent.

In January of 1858, eighteen months after the prince impérial's birth, Eugénie confirmed his assessment of her in a very public manner. She and the emperor were to attend the opera. As their carriage arrived, three grenades exploded, killing at least twelve people and wounding many others, including the emperor whose lip was cut by flying glass. One of Eugénie's eyelids was cut, too. Blood from the two injuries stained her white gown as she stepped out of the carriage. Police tried to hurry the imperial couple to safety. "Stop worrying about us," Eugénie told them. "This is our job. Take care of the wounded." She then pushed the emperor ahead into the theater where they received an ovation. Spectators said the emperor seemed unnerved, that one of his eyes was twitching uncontrollably, but that the empress appeared calm.

The explosions had been orchestrated by Fabrice Orsini and a group of Italians who were convinced Napoléon III had reneged on a commitment to support Italian unification. In truth, the emperor still favored unification but knew it would not be possible until Austria was forced to give up the Italian provinces it controlled.

In May of 1859, despite concerns about his lack of military experience, Napoléon left for Italy to lead the French army in support of Sardinia, the Italian kingdom leading the fight to drive Austria out of the peninsula. In his absence, Eugénie would be empress-regent for the first time. Knowing there would be complaints, Napoléon had named his uncle Prince Jérôme, youngest brother of Napoléon I, as coregent. Jérôme, flighty and frivolous, was essentially a figurehead placed to quiet the worst critics of female leadership.

Addressing the ministerial council at her first meeting, she acknowledged the difficulties ahead but vowed that with the ministers' help she would overcome them. The press was astonished to see a woman at the head of the council but would soon be impressed.

Over the course of the next two months, Eugénie chaired ministerial meetings—which could drag on for hours—at least twice a week. Among the items on the agenda was the assimilation of villages on the edge of Paris into the city itself. This meant she had to work with Baron Haussmann, the préfet of the Seine, with whom she often feuded. During her regency, however, she gained the baron's cooperation to nearly double the number of arrondissements, or city districts of Paris, from twelve to twenty. It was not a simple task. One village, Passy, was outraged to discover it was about to become the thirteenth arrondissement. Until then, unmarried couples living together were laughingly said to have been wed at the city hall of the fictional thirteenth arrondissement. "No way," said the righteous Passy villagers. "We don't want that onus on us."

Eugénie and Haussmann came up with a system that numbered the arrondissements like the shell of a snail. With the Notre-Dame Cathedral area number one, the arrondissements curled around, and Passy came up as the morally acceptable number sixteen. The area around the famous Gobelins Tapestry complex became (and remains) the thirteenth. No problem: Gobelins had become arguably the best maker in the world of tapestries by weaving diverse strands together. It could handle a tangle and still keep its reputation.

As regent, Eugénie pored over the weekly reports from the police and France's provinces and was pleased to find that the public generally approved of France's participation in the war for Italian unification. She also kept a close eye on it and saw news from the front as a public relations opportunity.

When Napoléon cabled her with news of a victory over Austria at Magenta, she ordered the cannons at Les Invalides fired and had his cable read out in the streets: *A great victory*, it said, *5,000 prisoners, 15,000 of the enemy killed or wounded.* Although the empress was shaken by the reports of casualties, she gathered up Clotilde, the Italian princess married to Plon-Plon, and drove with her through the cheering crowds on the streets of Paris, their way lit by bonfires and fireworks. She asked the archbishop of Paris for a *Te Deum* mass to be sung at Notre-Dame Cathedral and for parish priests to do the same throughout the country.

Three weeks later, Napoléon sent the colors of the defeated Austrians to Paris after the victory at Solferino, and this time Eugénie took the three-year-old prince impérial with her to Notre-Dame. They were nearly buried under the masses of flowers tossed into their carriage by the celebrating Parisians.

There was a more immediate concern, she warned—the increased militarism she saw developing in Prussia. She believed Prussia was taking advantage of the war in Italy in hopes Austria would weaken itself so Prussia could gain ascendancy in the German-speaking world. "No amount of assurances of peaceful intent on your part is going to satisfy Prussia," she wrote to her husband. The Italian unification movement was stirring up a call for a similar unification in the German states, she said, and Prussia was the chief protagonist. "End the war as quickly as possible and hurry home," she wrote, because it would be disastrous if Prussia were to join the Italian war on Austria's side.

At the heart of the Italian war, lay the question of the Papal States and Rome. Was it political or religious? Should the pope be the temporal ruler of part of the Italian peninsula or should his role be confined to governing the Church? Eugénie, like most French Catholics and the government itself, thought the Italian problem was religious. The pope's authority was spiritual and definitely not based on the amount of territory he controlled. It was only fair, she believed, that territories, such Emilia or Umbria, gain independence from papal control. Émile Ollivier, a republican and supporter of Italian reunification, who had worked with Eugénie on prison reform, recognized her objectivity in spite of her faith: "She was Catholic, but not a fanatic dominated by the Jesuits or the ultramontanes. She rallied to the official position of her husband and his government." (The ultramontanes were extreme conservatives who believed in the supreme authority of the pope.)

After a mere two months, the victorious French army returned home in July 1859, bringing with them a gift: the Italians had awarded France the territories of Nice and Savoy as a thank-you for its help, a small token for the lives of tens of thousands of French soldiers lost in the war. Napoléon led the army down the Champs-Élysées in a triumphal parade that Eugénie organized. Even Jérôme had to admit he was impressed with her accomplishments and "her clear, strong and so French judgment."

Many people were surprised that during her two months as regent, Eugénie had not reduced her commitment to the Ministry of Charity. Rather, she had expanded it, organizing a committee to collect and distribute funds to families of soldiers and sailors killed in the war.

She had enjoyed the work, she told Napoléon, and was eager to continue in a political role. When Napoléon scheduled a long official trip for them, she saw it as an opportunity to continue her involvement. The trip was designed to welcome France's new *comtés* of Nice and Savoy, but it also included a Mediterranean voyage that would take the imperial couple to Corsica, ancestral home of the Bonapartes, and on to French-controlled Algeria. Once the itinerary was set, Eugénie prepared a list of what she wanted to do at each stop, activities that would demonstrate her expanded role and carry her beyond the traditional accepting of bouquets and ribbon-cutting. Her goal was to meet with local people and learn their needs. She sent her list to General Émile

Fleury, Napoléon's longtime aide who was charged with organizing the trip.

It was a juggling act, Fleury acknowledged, with the distances to be covered, all the different means of transport—trains, boats, carriages—and the requests coming from towns and organizations who wanted the imperial couple's presence, in addition to the personal demands from the empress. "How can I find the means to satisfy all the exigencies?" he wondered. He produced a detailed itinerary that set the day and time for every event, and included tickets for those authorized to attend each.

Napoléon and Eugénie left the royal château at Saint-Cloud August 23, 1860, and boarded one of France's new trains to carry them to Chambéry, at the base of the Alps. Chambéry was the traditional capital of the county of Savoy, and there was a special satisfaction in arriving there as the Savoy had been pried away from France when Napoléon I was defeated. Now, his nephew, another Bonaparte, a victorious one, was there to welcome it back. In addition to the official events, the imperial couple wanted to see the glacier called the *Mer de Glace*. It had been named by two British explorers, William Windham and Richard Pococke, a century earlier, but it captured the public imagination fifty years later when Mary Shelley let Dr. Frankenstein's monster loose to wander the glacier. Eugénie would create her own sensation on the Sea of Ice when the short skirt she wore revealed her ankles.

From the Alpine glaciers, Eugénie and Napoléon descended via Grenoble and Marseille to the Mediterranean coastal village of Nice. It, too, was an appropriate destination as the city had been named after the goddess Nike, the one who brings victory. "You should come here in the winter," said Countess Mathilde de Cessole, one of the young women chosen to accompany the imperial couple on their visits. "When the rest of France is covered with snow, we have sunshine and palm trees." Although the city had been decorated and crowds were welcoming, it was a tense visit. Many residents preferred their connection to Italy and had moved out of the country. They resented having French named the official language when they had spoken Italian their whole lives.

Eugénie was fretting and exhausted by the time they arrived in Nice after numerous stops along the way, and she let Napoléon make the climb to a château alone. She was worried about her sister Paca, whom she had brought to Paris a few months earlier for medical treatment after she had been diagnosed with tuberculosis, and she was missing her son. She wrote to him, "My dear little Loulou, I am in Nice, a pretty little village that your papa has brought back to France. But everyone asks me about you and when you are going to come here. I tell them you will come when you are bigger." She went on to explain that she would next visit Corsica and the "modest house where your uncle Napoléon was born and from which he departed to conquer the world. You will also have to visit it when you're older because all the memories of our family are there."

The Corsican visit was emotional, with a raucous welcome of guttural cheers and clapping. Eugénie loved it, and it revived her: she smiled and enthusiastically waved to the crowd. After seeing the Bonaparte house, she returned alone to the carriage to rest, but there were people all around. She motioned them closer and once again was besieged with questions about the *chiuccu*, the little one, in the dialect of Corsica. "Do you want to see him?" the empress asked the crowd. She unpinned from her shawl the medallion with a painted portrait of the prince and passed it to the nearest woman who kissed it reverently and then it passed from person to person, each one kissing the likeness of the prince impérial. The empress was so touched, tears began to trickle from her eyes even as she smiled at her visitors.

On September 16, 1860, Eugénie and Napoléon arrived in Algiers on the yacht *l'Aigle*, the first European sovereigns to visit the country which had been conquered by France in 1830. Although the visit was to begin in Algiers on the Mediterranean coast, it was to be followed by a trip to the more rural, less Europeanized area of the country.

Algiers's population of 50,000 was such a mixture of ethnicity—Arabs, Kabyles or Berbers, Jews, Europeans—and languages that it startled the journalists traveling with the imperial couple.

Its cosmopolitan mix must have reminded Eugénie of Granada, and she quickly zeroed in on the women of the town. When the veiled Muslim women came to call on her, she sent away the male guards and invited the women to unveil so they could talk freely.

Jewish women came to see her, as well. They had a fondness for Bonapartes as Napoléon I had made the Jews of France citizens. They brought the empress an engraved fan of ostrich feathers and pearls which she treasured (now on display in the château de Compiègne).

On September 18, Eugénie was scheduled to be the star of the day for the inauguration of the Boulevard de l'Impératrice, a mas-

Fan offered by the Jewish women of Algiers to
Empress Eugénie in 1860. *Musées de Compiègne,
GrandPalaisRMN (Compiègne) / Christian Jean*

sive development of parks, promenades, shops and other buildings along a broad street that linked the port to the center of Algiers.

But all the joy went out of the day when she was told there had been a telegram saying her sister Paca had taken a turn for the worse and was gravely ill. The Algerian visit would be cut short and the trip to the interior canceled so that Eugénie could immediately return to Paris. A storm had risen in the Mediterranean, but the empress was in a panic to get home, so as soon as the emperor completed the last formalities in Algiers, they were gone.

What the empress did not know was that it was already too late. Paca had died just as they reached Algeria. The emperor had been told days earlier about Paca's deteriorating condition but had kept the news from Eugénie. He also withheld another telegram asking that Eugénie return immediately because her sister was dying. And when the third telegram arrived, this one saying Paca had passed away, he kept that from his wife as well.

It was not until they arrived back in mainland France that Eugénie learned the truth.

The empress was distraught. Shock, grief, anger, all rocked her frame. How could her husband have let her bask in the cheers of the crowd as her sister lay dying? How could he have denied her the chance to be with her sister at the time she needed her most? How could she ever stand to look at him, talk to him again?

What would she do without Paca? And Paca's children, what now for them?

There was another shock waiting for Eugénie when the couple arrived in Paris. Paca's funeral had taken place just two days earlier, and she had already been buried.

The empress could no longer face her husband. She had to leave, get away from him, from Paris, from France, from everything they represented.

She fled to Scotland, home of her mother's family. She may have been considered Spanish, but she also had the blood of the strong, resilient Scots running through her veins. Nonetheless, she was also worried about her own health. She was coughing a great deal and unable to sleep. The specter of Paca's illness hung over her. Was she about to suffer the same fate? Her first stop, however, was London, where she visited Queen Victoria and Prince Albert. They avoided politics and hardly mentioned Napoléon. Victoria later wrote, "She gave me such a melancholy impression as if some deep grief and anxiety weighed upon her."

Napoléon and the court propaganda machine worked to make the best of it. The empress is concerned about her health in the aftermath of her sister's death, so she is going to visit a specialist in Scotland, they announced to the press. The emperor wrote to her daily telling her their four-year-old son was asking when Mommy was coming home. When those appeals produced no results, he began writing her about day-to-day business, adding, finally, that he hoped she was in a better frame of mind and had forgiven him.

Eugénie visited a cousin in Scotland, then a doctor who reassured her that her cold was not tuberculosis and that she was not suffering from what had afflicted Paca. She could relax: her health was good.

She knew she could not stay away forever, and a separation from her husband was out of the question. She was a mother and she missed her son. Besides, Eugénie was still empress of the French. However, she needed to find peace of mind. When she returned to France, she knew it had to be on her own terms.

She gathered strength as she headed back to London. All along the way, people turned out to greet her and cheer her. Her, not the emperor, just her.

Eugénie remained there another week, staying at Claridge's hotel. Victoria and Albert came to pay her a visit. The queen was happy to see Eugénie in "much better spirits and looking very pretty." Eugénie chatted about all she was doing and seeing in London but carefully avoided any mention of her husband. "Altogether very strange," wrote a puzzled Victoria. The British press, which had followed Eugénie's trip in Scotland, noted her arrival:

"The Empress looks much better since her journey, and has expressed warmly the kind reception she met with, particularly in Scotland. She wears a tartan shawl which I suppose she bought in Glasgow."

There are no records of what might have passed between the imperial couple privately when they were finally reunited, but Napoléon was on the dock to welcome her when she landed in France, five weeks after she had left. He kissed her, and they boarded a train to Paris.

But Eugénie was not quite finished. She arranged the transfer of her sister's remains to Spain and then had one more thing to accomplish before her grief and anger could be played out: she demolished the house she had built for Paca.

When she returned from her escape to Scotland in December, seeing Alba House where Paca had died was like a slap in the face. Her sister, her freedom, her husband's fidelity, her youth, even her ability to have more children—they were all gone, but Alba House was still standing, a baleful reminder that she had not been there when her sister needed her most at her side, when she herself needed most to be there.

Her response was visceral.

"Tear it down. Nobody will ever inhabit Paca's bedroom," Eugénie wrote to her widowed brother-in-law, the Duke of Alba.

In a paroxysm of guilt and grief, she went through the house frantically removing personal objects and cherished items, and by February 1861, just three years after it was completed, nothing was left. All traces of Alba House had been erased. The land on which it had stood was sold, and the money she had borrowed to build it was repaid.

IN THE MONTHS THAT FOLLOWED, EUGÉNIE BEGAN TO REGAIN HER COMPOSURE. SHE SPENT hours playing with Loulou and looked carefully at the lives of other people, especially women. She was determined to regain her own "sense of meaning" by doing more to help them and by moving beyond her own pain and anger. Her hopes found expression in a prayer she wrote during that time for her son: "Only in putting the past behind me can I find happiness."

Eugénie had always had strong charitable impulses, but now her ecumenical outlook also became clear in her work. She continued her support for the pope's temporal powers but said "It is more against *unbelief* that we should fight, rather than differences in belief."

Her American dentist, Thomas Evans, remembered her telling him, "There is but one justice before God, and it belongs to all men alike, rich or poor, black or white, Catholic or Protestant, Jew or Gentile." She worked closely with the Grand Rabbi of France and donated large sums of her own money to Jewish charities.

She took on a more militant character in all aspects of her life, from her quest for jobs and better pay for women to her involvement in the foreign policy of the Second Empire. She seemed to be on top of everything, following world events closely, including the upheaval in Mexico, as well as the Civil War in the United States. When she learned of the assassination of President Lincoln, she immediately wrote to Mary Todd Lincoln with her condolences.

Napoléon consulted her about nearly all his decisions and admitted, once again, that she had her finger on the pulse of the public and understood its concerns.

CHAPTER TEN

DESIGNING A DISASTER

FRANCE, IT SEEMED, WAS "STANDING ON TOP OF GOLDEN HOURS," AS THE ENGLISH POET William Wordsworth wrote. The economy was thriving, and Paris was sparkling with shiny buildings, lush parks and spacious boulevards orchestrated by Baron Haussmann. It had become the dream destination of tourists everywhere. New railroads, new streets, new fashions—everything was new. Including the empress, it seemed. She glowed in new gowns of silk and wore around her neck "the wealth of the empire," jewelry that was a gift from her husband, the Emperor Napoléon III. He might have looked old, ill and tired—the result of his debilitating gallbladder stones—but at his feet sat a handsome little boy, their son, the prince impérial. The future looked bright.

It was time, Napoléon thought as he surveyed the splendor he had engineered, to move forward with the next step, a plan he called the Grand Design. Under his plan, the emperor would counteract the growing influence of the United States in the Americas by establishing a French sphere of influence in North America to reclaim what Napoléon Bonaparte had lost more than half a century earlier.

Selling the Louisiana territory to the US in 1803 had been his uncle's biggest mistake, he believed. Known as the Louisiana Purchase, it was the greatest land bargain in history involving 530 million acres of territory. For $15 million, less than 3 cents an acre, the size of the United States was doubled, the country was strengthened materially and strategically, and it was provided with a powerful impetus for westward expansion.

Napoléon III planned to counteract that transaction with his Grand Design of a vast commercial empire extending from the Gulf of Mexico to the Pacific Ocean, including part of Texas. He had been planning it ever since he was imprisoned in Ham following his failed coup attempt in 1840. He'd discussed the plan with Eugénie, who was enthusiastic; he also mentioned it to British Prime Minister Benjamin Disraeli, saying it was of "high importance" to establish a European dynasty in the Americas.

That was in 1857, about the same time Eugénie, vacationing in Biarritz, was meeting a conservative Mexican politician named José Manuel Hidalgo y Esnaurrízar. Hidalgo, who recently had been dismissed from his diplomatic post, described the political upheavals wracking Mexico and explained how his compatriots longed for a monarchy to bring stability to the country.

Hidalgo's report to Eugénie was only part of the story, however. Mexico's liberal government, now under its first Indigenous Mexican president, Benito Juarez, had confiscated Catholic church lands and sold them off. Monasteries had been disbanded as well. Nunneries were allowed to remain as long as they did not accept new novices—which guaranteed their eventual demise. All these things were alarming to the conservative land-owning aristocrats and Europeans in Mexico. They feared their properties would be the next to catch the government's eye.

Hidalgo neglected to mention that or the concerns of ordinary Mexicans and instead assured Eugénie that Mexico would welcome a European ruler who would reverse these changes and restore what he and his fellow conservatives saw as *order*.

His words had a profound effect on the empress. Not only was Mexico a Catholic country, it was also one that spoke Spanish and had been a Spanish colony until 1821, just five years before Eugénie was born. Many of her Spanish friends had family connections to Mexico, and she could feel the distress Hidalgo described.

She said she would try to help and would encourage her husband to do so, as well.

In 1861 two events converged to convince Napoléon that the moment to launch his Grand Design had arrived: the United States became engulfed in its civil war, and Mexico, under the recently elected Juarez, declared it could not afford to repay the loans it had received from European countries and would default on them. France and Britain, two of the lenders, promptly severed diplomatic relations with Mexico and then, joined by Spain, which had also loaned money to its former colony, dispatched a military force to collect the debts.

Battles ensued. Britain and Spain worked out deals for repayment and sailed home. France stayed. Napoléon rushed to explain why: "America supports our manufactures and keeps alive our commerce." But, he added, a United States involved in the region constituted a threat "if it takes possession of the Gulf of Mexico and governs the West Indies and South America, thus controlling the entire produce of the New World." He had reason to worry because the US, which formally recognized the Juarez government, had been pursuing rights to build a canal across Mexico to facilitate shipping between the Caribbean and Pacific. In addition, the recent westward expansion of the United States had come primarily at the expense of Mexico and Spain as the territories such as Texas and California were absorbed in the US's belief in its "manifest destiny."

Napoléon acknowledged that the US played a vital role in France's economy by supplying cotton for its textile industries. But he also emphasized that "If a firm government is established in Mexico with help from France, we shall give to the Latin race beyond the ocean its ancient strength and power. We shall have guaranteed the security of our colonies in the West Indies and extended our benevolent influence to the center of America."

The Latin race? Napoléon was again showing the influence of Saint-Simonianism. It was his economic adviser Michel Chevalier, an engineer and Saint-Simonianist, who, during spent time in Mexico in the 1830s, developed the theory that Mexicans and those in Caribbean and South American countries shared a "racial and cultural affinity" with Europeans in countries that spoke Romance languages, such as French and Spanish. This meant, Chevalier said, the Latin people could be seen as natural allies in the struggle against the Teutonic world. His theory found numerous sympathizers in the government of the Second Empire, and Napoléon took advantage of it for his own ends. The label *Latin* attached to peoples from South America and the Caribbean and its derivatives—for instance, Latin America and Latinos—stuck and remains today even though Chevalier's racial theory has been debunked.

Napoléon's plans were welcomed by the Mexican Catholic Church, Mexican conservatives and much of the upper class who had seen their privileges erode when Juarez came to power. These were the people Hidalgo had described to Eugénie.

But from the moment French troops set foot on Mexican soil in 1861, things began spinning out of control. On May 5, the French were soundly defeated in the Battle of Puebla by forces loyal to Juarez's liberal government. It would take the French nearly a year to reach the capital of Mexico City from their coastal base, and they were unprepared for the land that met them as they marched inland. There were deserts, mountains, unbearable heat, dirt roads, rivers with no bridges and, most surprising and alarming, hostile Mexicans. These were not the people Hidalgo claimed to defend or the wealthy conservative politicians of Spanish descent who had slipped off to Europe when they were displaced by Juarez's reforms. These were Indigenous Mexicans, or *Indians* as the Europeans then called them, and peasants, who had already rid themselves of European domination forty years earlier when they'd won independence from Spain. They had no desire to have another group of Europeans tell them how to live.

No one, it seems, had really thought matters through. Not Napoléon who had already picked Archduke Maximilian, younger brother of Austrian Emperor Franz Josef, to sit on the Mexican throne. Napoléon had no idea how strongly the Indigenous Mexicans resented European domination.

Not the conservative Mexicans who said they were looking for a monarch. They hadn't noticed Maximilian's liberal leanings or the reforms he enacted during his time in charge of the Austrian navy when they agreed he should be their emperor. Nor had they listened to what he said after witnessing the brutality used to quell the European unrest in 1848. "We call our age the *Age of Enlightenment,* but . . . in the future, men will look back in horror and amazement at the injustice of tribunals, which in a spirit of vengeance condemned to death those whose only crime lay in wanting something different to the arbitrary rule of governments which placed themselves above the law."

And certainly not Empress Eugénie. She had not thought it through either, and she failed to grasp how little her informants knew of Mexico beyond their own interests.

The doomed enterprise moved ahead. The French public was indifferent to the so-called rescue mission, but the French military was eager for action.

Filled with evangelical zeal to see the Catholic Church restored to its former power in Mexico and clinging to a romantic view of the former Spanish colony, Eugénie went to Madrid to see Queen Isabella of Spain, whom she'd known since her childhood, to obtain her blessing for the Grand Design. Mexico would once again be linked to Europe, Eugénie explained, and, under Napoléon's plan, the Americas would again provide commercial opportunities for the Old World.

Isabella refused. An Austrian monarch on the throne of a former Spanish colony? Never! Spain had had its own problems with the Austrian Habsburg monarchs who had ruled the country for nearly two centuries, from 1516 to 1700 and, as far the Spanish were concerned, had led it into economic and political decline before being booted out. Spain wanted nothing more to do with them. Eugénie pointed out to Isabella that it would be impolitic for Britain, Spain or France to pick a ruler from one of their own countries: the new monarch had to come from a nation not involved in the financial skirmish over debts. France would, however, protect Spanish interests. France, Isabella responded, was arrogant beyond reason if it thought it could "guarantee the security of *Spanish* colonies."

Eugénie went home disappointed but undeterred. She was more determined than ever to see the Grand Design completed.

In the summer of 1863, however, the project received another blow when the US government, worried about French aid finding its way to the Confederacy via Mexico, provided financial aid to reaffirm its support for the embattled government of Benito Juarez.

Although France was officially neutral in the Civil War, its sympathies toward the South were clear. Cotton kept its mills running—not just running but also making uniforms for the Confederacy, a fact that sparked outrage in Washington when it was revealed. Nor was it any secret that Napoléon had offered the South use of French shipyards for building warships. "If the North wins the war, I'll be happy, but if the South carries it off, I shall be overjoyed," he said. Part of his reasoning rested with the fact that the Southern way of life resembled the way European aristocracy lived—in beautiful, large houses on vast swaths of land run by laborers.

The fact that the South was sustained by slavery was ignored completely or glossed over. Many European aristocrats and business people were involved in the slave trade through ownership of slave ships or properties in the United States, and more owed their wealth and incomes to products produced by slave labor. Many others wore blinders, seeing only the elegant homes and the gracious style of life without paying attention to the slaves whose labor created the illusion of beauty. The busy factories of the North, on the other hand, were noisy and dirty, not gracious or charming, even though those factories made many of the products France needed and bought.

On several occasions, Napoléon had hinted that France might intervene in the Civil War if the situation warranted. The Lincoln administration warned of severe consequences if it did. Officials in Washington considered the emperor a loose cannon, a dreamer with flights of fancy who acted on impulse and could not be trusted. "He's a perpetual nightmare," warned Washington's ambassador to Belgium, Henry Sanford. "The emperor is at the center of nearly every international problem."

Napoléon and Eugénie heard the rumblings, and their own embassies warned them "that, amongst the Mexican people, the idea of a monarchy was bound up with hateful memories of Spanish absolutism and clerical tyranny . . . that the United States, whatever their discords at the moment, would never ratify or tolerate the sovereignty of a Habsburg [the Austrian ruling family] on the continent of free America."

The emperor and empress began to have doubts about their enterprise. Was the Grand Design unraveling? How far should they go? Who would win the Civil War? Hundreds of young Frenchmen, acting on their own, had already crossed the ocean to join the Southern cause. Should the French government follow suit and intervene?

Napoléon and Eugénie sought an opinion from someone they could trust, their American dentist, Dr. Thomas Evans. He was a family friend and confidant; Eugénie had known him since her youth and had introduced him to Napoléon. Go home to America, Napoléon told him, find out what's really going on and who's going to win the war.

Although using a dentist as a diplomat was unconventional, Evans, who was from Philadelphia, was hardly the average dentist. He'd built an international business for his medical products and developed revolutionary dental treatments such as gold fillings. He also had worked on the teeth of nearly every crowned head in Europe and was friends with many of them. He was invited to their homes and often made the social rounds with them. His contacts were legion.

Evans was respected in America, too, and had no trouble getting a meeting with Secretary of State William Seward as well as with President Abraham Lincoln. They both told him: "We [the North] shall succeed." Seward gave Evans a pass to meet General Ulysses S. Grant in Virginia so he could assess the state of the war firsthand. Evans looked around the camp and noted the relatively good health of the men there and the high quality of care for the sick and wounded. And he saw something else: the modern military equipment of the Yankee armies. Evans carried his information back to France, telling the emperor he was convinced of a Union victory. "Feeling myself entirely convinced that the end of the war was not far distant, I so informed the Emperor," Evans wrote. Napoléon's reaction was "typical of a military mind."

"When the plan of campaign arranged between Grant and Sherman was reported to me, I saw by my maps that it was the beginning of the end [for the South]," the emperor later said.

Meanwhile, the South, in a last-ditch effort to garner French support, aimed at Napoléon's well-known weakness for women. It sent Rose O'Neal Greenhow, a beautiful and witty spy, to tempt the emperor. He received her in his private study. Napoléon was "polite but careful," talking with "ashes dribbling from his incessant cigarettes," Greenhow reported. He resisted her charms. She was then invited to a ball by Eugénie, but the invitation was all Greenhow gained from the visit. There was no endorsement of the Confederacy, and the intelligence Evans brought back to Paris held sway. France remained neutral in the war.

PLANS FOR MEXICO LOOKED INCREASINGLY BLEAK, BUT NAPOLÉON AND EUGÉNIE FELT IT was too late to turn back. Archduke Maximilian, the designated ruler, was informed that the people of Mexico had voted to make him emperor and, with his wife Charlotte, had already set sail for the country. Maximilian was not told the plebiscite was bogus, that it was held only in an area occupied by the French army. Whether the emperor knew the details of the vote is unclear, but whatever doubts Napoléon and Eugénie harbored were swallowed or faced with defiance. When William Lewis Dayton, the

American ambassador to France, went to see Eugénie with a last-minute appeal to end the Mexican adventure, she promptly rejected it. "But Madame," he said, "the Civil War is getting to its end. France should abandon its plans for Mexico. If not, the Archduke will be in trouble."

The Empress responded haughtily. "Sir, if my son was of age, I would put him at the head of the army to write one of the most prestigious pages in history."

"Then Madame, you should thank God that your son is still brandishing only wooden weapons," Dayton replied, not bothering to mask his anger.

Nonetheless, when Charlotte, or Carlota as she was known as the newly installed empress of Mexico, enthusiastically wrote to Eugénie, whom she idolized, and invited her to come visit, Eugénie pointedly ignored the invitation. Eugénie also began to question the elaborate court the new rulers were setting up to replicate France's, they said. The young couple—both Maximilian and Carlota were in their thirties—had spent their voyage from Europe to Mexico planning the details of their new court's etiquette. Eugénie advised Carlota to pursue more serious issues and to keep a "hand of steel in her velvet glove."

Maximilian, at the same time, had angered those who had put him in power when he announced he was continuing some of Juarez's liberal policies and would not be returning confiscated properties to the Catholic Church. When the papal nuncio came running to Eugénie for help, he was shocked when she told him she would not help him and that she supported the emperor of Mexico. Maximilian and Carlota are the only things standing in the way of corruption and Protestantism, Eugénie said. They were the "anchor of salvation," and the pope should be pleased they were defending the "moral side of the country" against financial privileges. The nuncio spluttered and fumed and reminded Eugénie that she had supported the war *because* she wanted a return of church property. It did no good.

As things continued to slip out of control, Maximilian called on France for more money and military support. His policies had cost him the support of the only segment of the Mexican population that backed him—those of European descent—and left him in dire need of assistance. His army faced constant attacks by militias and guerrilla units loyal to Juarez, the Mexican president that Maximilian thought he had replaced. But Juarez had not been defeated. He escaped to the northern part of Mexico and, with ongoing support from the United States, continued his battle to hold on to his rightful place as president of the country.

Emperor Maximilian issued a "black decree" targeting the guerrillas and Juarez's militia, stating that any Mexican bearing arms against the imperial regime, that is, Maximilian's own rule, and refusing to surrender would be executed. His stance only worsened the situation and soured relations with French forces who were there to defend him. They had begun to grasp the true situation in the country, and many deserted, unwilling to fight those they saw as the rightful citizens of Mexico. The remaining troops suffered the brunt of the attacks by Juarez's supporters.

In France itself, many now lamented how its treasure and military manpower were being drained by the Grand Design. What's more, they pointed out, with the North emerging victorious in the Civil War, the reunited United States could turn its attention to other problems, such as the threat posed by a European power on its borders.

Reading reports of casualties and losses, Eugénie felt her heart squeezed. The price of political power was high. "For me," she was to say later, "the most painful thing in the world would be to find myself face to face with those whose grief I have contributed to by the instigation of the Mexican expedition." But, she added, "the honor . . . of France was pledged."

More aid for veterans and their families had to be given immediately, but how long could this faraway venture be allowed to continue robbing France of its most valuable assets?

In search of answers and comfort, Eugénie retreated to the Basque country once again and began building a chapel dedicated to the Virgin of Guadalupe, patron saint of Mexico. Her worries, her confusion, her contradictions, her hopes—all were manifest in the project. Its construction was perhaps an instinctive reaction for Eugénie, who was overwhelmed with the need to do something, to take some sort of action. She would have been familiar with the shrine to Our Lady of Guadalupe in Extremadura in Spain and remembered that many of the Spanish conquistadores who went to the New World came from there. She could easily have associated the two, feeling her connection to both Spain and Mexico when she ordered the building of the chapel.

Its focus was a large copy of Mexico's Our Lady of Guadalupe, painted by the Alsatian Louis Charles Auguste Steinheil. It was to Our Lady of Guadalupe that the empress now prayed and poured out her heart in hopes of finding comfort and consolation, perhaps expiation. The chapel, located in Biarritz where it still stands, became the imperial family's place of worship, a site of penance, in a way, for the war in Mexico.

Recognizing the failure of his Grand Design, Napoléon announced he would bring French troops home, and he advised

Chapel Notre-Dame-de-Guadalupe, built by Empress Eugénie in Biarritz. *Biarritz, Wikimedia Commons, Johanna Daniel, Peccadille, 2017*

Maximilian and Carlota to leave, as well. With relief, Eugénie endorsed her husband's decision, but Maximilian and Carlota refused, determined to hang on to their thrones. They begged for more men and money. When that was not forthcoming, Carlota sailed to France to personally appeal to Napoléon and Eugénie.

It was July 1866, a grim and fractious time for the imperial couple. Napoléon, already in poor health, had suffered a painful attack from his bladder stones; his doctors treated him with the opiate tincture laudanum, which left him nearly insensible. Eugénie suggested her husband abdicate: she would take over as regent until the prince impérial, then ten years old, reached his majority in eight years. Napoléon reacted with fury, and the couple's relationship frayed. Observers said they were barely speaking to each other.

In a pain-free moment, the emperor agreed to see Carlota, even though he had been warned about her "difficult personality." He told her he respected her courage and generous nature but that no more French aid would be forthcoming. She left in a rage. "What after all, should I . . . have expected from the word of a Bonaparte!" Carlota had no better luck when she went to Eugénie, who had grown impatient with her nonstop demands.

Signs of Carlota's instability were evident in a long, rambling letter she then wrote to Maximilian, but she was correct in her assessment of the imperial couple. They looked "tired and older," she said, and were "dazzled by their own splendor," unable to admit their power was fading.

Despite a continuing decline in her mental health—Carlota had begun showing signs of paranoia, fearing assassination and believing her food was poisoned—she went to see Pope Pius IX seeking support for Maximilian. The pope refused. Carlota suffered a complete mental breakdown and refused to leave the Vatican. The pope finally ordered a bed moved into the pontifical library. She was the first woman known to have slept in the Vatican. Her brother, now King Leopold II of Belgium, was contacted to take charge of her. Carlota would spend the rest of her life in confinement.

Meanwhile, Napoléon, having recovered from the worst of his pain, convinced Eugénie that they should concentrate on liberalizing the government to prepare it for their son's reign. She said she understood and agreed. He ordered the last of the French troops home.

In Mexico, Maximilian now found himself on his own. His wife was incapacitated in Belgium, and France had refused all calls for help. As events moved toward a climax, the Austrian archduke, in a desperate move to crush his opponents and cling to power, took personal command of his army against Juarez's supporters. His forces were defeated in the battle of Querétaro, and he was taken prisoner. "I should never have come here," the captured emperor was heard to say.

On June 19, 1867, at six forty in the morning, Maximilian was led from his prison cell to a courtyard in what is now the Cerro de las Campanas National Park in Santiago de Querétaro and placed in front of a firing squad. He handed each member of the squad a gold coin. "Aim for the heart," he told them.

Then he stood at attention before them. "I forgive everyone, and I ask everyone to forgive me," he said. "May my blood which is about to be spilled end the bloodshed which has been experienced in my new motherland. Long live Mexico! Long live its independence!" They fired.

Six months after his execution, his body was repatriated to Austria.

The following year, French artist Édouard Manet reproduced the scene in a dramatic painting.

CHAPTER ELEVEN

"A WAVE OF INSANITY"

IT WAS A PARTY AND THE WHOLE WORLD WAS INVITED—THE 1867 EXPOSITION UNIVERSELLE, or World's Fair. More than 11 million people accepted Napoléon III's invitation and came to Paris to see the glories of France displayed over 119 acres on the Champ de Mars, the parade grounds near the country's military academy. Among them was the head of every royal house—even the Russian czar and the Turkish sultan. The only exception was the widowed Queen Victoria, now living in seclusion at Windsor.

If there was a face of the Exposition, a brand ambassador, it was Empress Eugénie. She was everywhere, and her gowns, jewels and gracious behavior won rave reviews from virtually everyone.

Behind the glittering facade, however, cracks were beginning to show. Emperor Napoléon III looked shrunken and old, especially compared to the vibrant Eugénie.

At the same time, life for the average French person was becoming more difficult. Recent bad harvests prompted agricultural workers to leave farms and flee to the cities in search of jobs. The cost of living had spiraled upward, and people poured into the streets in protest.

Those attending the Exposition had two feelings, according to one writer, "a feeling of dazzling brilliance and a feeling of fear. Never have people enjoyed themselves more frenziedly or more uneasily." Another said that "a wave of insanity" had swept over the country.

Who's responsible for all this "unnecessary extravagance" while the poor suffer? people asked. There was an easy answer: *L'Espagnole*, the Spanish woman, Eugénie. It's all her fault: she's a spendthrift and ostentatious; she wants all the attention; she's bullying the emperor. The empress's popularity began to wane.

In an effort to calm nerves and divert attention away from France's problems, Napoléon moved to liberalize the government and create a constitutional monarchy. Eugénie recognized the need for change but objected strenuously to Napoléon's timing. Don't do it now, she pleaded. It would be disastrous to make changes from a weakened state. Wait until we're in a stronger position.

The emperor, physically depleted and torn by political pressures and the need to keep peace in the family, must have felt as though he were juggling lit firecrackers.

THE 20,000 GUESTS AT THE OPENING CEREMONY OF THE 1867 EXPOSITION COULD WELL have imagined they were looking at an allegory as they gazed at the platform. There stood the emperor with his wife the empress beside him, her hand resting on the shoulder of their son, the young prince impérial who stood slightly in front of them—the past, the present and the future.

Emperor Napoléon III, fighting chronic pain and struggling through the haze created by the painkillers his doctors fed him, stood resolutely in his bemedaled uniform at the entrance to the Palais de l'Industrie. Visitors could see his time was in the past.

His son, the eleven-year-old prince who was honorary president of the Exposition, was also dressed in a uniform. He looked shy, but eager to please—the future in a charming form.

But it was the empress who commanded all eyes. Despite the cold of that gray April day and its rain, she lit up the massive hall. In her shimmering white gown, pearl necklace and diamond tiara sparkling against her auburn hair, she dominated the scene. She radiated strength, energy and pride. And that hand of hers on the boy's shoulder as they stood on the stage together? A loving bridge to the future? Or was it a tight grip? It hardly mattered: this party was all about the present.

Let the celebration begin.

IT HAD TAKEN MORE THAN THREE YEARS TO GET TO THAT POINT. NAPOLÉON HAD BEGUN plans for the Exposition in 1864 when his Grand Design was moving forward. At home, changes Baron Haussmann had made in Paris were nearly complete. Prosperity was in the air. The emperor wanted to show off his successes and do a little bragging: the Second Empire is even better than the First; my Exposition will be better than the paltry one Britain had in 1862; this World's Fair will be good for business, good for France and good for my image.

Knowing thousands, probably millions, would flock to Paris to see exhibits from France and thirty-two other countries, the city and the state agreed to foot the bulk of the bill, and a public subscription brought in a supplemental $2 million to cover preparation costs. That, along with admission fees, charged for the first time at the Exposition of 1855, would help turn a profit.

Napoléon appointed an imperial commission to organize the fair and, ever loyal to his family, named his feckless cousin Plon-Plon as director. But most of the power was given to an engineer named Frédéric Le Play who knew how to work with Plon-Plon after the two of them had held dual responsibility for the 1855 Exposition.

Le Play vowed to use everything he had learned from mistakes made at earlier fairs to make this one the success the emperor demanded. It would show off French progress in several fields including education, one of the empress's key interests. This Exposition will be, said Michel Chevalier, the emperor's economic adviser, "a happy marriage of industry and art." Even Victor Hugo, who said he considered Napoléon III a traitor and was living in self-imposed exile on the Channel Island of Guernsey, couldn't resist the pull of the "happy marriage" and agreed to write a *Paris Guide* for the Exposition.

The commission ordered that the Champ de Mars be leveled and then an enormous oval-shaped building called the Palais du Champ de Mars installed to house the exhibits. The palais was a 1,600-foot-long structure with gardens and a pavilion topped with a dome at its center. Despite its size, it did not provide enough room for everything that was planned, so the commission commandeered the Île Saint-Germain, an island in the suburb of Billancourt, to gain another 52 acres for agricultural exhibits.

Opening day, ironically April Fools' Day, 1867—*poisson d'avril*, when the French play jokes by pinning paper fish on unsuspecting people's backs—was cold and wet, but the imperial family put its best foot forward to welcome guests at the Palais de l'Industrie (site of today's Grand Palais), a monumental relic of the 1855 Exposition. Not everyone was impressed. The building looks like "an ox galloping through the roses," said one critic. The ventilation was terrible, rendering the structure unbearably hot or cold (depending on the outside temperature), but it was one of the few buildings ready for opening day. Construction on others had faltered in the miserable weather that had hung over northern Europe throughout March.

The huge space behind the building's Gothic facade lent itself to the gala opening, and on hand to hear Napoléon's welcoming wish "to honor workers" and his hopes that "nations and people learn to live in peace" were sovereigns and distinguished representatives from most of the thirty-two countries exhibiting at the fair.

What they were exhibiting, however, had been a source of contention. When Eugénie learned that the commission wanted to ask countries to send people to display racial and cultural differences in a sort of human zoo, she was shocked. "You can't exhibit people like animals!" the empress exclaimed. The commissioners backed down.

There were plenty of other exhibitions, though, 50,000 of them organized in 10 different groups. Each group was subdivided into several "classes" for what was announced as a celebration of know-how, industry and labor, not merely as economic assets but also as "cultural facts." The goal was extraordinary: "To cover everything everywhere: Europe, the Americas, Africa, and Asia . . . in all fields of endeavor, from industry to fine art but also cultural heritages" and to see "the bounty of nature transformed into universal harmony for the human race."

Even more extraordinary is how close it came to reaching that goal, especially as it occurred against a background of intense national and international tensions.

Opposition politicians continued to rail against Napoléon's authoritarian rule. The general public protested what it believed to be increased activity of government agents, secret police, spying on the public. At the same time, workers called for equality of the kind Karl Marx had described in "The Communist Manifesto" in 1848; demonstrations against the high cost of living erupted in cities across France.

At the same time, countries and territories were being shuffled like a deck of cards. In 1867 alone, France bought Luxembourg from the Netherlands, then Luxembourg split, sent one duchy back to the Netherlands and claimed neutrality for the rest; the provinces of Canada joined to become an independent dominion, not a colony of Great Britain; Austria and Hungary linked together to create the Dual Monarchy; the United States bought Alaska from Russia; Singapore became a British crown colony; Cambodia won independence from Siam but became a protectorate of France and Britain; the United States grabbed control of Midway Island; Native Americans of Great Plains tribes were forced onto reservations; Prussia under Bismarck's leadership maneuvered a group of independent German states into the North German Confederation; and the Russian partition of Poland turned that kingdom into a province of the Russian Empire.

The game Parcheesi also made its appearance . . .

. . . and Alfred Nobel invented dynamite.

But the only explosions fairgoers were hearing were merry and musical ones. Jacques Offenbach, famous for the cancan music, made the city chuckle with his parody of royalty and the military, *The Grand-Duchess of Gérolstein*. Johann Strauss II made it dance with the new orchestral version of "The Blue Danube" waltz he wrote especially for the Exposition.

Most of the 11 million visitors were so entranced by the endless sights and sounds that they paid little heed to anything else. They were getting around the city easily, thanks to a new means of transport—the Bateaux Mouches on the Seine. The boats were named in honor of their place of origin, a section of Lyon called La Mouche. They attracted the American singer Lillie Moulton, who had become a favorite of the imperial family after they admired her ice-skating. She joined the heir to the Swedish throne, Prince Oscar, to sing duets as they cruised on the river in the new boats. Lillie had bought a season pass to the fair and was there nearly every day because "it is always a delight." In her letters home, she raved about everything from "handsome Hungarian zitheriths" [zither players] to the "delicious rolls hot from the oven" at a Viennese bakery, one of hundreds of international food stands that surrounded the main building and presaged the modern food court. The American stand did not do well, save for its soda fountain which was a success even though the rye grass straws served to sip the drinks turned mushy in the beverages. Still, people said they were impressed that the United States was able to produce such a good exhibit a mere two years after the end of the Civil War.

Food stands, musicians and other performers were, however, treated with scorn by "serious" critics and fairgoers who felt they turned the Exposition into nothing more than an amusement park that distracted people from the important exhibits of scientific and technological advancement, such as the display on the history of labor and the presentation of a new light metal called *aluminum*. Or even the working model of the yet-incomplete

Suez Canal. Nonetheless, most eagerly tried the technological invention two American brothers named Otis were showing—an elevator—even if they did not spend too much time analyzing the massive cannon the German manufacturer Krupp had on display. Little did they know that three years later that 50-ton giant would nearly destroy the city in which it was now merely a curiosity.

One category of exhibitors included "articles whose special purpose is meant to improve the physical and moral conditions of the people," which got special attention when Napoléon himself entered the competition with a design for a workers' housing project. To the surprise of no one (except perhaps Napoléon), the emperor won a gold medal for his submission.

It was Eugénie, however, who seemed to be winning the public's regard. She was the vibrant star of every party, every ball, every event. Yet she stayed focused and concentrated on the success of what was happening. Princess Pauline von Metternich remembered seeing her in the gardens of Versailles at the end of a major fete the empress had organized with water pageants, dinner for 600 and fireworks. Eugénie was gowned in white and gold and had a trail of partygoers in her wake, showering her with compliments on her appearance. She hardly noticed their presence, but when she saw Pauline, she stopped her and wanted to know only one thing: Was the fete okay?

The party, with its gondolas on the Grand Canal of the Château de Versailles and orchestras concealed in the shrubbery to make sure there was always music, was definitely okay, but no matter how successful the party was, it was still Eugénie everyone wanted to see. She made very public and visible shopping trips to the exhibition, visiting it more than thirty times.

Eugénie's concerns, however, went beyond her public relations work as the personification of the Second Empire. She was spearheading the move to show off French progress in education, particularly education for women, and she was determined to make sure grants were forthcoming and money was raised so schoolchildren, their families and their teachers could attend the

Exposition either for free or at reduced rates. The empress set about rewarding the students with special conferences, museum trips and even private visits to the Tuileries Palace, where, according to one newspaper, she and Napoléon greeted them "like they were ambassadors of a great country."

Two major events were to be the highlights of the Exposition Universelle. The first was the annual Revue de Longchamp, a military display much like today's parades on the Quatorze Juillet, Bastille Day. It was traditionally a colorful, joyous, self-congratulatory event with marching units and mounted ones, all displaying their well-pressed uniforms and well-polished equipment. But for the 1867 Revue, extra shining and ironing were done, and units from every part of the French Imperial Army—more than 60,000 men—were gathered at the large racetrack on the western edge of Paris and in the newly redeveloped Bois de Boulogne. Eugénie, radiant and waving to the crowds, led the procession to the track in a gilded carriage. Napoléon and visiting sovereigns followed on horseback, and then all mounted the steps to the reviewing stand.

"When squadron on squadron charged with drawn swords upon their sovereign and their escorts, and halted but a few paces from them with the cry of 'Long live the emperor,' the thrill was magical," wrote one journalist. "At that moment there swept through the people and the army a conviction that French power was irresistible."

They could not have been more wrong. Sharp-eyed visitors, like Bismarck sitting alongside the Prussian King Wilhelm, saw that the artillery equipment was out of date and the field organization was old-fashioned. Furthermore, France's refusal to impose conscription meant that although the numbers looked impressive in a revue, they were not nearly enough for a real war. Those handsome uniforms with their red trousers, no matter how well-tailored, made their wearers easy targets.

"The scenery," one general was to say of the 1867 Revue, "overshadowed an army in crisis."

Nevertheless, the crowds loved it, a celebratory atmosphere that later would be captured in a popular song called "Coming Home from the Revue."

Returning home from Longchamp, our hearts at peace,
We cheered the Army of France nonstop . . .

But on the return from Longchamp on June 6, the real world crashed the party. A Polish refugee, angry about the Russian partition of his country, fired a gunshot at the Russian czar, Alexander II. He missed. Napoléon, who had been the target of more than one assassination attempt himself, made a try for royal bonhomie. "Sire," he said to the czar, "we have been under fire together, which means that now we are brothers-in-arms."

The czar, nursing a grudge against Napoléon because he had favored Polish independence rather than the Russian partition of the country, was angered and offended by the attack. He was not in the mood for brotherly love. "Our lives are in the hands of Providence," he snapped.

Alexander's temperament did not improve when a group of young lawyers poured out of the Palais de Justice with cries of "Long live Poland" and "Get out!" The furious ruler stormed back to his quarters at the Élysée Palace and announced he was leaving France.

It was Eugénie who rushed in to calm the diplomatic waters. She went first to see the czar to placate him and then to the Spanish exhibits where she chose gifts for him. That evening, she organized a *Te Deum* mass at the Russian Orthodox church in Paris to be sung in thanks for Alexander's safety. On top of this, she added an extra ball at the Tuileries Palace in the czar's honor just three days later. It was done with such pomp that even Mérimée, who was usually blasé about court events, had to admit he was impressed. So, too, was Pierre Tetar van Elven, an artist who produced an evocative, sensuous and dreamy painting of the ball that reflected everything Eugénie was trying to convey to the disgruntled czar.

The czar preened under Eugénie's charm, flattered by the gifts she had obviously purchased personally for him, and the extra attention she showered on him alone. Nonetheless, he had to make clear his royal standing had been offended, so he gathered up his sons and left just a day earlier than planned. But the fact that he had stayed that long was a triumph for Eugénie.

The czar's departure was the cue for the entrance of the Ottoman ruler, Abdulaziz, the first Turkish sultan ever to visit western Europe. He had been traveling in Italy and southern France to avoid the ruler of Russia, his traditional foe. With the Russian czar now gone, Abdulaziz, sparkling with diamonds, swept into Paris. To some degree, he may have felt he was coming to a family reunion. His grandmother was said to be Aimée du Buc de Rivéry, a cousin by marriage of Empress Josephine, Napoléon's grandmother and first wife of Napoléon Bonaparte. Du Buc had disappeared at sea but was rumored to have been captured by Barbary pirates and sold as a concubine to the sultan, becoming his favorite wife. Although no evidence has been found to validate the claim, both Abdulaziz and Napoléon III were content to take advantage of the legend when it was politically useful.

Abdulaziz made his grand, bejeweled entrance at the pinnacle of the Universal Exposition—the prize-giving ceremony on July 1 when the prince impérial, honorary president of the Exposition, would hand out medals. His mother and father, the emperor and the empress, would be there as well to congratulate the winners. Once again, the imperial family would appear at the Palais de l'Industrie, now hung with banners and draperies topped by gilded imperial eagles perched on the upper cornice.

But just as the emperor and empress were set to leave the Tuileries Palace for the ceremony, disaster struck: they received word that Maximilian, the emperor of Mexico, had been executed by firing squad. The Austrian archduke had been shot nearly two weeks earlier, but the news had been slow to arrive. Eugénie and Napoléon were staggered and horrified.

For Eugénie, who had backed the Mexican incursion in hopes it would lead to a closer alliance with Austria as a bulwark against growing Prussian power, it was a personal blow. Her friend Prince von Metternich, the Austrian ambassador, also had been devastated by the news of Maximilian's death. "He cried like a baby," she was told. She was desperate to get to Biarritz and the chapel she had built there to pray to Our Lady of Guadalupe for forgiveness, understanding, guidance and peace.

But before they could do anything else, she and Napoléon had to get through the prize-giving. They would withhold the news of Maximilian's death from the public until afterward, but Eugénie changed her dress to one more sober. She still had to look like the empress, after all, and one of the people she had supported—Julie-Victoire Daubié, the woman whom she had worked with to get French women the right to earn degrees—would be getting a medal. The empress could not, would not, miss that nor would she downplay its importance.

She redid the kohl she habitually used to underline her eyes—her only concession to makeup—and drew on her gloves. Then she slipped her hand into the crook of Napoléon's arm, and leaving the shards of their dreams behind, together they walked toward the carriage standing in readiness to carry them to the eager crowds waiting for them at 1867 Exposition Universelle.

Tears would have to wait. Empresses do not cry—at least, not in public.

CHAPTER TWELVE

MADAME LA SULTANE DE FRANCE

EUGÉNIE RAISED HER HAND TO HER FOREHEAD TO BLOCK THE SUN AND LOOKED STRAIGHT ahead. "There was a true Egyptian sky, that enchanting sunlight that has an almost hallucinating clarity," she said, standing on the deck of the yacht *l'Aigle* as it prepared to enter the Suez Canal. "Fifty vessels, all flying their flags, were waiting for me. The sight was one of such magnificence and proclaimed the grandeur of the French Empire so eloquently that I could scarcely control myself. I rejoiced, triumphantly."

What a contrast to what she'd left behind when she headed off to officially open the Suez Canal in November 1869. Back home in France, violent protests about the cost of living were increasing, and recriminations about the disastrous Mexican venture continued unabated. There were unending palace intrigues and bitter arguments with her husband about liberalizing the regime.

But, for now, she was free of all that as she sailed toward the canal aboard the imperial yacht.

Napoléon was supposed to be there, too, but his deteriorating health kept him in Paris. Ministers speculated that the real reason he stayed home was a desire to get his wife out of the way so he could reorganize and liberalize the government the way he wanted without her interference. That may very well have played a part in his decision, but Napoléon also knew Eugénie was the best person to handle the trip and deal with the difficult personalities involved. She'd already proved she could manage the egos of skittish potentates; plus, she had a personal stake in the canal.

It was Eugénie who had argued her cousin Ferdinand de Lesseps's case with Napoléon to gain his support for the canal. The canal would allow ships to sail directly from Europe to Asia, foregoing the long voyage around the tip of Africa. It was not difficult to make the case to the emperor. Although he knew it would be hugely expensive, he had no problem seeing the economic advantages of a shorter trade route. Napoléon was close to the Saint-Simonians, a group that believed in a merger of technology and the arts; although it had a utopian philosophy, it also had its feet on the ground. In their balance of ideals and practicality, Napoléon, working with his economic adviser who was one of its leading members, had found the basis for his decision to renovate Paris. The emperor also knew the Saint-Simonians had themselves tried to instigate the building of a canal a few years earlier. As a result of his sympathies for the group and his own interest in progress, Napoléon listened to his wife with a willing ear and gave de Lesseps the necessary backing to make the canal a reality.

Like Eugénie, Napoléon also had a personal reason for his interest in the canal. He knew that his uncle, Napoléon I, had a canal in his mind seventy years earlier during the Egyptian campaign when he had found remnants of one from the time of the pharaohs. But the waterway between the Mediterranean and Red Seas had been an unreached goal until now, condemning shipping between Europe and Asia to long trips around the Cape of Good Hope. The new canal would cut 8,900 kilometers (more than 5,500 miles) and 10 days off the travel. The financial impact would be enormous.

In opening the canal, Eugénie would not as much be cutting a ribbon as tying international economic and political interests together with family history. It would slice apart Africa and Asia but would bring the world together.

First, however, the empress needed to do some packing.

Her wardrobe for the trip was to be a weapon, as much a tool as any in the diplomatic briefcase. All eyes would be on her, and she and Napoléon intended to make sure that when the world looked at her, they saw the grandeur of France and its power. She called the designer she most trusted—Charles Frederick Worth— and together they planned outfits for every event and eventuality. For two months of travel, dinners, ceremonies, meetings and different cultures, Worth would have to create more than a hundred gowns and accessories for all of them. There would also be jewelry, hats and scarves. Louis Vuitton was commissioned to make trunks—nearly two hundred—to accommodate the special designs. Eugénie had spotted the work of the young leatherworker— one of many craftsmen carrying out orders from the imperial palace—when he solved a packing problem that bedeviled her and other travelers: how to cram their numerous trunks into the small spaces of ships' holds and carriages. The trunks were all made with rounded tops. Vuitton had another idea—he made them flat, easy to stack. Thanks to Eugénie and the flattop trunks he created for her, Vuitton made his name.

Then Eugénie faced her biggest diplomatic challenge: choosing her traveling companions. The Tuileries Palace was overwhelmed with requests to be included; politicians, artists, writers, chefs, friends, and friends of friends fighting to get their names on the list to attend what newspapers proclaimed as the "event of the century." One person, however, said *non*, her friend, Prosper Mérimée, then sixty-six, who told her his health was too fragile. He suffered from severe respiratory problems and said he had been exhausted by all the travel he'd done and the ceremonies he'd attended. He did not want her to go either and expressed a wish that something would happen to keep her in France. It was the wrong time and too long a time to be away, he said.

Eugénie was saddened by his refusal, but she surrounded

herself with other friends and family: Paca's children, some of her ladies-in-waiting, as well as the dentist, Thomas Evans. Her cousin, de Lesseps, naturally would be there, too. While she wished Loulou, her son, could come along, his schooling kept him in Paris. Eugénie was nonetheless buoyed by the knowledge she was doing something for his future—and what's more, something significant for her country.

She made one more addition to her entourage: her pet turtle Reine, or Queenie, would come along to the opening of the Suez Canal. Her ladies-in-waiting, used to the empress's quixotic behavior and love of animals, probably just shrugged and hoped they would not be the one delegated to care for the little reptile. Eugénie may have seen Reine as a mascot. She knew Egyptians viewed the turtle as a powerful creature, one capable of warding off evil, and there were images found in the ancient tombs that showed the beasts on the wands of magicians. She would welcome any extra help.

Even with all the work and diplomatic hurdles that lay ahead, Eugénie viewed this trip as almost a vacation and was eager to take it on.

The empress and her entourage departed from the private rail station at Saint-Cloud, taking the train to the port city of Toulon, then boarding a ship that would carry them to Venice where *l'Aigle,* the imperial yacht, was waiting for the empress. It would be her home for the next six weeks, and with her love of the sea, she was delighted to settle into the lovely green stateroom and suite prepared for her.

Even though it was the middle of the night, two o'clock, when she arrived in Venice on October 2, excited crowds were wide awake to greet her. A beautiful gondola arrived to ferry her to *l'Aigle,* and hundreds of other gondolas packed with people were poised to escort her on the short voyage. Venetians hung out of their windows and jammed the streets, cheering and singing. When she finally entered her cabin after waving to the crowds, she could still hear their voices. Their *canzoni* (songs) were her lullaby.

The next morning, Eugénie personally greeted the 180 sailors and their officers who had assembled. Her love and knowledge of the sea and sailing were well-known, as was her fearlessness in storms, so the men had convened to salute her as their "godmother."

A few hours later Eugénie faced her first diplomatic challenge when the Italian king, Victor Emmanuel, boarded l'Aigle. She braced herself, for he had never been one of her favorite people. She remembered his snide comment about her being named regent of France—"I'd show her what a woman is good for." Eugénie found him rude and inconsiderate. Nonetheless, she had a message from Napoléon she intended to pass along: the Italian peninsula must be united. The king responded that she should move from her yacht to his royal palace so they could have further discussions in private. She declined saying she wanted to remain incognita, a polite fiction for an empress surrounded by an entourage of 120 and the pomp of royalty.

The king was gone within fifteen minutes, but he wrote to Napoléon that he was "delighted" by their meeting, even though the presence of witnesses prevented him from sharing more information with the empress. Eugénie scoffed: "It did not stop him from whispering in my ear things that would make your hair stand on end!" she wrote to her husband. "I will tell you the details when I am back." The emperor and empress were staying in touch daily by telegraph, but whatever was whispered in Eugénie's ear is lost to history.

But Victor Emmanuel was easily put out of her mind in the clamor of welcome she was given. Over the next four days, she played tourist in Venice with its mayor acting as her personal guide. He took her to the city archives where the director gave Eugénie a chance to indulge her love of antique manuscripts and autographs and thumb through 193 volumes of correspondence between the Venetian ambassadors and the Spanish court. The mayor also made sure she saw everything from the churches and museums to the gondola of the last doge. Although it was a private visit, they were never alone. Excited crowds followed them everywhere and cheered her; at the same time, hundreds of gondolas surrounded her yacht, their passengers eager for a glimpse of the empress.

"A strange city," Eugénie wrote to her son. "Venice keeps the memory of its past glory. No one can fear it now, but one can yet be captured by it—captured by its charm."

Still heartsick by the tremendous loss of life in the Mexican campaign, Eugénie made a pilgrimage to a cemetery to lay flowers on the graves of French soldiers killed at the battle of Magenta ten years earlier when Napoléon III's army had liberated part of Italy from Austrian control. "They rest so far from home, their family and friends," she wrote Loulou, feeling melancholy with her own distance from home and family. "They deserve our prayers more than anybody."

AFTER FOUR DAYS IN VENICE, EUGÉNIE AND HER ENTOURAGE WITH ITS FORTY SERVANTS SET sail for Athens—and were suddenly caught in a storm. She was thrilled. She stayed on deck, enjoying the show the sea played out for her and the spray that hit her face. "The Empress was the only one who did not get sick," the admiral in charge of the small fleet reported to Napoléon. "She looked perfectly happy and her love for sailing just increased."

Athens was less enjoyable. Eugénie was not a fan of the ancient Greeks. "They were windbags, unfriendly, unbearable," she said, looking back on them from a ruler's viewpoint, "always fighting with each other—in one word, ungovernable." Her opinion was not improved when Greece's King George and his wife, Queen Olga, "dragged [her] through the Acropolis under a gray sky."

But then, reinvigorated by traveling through another storm at sea, she was in Turkey and Constantinople where, according to one of her ladies, "she looked happy to see the brilliance of the Middle East." The architecture and mosaics no doubt reminded her of the Moorish style of her native Granada, and the welcoming salvos of warships gathered in the Bosphorus Strait combined with the cheers of thousands of people on the docks were to give Eugénie a glow of happiness.

She was also impressed by the Beylerbeyi Palace with its two beautiful bathing pavilions. The Beylerbeyi, Sultan Abdulaziz's summer residence, was where she was to stay on her trip, and it was already clear he had pulled out all the stops to make the empress feel at home. Beylerbeyi was only four years old when she stepped into the massive entrance hall with its pool and fountain. It was appointed with French furniture and chandeliers, although the sultan made sure the private apartments for Eugénie in the harem were decorated in Eastern splendor.

Eugénie was the first Christian woman to be welcomed there. She was also the first Christian monarch to visit the city in more than three centuries.

Unlike Venice and Greece, however, her trip to Turkey was not for pleasure or sightseeing. This was a pivotal diplomatic stop aimed at convincing Abdulaziz that he should firmly ally himself with France and that, by doing so, he was guaranteed French support in Turkey's international conflicts. She may have read Mark Twain's description of the sultan in *The Innocents Abroad*, which had been published earlier that year, and in which he called Abdulaziz a "weak, stupid, ignorant [man] who believe[d] in gnomes and genii and the wild fables of the Arabian Nights." Eugénie knew different. Twain had misread the sultan; he was intelligent and wily and had haggled with France for years over the Suez Canal, successfully gaining most of the concessions he wanted. In the eight years since he had taken power, he had built the Ottoman navy into the third largest in the world, behind only Great Britain's and France's.

Eugénie was well aware she had her work cut out for her because there was also some unpleasant history between them. Two years earlier, when Abdulaziz was attending a ceremony at the Universal Exposition in Paris, he refused to give the empress his arm, making her feel he was standoffish and chauvinistic. He may have just been following precepts of his Muslim faith which limited physical contact between the sexes in public, but the public gesture looked like a snub.

Now, however, Abdulaziz knew he needed France to help him keep Egypt's ruler, Ismail Pasha, in line and his traditional enemy, Russia, at bay. Russia, smarting after its defeat by European powers allied with the Ottoman Empire in the Crimean War thirteen years earlier, was squeezing him to regain its prestige and expand its empire south for greater access to the Black Sea. The sultan knew he was vulnerable and had to keep his allies happy. But he was under no illusions. He realized Eugénie's ten-day visit to Constantinople was a last-minute addition to her itinerary and was a diplomatic bribe meant to flatter him and keep him from sending troops into Egypt. Egypt was then a province of the Ottoman Empire and was governed by his ambitious cousin Ismail Pasha who, during his visit to the 1867 Universal Exposition, had convinced the European powers to recognize him as the khedive, essentially viceroy of the Ottoman Empire, giving him a status second only to the sultan in the empire.

Abdulaziz was angered. As far as he was concerned, Ismail was nothing more than a bureaucrat, governor of just one of his provinces, or a *wali*. The Suez Canal might have been in Egypt, but Egypt—and the canal—was part of *his* Ottoman Empire.

With its imminent opening, the sultan realized that the eyes of the world would be watching, but still, the idea of sharing the spotlight at the canal ceremonies with Ismail was intolerable. Sultan Abdulaziz was not about to play second fiddle to a *wali*. He knew full well that the French-educated Ismail had outmaneuvered him in Paris at the 1867 Exposition when he connived to get the title *khedive*. And now Ismail was flexing his muscles as head of the country, which was home to the Suez Canal, by trying to impress the Europeans with his own modernization program. Abdulaziz chafed at Ismail's aggressive defiance of the sultan's authority.

Europe recognized the potential for the family feud's turning into something bigger, and it was desperate to prevent any internecine battles. Part of Eugénie's job was to keep the lid on by serving as an unofficial peacemaker between the squabbling cousins. She was to make sure the world noticed her visit to Turkey and, hence, give the sultan front-page exposure in newspapers around the world. Publicity from the glamorous visit would be his reward for keeping his armies bivouacked at home and not sending them to Egypt to teach Ismail a lesson. It was also a signal that France would live up to its promises and do whatever necessary to keep Russia from interfering in the region and getting its clutches on the canal.

Abdulaziz put his all into impressing his visitor, sending a barge manned by forty oarsmen to collect the empress and bring her to the royal palace for a sumptuous banquet.

Eugénie was equal to the occasion, calling on her sartorial tools to make clear the power and strength of France to this wary ally. Dr. Evans recorded that she'd chosen a gown of bright yellow silk and, in deference to Islamic practice, wore "a light mantilla over her head," as well as "a diadem and many rich jewels." The sultan seated her alone under "a dais or canopy of crimson silk."

Her strategy worked. The sultan, like the Russian czar before him, was charmed by the empress and raved about her wit and conversational skills. She seemed to bring him out of his shell. Instead of his formerly reclusive style, he organized a social program for Eugénie, including a series of dinners with more than a hundred guests. He then surprised European ambassadors, who were used to his aloof behavior, by spending time talking to both the men and women attending. He even took the empress on a visit to the harem where he demonstrated his awareness and acceptance of European customs by letting the unveiled Eugénie now take his arm. His mother was not pleased. When the Sultana Valida saw the two of them approach, she was horrified by Eugénie's flaunting of Islamic religious mores. In her eyes, the empress was misbehaving.

To put her in her place, the sultana Valida defiantly strode out in front of Eugénie and punched her in the stomach, nearly knocking the stunned empress to the ground.

The sultan reacted angrily and scolded his mother as Eugénie, bent over, struggled to catch her breath. He had been trying to convince the empress that the Ottoman Empire was civilized and becoming modern, but now, with that literal blow to the gut, he feared his mother had set back his campaign.

Eugénie's ladies-in-waiting, following behind, had a much different reaction: they burst out laughing. Within a few minutes, the empress had caught her breath and began laughing, too. Her surprising response managed to restore calm and ease the Sultan's fears. Women in the harem, after witnessing how Eugénie had handled the situation light-heartedly but with dignity and not a single word of complaint, began referring to her as Madame la Sultane de France, a sobriquet that caught on.

Her "meeting" with the Sultan's mother, however, was just one more diplomatic hurdle, albeit an unexpected one. Earlier, she had met with members of the French community in Constantinople where she was also caught off guard when the French ambassador asked her to make a response to his welcoming speech. Embarrassed and unprepared, the empress felt tears gathering in her eyes as she battled for composure, unsure what to say or do. She disliked and even feared public speaking but thought she had mastered self-control and learned how to act in front of an audience after her lessons with the actress Rachel. Yet here she was, trembling in front of a friendly audience, unable to say a word, unable to control her reaction. For a few minutes, the room was silent . . . and then, the crowd stood and began applauding, cheering a woman who had braved storms both diplomatic and maritime, but who was now humbled before them. Eugénie recovered with smiles and gratitude. Her *thank you*s poured out easily.

The sultan, meanwhile, was anxious to paper over the incident with his mother and take full advantage of Eugénie's visit. The Russian ambassador had already grasped that her trip represented France's support of not just the Suez Canal but also of the

Ottoman Empire. As a result, the irritated ambassador snubbed her and, by extension, France, staying away from the official welcome accorded the empress by the diplomatic corps. He did send his wife, however, and Eugénie soon spotted her. "I'm so sorry my arrival made your husband sick," the empress said with a disingenuous smile. She and the sultan then moved on, speaking to everyone else and leaving the wife of the Russian ambassador standing dismayed by herself. Message sent.

The Russian ambassador, cowed by Eugénie essentially issuing a challenge in reaction to his snub, conspicuously arrived at the official dinner at the end of the empress's visit. Message received.

Message received in Paris, too. Napoléon hurried to praise his wife. "They [your successes] are due above all to your personal talents and not only to your position," he wrote.

Abdulaziz, a cunning operator himself, made sure to seize the center stage whenever he could as Eugénie's visit drew to a close. He publicly and lavishly expressed his thanks to Madame la Sultane de France with parting gifts of rare and valuable textiles and rugs.

One gift, however, stretched Eugénie's diplomatic talents and self-control to the maximum. It was a tapestry portrait of Napoléon III, with his hair and mustache worked in real hair. One of her ladies-in-waiting burst out, "How ugly!" but the empress, relieved that the Turkish women who had made the gift spoke no French, turned to them with a smile and complimented them on the "wonderful resemblance to the original."

Nonetheless, Eugénie was pleased with her visit. "Now that I've seen the Bosphorus, I can understand why Russia wants it so much."

As thrilled as Abdulaziz was about the empress's visit, he would have been less enthusiastic had he known how enthralled she was with Egypt. In the months before her trip, she had called in Gaston Maspero, France's leading Egyptologist and famous as the one who had unwrapped the mummy of Ramses II, to tutor her and the ladies who would be traveling with her. "The task was difficult," said Countess Marie des Garets, one of the ladies-in-waiting. "We were taking notes, the empress was asking many questions. He certainly never had a more attentive and . . . ignorant audience." But Eugénie was greedy for the knowledge, reading almost non-stop about the country and peppering Maspero with questions.

The empress was, in part, caught up in the wave of Egypto-mania that surged when work on the Suez Canal began, but she also felt her youthful enthusiasm for Napoléon Bonaparte and his triumphs stirring again. She would be treading in the first Napoléon's path in Egypt, seeing the same wonders, and then, making the gesture that would bring his vision of a canal to reality. It was all part of her son's heritage now, and she reveled in it.

Another thing working against Abdulaziz was that Ismail Pasha, the khedive, was enamored of the empress. He would do everything he could for her, including building her a palace. And, unlike Abdulaziz, he was not only after a political alliance, he was on a personal quest. He wanted to win her respect, if not affection, and he had another weapon the powerful sultan lacked: Ismail spoke French. He would need no translator to express his admiration. "My eyes fancy looking at you for a lifetime," he said to her.

When *l'Aigle* sailed into Alexandria with the empress onboard, Ferdinand de Lesseps, the French consul, and several dignitaries of the Ottoman government were on hand to welcome her. So, too, was the khedive, who took charge and personally escorted her to the train for Cairo and the 300-room palace he had built for her on an island in the Nile. He had hired European architects to create a building that he wanted to resemble the Château of Versailles and capture the elegance of Eugénie's rooms at the Tuileries Palace. But Ismail did not want his architects to forget Eugénie's own background, so he made sure they added interiors that recalled Granada's Alhambra and its Moorish detailing. Then he added Egyptian designs and materials, as well as extensive gardens and a zoo. Work on the palace was slow, and Ismail called in more workers, determined it would be ready for the empress. Ismail succeeded, and the building became one of the landmarks of Cairo. It would go through a series of owners, financial problems and renovations before becoming today's Cairo Marriott Hotel.

Ismail did not stop at building a palace for the empress. He had four days of parties and visits planned for her and shuttled her from place to place. Knowing her eagerness to see the real Egypt, he arranged for her to attend an Egyptian wedding, where the delighted Eugénie, clad in an Arab dress, watched belly dancing. She told Ismail that it reminded her of Spanish dances, "if perhaps more indecent."

The khedive was also eager to show off the remodeling he was doing to "make Cairo like Paris," he told her. He had hired French architects, landscape designers and gardeners. He'd even created a new quarter of the city with long avenues ending in squares, and a pattern of radial streets with monuments and public buildings that defined vistas, just like in Paris, Ismail said. Unburdened by modesty or restraint, he'd named the new city division Ismailiyah.

It was clear he had had to borrow heavily to spend so lavishly to modernize the country. There were new railroad lines "just like in France." Miles and miles of telegraph lines "just like in France." New schools "just like in France." On and on it went, but Eugénie had begun to question the proliferation of projects. They looked like a veneer; plus, she had no need or desire to see everything "just like in France." Her interest was Egypt. She'd even thought briefly about creating an Egyptian museum like her Chinese Museum in Fontainebleau. She had seen the jewelry of Queen Ahhotep II when it was displayed at the Universal Exposition and considered asking Ismail to give it to her for a possible display. Ismail knew her interest in the pieces and said she should talk to Auguste Mariette, the resident Egyptologist in Cairo and the man who had discovered the tomb of Queen Ahhotep II in 1858.

Mariette, who was developing a museum of Egyptian antiquities in Cairo, told her he believed the jewelry belonged in Egypt. Seeing the pyramids, museums and temples, she realized he was right. Mariette, however, thanks to an agreement he made with the French government to fund his work in Egypt, sent half of the antiquities to the Louvre with the other half remaining in Egypt. It would be another 150 years before pressure to repatriate antiquities began to see artifacts restored to their countries of origin.

At the khedive's request, Mariette also used his knowledge of Egyptian lore to outline an idea for an opera to celebrate the opening of the Suez Canal. He sought help from Camille du Locle to refine his idea, and the two of them proposed it to Guiseppe Verdi. The result was *Aida*. Even though Mariette and du Locle designed the costumes and stage sets, it was not finished by the time the canal was opened, forcing the disappointed khedive to stage Verdi's *Rigoletto* instead.

Eugénie, meanwhile, was determined to see and learn more of the country, not just what the khedive had chosen. Tell me about the real history and civilization of Egypt, she told Mariette, and, then, as with Maspero, she proceeded to bombard him with questions, her ladies remembered. "Was there really a Queen Nitocris?" she asked. "Was she regent of Egypt? And Ramses II—did he really have 170 children? How were the pyramids built? How did such a grandiose civilization become a vassal to the Roman Empire and the Turks?"

Mariette was taken aback, struggling to keep up. Finally, either having a brilliant idea or looking for relief, he said, "Would you consider a cruise on the Nile so you can see for yourself?"

Cruise was the magic word for Eugénie, and combining it with the opportunity of seeing more of Egypt made it even more alluring.

A beautifully outfitted *dahabiyah*, a large houseboat, became her quarters for nearly two weeks as she began a languid trip up the Nile with only her nieces and nephew, two of her ladies and a soldier. The khedive sent other boats with his guests along behind, but they were told to leave Eugénie and her party alone unless approached by the empress. Ismail said he respected her desire to travel incognita and provided everything he could to protect her privacy. The ever-active empress, however, insisted she would not spend her time sitting on deck; she would ride daily, as she always did. The khedive quickly added to the entourage his best horses and a white camel the empress had loved, as well as his own soldiers to assure her safety during her rides.

It was the vacation Eugénie had been longing for. It gave her time to explore new places and ideas and reflect, but she could not escape her worries, which often led to sleepless nights. The political situation and Napoléon's health nagged at her, and her concern had increased with her distance from Paris. The emperor's daily telegrams about the problems did nothing to allay her fears. Seeing the pharaohs' tombs and talking about their embalming methods only intensified her anxieties and, worse, brought back painful memories of her sister's death.

One night, she went to the cabin of her lady-in-waiting, Marie des Garets. The idea of a body's decay after death had always bothered her, especially after the rapid burial of Paca after her death. Perhaps embalming in the Egyptian manner was a good solution, something we should do, she said to her lady-in-waiting. Marie was surprised by the late-night visit from the empress, but

Empress Eugénie on her camel, visiting the pharaohs' tombs. *Painter Charles-Théodore Frère, Musées de Compiègne, Creative Commons*

said she had no desire to be embalmed so she could be dug up in 2,000 years and put on display. Eugénie agreed that was an unhappy outcome but, she said, the Egyptian way of death "gives a real grandeur to their nation."

Grandeur in Egypt was not lacking in any case, she realized. Every day the Nile was showing her more: Boulaq, Minieh, Denderah, Luxor, Thebes, Edfou, Assouan and Philae Island. Ismail's promises of incognita travel were an affable untruth: every village along the way was adorned to welcome her. But Eugénie had no complaints. At night all the boats were illuminated, and their lights reflected as twinkling stars in the water. She thrilled to hear jackals yapping in the distance.

In Luxor, the empress attended a banquet under a tent of palm leaves with some of Ismail's guests from other boats. Upon reaching Philae Island, revered by the goddess Isis and seen as the burial place of Osiris but also known for its early Christian connections, Eugénie asked to visit alone. The temples were located on the island at the First Cataract of the Nile. Crossing to it was nerve-wracking. Her ladies-in-waiting were delighted to be left behind and let the empress enjoy another turbulent moment on water.

The rowers chanted slowly as they fought the rapids and maneuvered around outcroppings of rocks. Eugénie was enchanted, finding nature's caprices and the river more awe-inspiring even than the ancient buildings with their vivid images. However, once on the island, a stone in the Tiberius Kiosk, often called Pharoah's Bed, caught her attention. The kiosk had been built as a temple to Isis, goddess of birth and magic. Eugénie was probably drawn to Isis's legend as the mother of Horus who had given birth to him only after a long pregnancy and difficult labor. The huge, ornate structure, which had been begun in about 280 BCE, contained some of the best-preserved carvings of the early Egypt period. It also held a stone that had been carved by one of Bonaparte's generals, Louis Desaix, in March 1799 to memorialize his army's arrival at the cataract. When the entire complex was threatened by the high waters created by the Aswan Dam, it was dismantled and moved to the nearby Aglika Island where it remains today.

Seeing the carving by Desaix, however, Eugénie felt as though she had been given a sign directly from the first Napoléon, a sign that, despite all her worries about her husband's health, the regime would last until their son came of age. She returned to her dahabiyah elated.

As the boat drifted onward, she spent hours on her daily rides, often atop the white camel Ismail had sent for her. "This climate makes me feel so good," she wrote to her husband. "Despite the heat, the air is light and we can breathe easily."

With Marie des Garets, another devoted equestrian, she ventured beyond the fertile strip of land alongside the river into the neighboring desert. There she saw for herself what she had suspected from the moment of her arrival in Egypt: the modernization the khedive touted was a facade, a sham that veiled extreme poverty. Eugénie was shocked, especially by the wretchedness of the women, most of whom appeared half-naked and lived in "miserable huts." Reaching into her pouch, Eugénie gave all the money she was carrying to them. In return, they blessed her, bowing and smiling. Their dignity touched Eugénie deeply.

Her own ladies, however, had grown restive with the slow pace of travel and were bickering. The heat, which Eugénie found reminiscent of her native Granada, made them nervous and uncomfortable. She turned nursemaid, handing out bananas, telling them to quit drinking so many iced beverages and sent them to bed early.

It was probably not surprising that in the atmosphere of such discomfort and complaints, Eugénie's own worries came flooding back. At the height of her anxieties, she wrote Napoléon that she had decided to come home immediately, that she should be there for the opening of parliament and help deal with questions facing the Second Empire.

Even tired and ill as he was, Napoléon was thunderstruck. How could she possibly think of skipping the inauguration of the canal? It was the work of her own cousin. It had taken fifteen years to get it to this point. It was a major triumph for France.

With Russia and England both looking for an opportunity to get their hands on the canal, the emperor, in a hastily drafted message, pleaded with Eugénie to stay put. Our being in two different places at this crucial time makes France look stronger, he said. You are representing the prestige of France at a key international event and should finish the trip as planned. "Besides that, I need you there as my eyes and ears," he wrote.

Eugénie relented and agreed to stay, ordering her dahabiyah back to Cairo. She wrote Napoléon that she now completely agreed with him and believed that the empire should be liberalized immediately. They did not have to wait for a better moment or leave it for their son to accomplish.

Eugénie was happy to be "home" again on her yacht and declared the day after her arrival a holiday for her sailors. There would then be a short trip to Port Saïd, a prequel to the main event, the opening of the Suez Canal.

On the morning of November 16, *l'Aigle* sailed through a phalanx of yachts, sailboats, naval vessels and nearly every other kind of seafaring conveyance to berth itself between the *Maroussia*, Khedive Ismail's opulent yacht, and the *Greif*, the elegant two-masted brigantine that was the personal sailing ship of the Austrian Emperor Franz Joseph.

As usual, it was Eugénie who was the undisputed star, the one person everyone wanted to see. There would be two long days of celebrations. She first welcomed the khedive onto her yacht and then king after king, prince after prince, followed by a never-ending stream of rulers and magnates. Each arrival was announced by the firing of cannons. That afternoon, when Eugénie emerged from her cabin to attend ceremonies on the beach, the whole world seemed to catch its breath. Emperor Franz Joseph, who had been impatiently pacing the deck of his yacht as he waited for her, nearly tripped over his feet in his hurry to escort her down the gangway to the ceremony. The empress was resplendent in a gray ribbed-silk taffeta gown, richly trimmed with white Alençon lace and jewels that brilliantly reflected the Egyptian sun. In a salute to Egypt and its history, she wore a small black hat with two ostrich feathers, symbol of the god Osiris and favorite ornament and mark of status for the pharaohs.

There was a Christian blessing, which went on too long in the heat, Eugénie thought, then a Muslim one, which was blessedly short. It was the prelude to the festivities which followed— banquets, music and fireworks over the water.

At the end of the evening, the empress, gratified by the events but needing time on her own to absorb the spectacle, slipped away from her bodyguards to walk in the soft air of the starlit night. She caught snatches of conversations in different languages and rejoiced in the unexpected pleasure of eavesdropping on regular people and hearing how excited they were about the event. The next day was only hours away, and it would be the most important one, the pinnacle of years of work and her own trip. She would open the Suez Canal.

It was around that time that Reine, Eugénie's turtle, slipped

View of the Suez Canal the day of the inauguration. *Édouard Riou, Jules-Descartes Férat, Charles Barbant, GrandPalaisRMN (Château de Versailles) / Gérard Blot*

away to enjoy the sand and warm water of the Nile. Despite numerous searches, the animal could not be found before Eugénie left for the opening of the Suez Canal. A few days later after Eugénie had sailed home, Reine was spotted on the road to the pyramids. She was retrieved and given a new home in the zoo Ismail had created around the Gezirah Palace he had built for Eugénie. Reine evidently found her new life comfortable and lived to be ninety. Her death in 1949, nearly thirty years after her mistress passed away, was noted in an obituary in *The New York Times*.

IT WAS EIGHT O'CLOCK IN THE MORNING OF NOVEMBER 17 WHEN EUGÉNIE'S YACHT LEFT ITS berth and took its place at the head of a seemingly endless flotilla. "I can never forget her radiant figure," wrote Dr. Evans, "as she stood alone on the bridge of the *Aigle*, while the imperial yacht slowly passed by the immense throng that had assembled on the banks of the Canal."

Passage through the new waterway was not entirely smooth, however. There was debris left by construction, and at least one beached boat to skirt and sections where the water level was dangerously low for passage of the yacht. Captain Charles-Jules de Surville, chosen by Napoléon to pilot *l'Aigle* on its most auspicious voyage, admitted he was nervous and moved with caution through the canal.

After several anxious hours, the great camp Ismail had set up at Ismailiyah at the end of the canal finally came into view, and with it a sense of relief, then exhilaration.

She had done it! Eugénie had made the trip generations had dreamed of, longed for. She had traversed the Suez Canal: East and West were now true neighbors. For the second time in a matter of days, she was overcome with emotion, her eyes brimming with tears. The excitement, the triumph, it was almost more than she could take. Cannons were firing, people amassed along the canal were cheering deliriously, crying in each other's arms, men tossing hats in the air.

Eugénie looked to the shore and saw the large tent of the khedive along hundreds of other tents representing different tribes and groups. Dignitaries, aristocrats, politicians, nomads, people of all backgrounds and nationalities, including the Norwegian playwright Henrik Ibsen—all of them brought together by the canal. There as well were the workers, those who had begun building the canal with nothing more than picks and shovels, laborers like their ancestors who eons before had built the pyramids. As many as 30,000 people would have been working on the canal at any given moment. Many, perhaps thousands, had lost their lives in the years of toil to accomplish what the world was now celebrating.

Celebrations spilled into the next day, becoming even more colorful and exhilarating. Eugénie, even though besieged by crowds, took her family and ladies-in-waiting to a fantasia of a thousand horsemen, whirling dervishes and even a donkey race. Finally, escaping the throng, Eugénie found her favorite white camel again and rode to the top of the dunes to view the camp and the festivities. She visited the small shops and cafés, saw the animals and even played with the children. "It was such a party," recalled Marie des Garets. "After spending so many days exploring the ancient Egypt, it was a pleasure to joyously discover a young, happy and vibrant country."

The day was not over, however. The khedive had some more showing off to do and some one-upmanship to tweak Sultan Abdulaziz's nose. He wanted to advertise to the world that the Suez Canal belonged to Egypt.

Ismail had gone shopping when he was at the Universal Exposition in Paris two years earlier, and he was about to display his and his country's importance and wealth by parading the purchases he'd made. That night he hosted a state dinner and ball where everything—tables, chairs, tableware, candlesticks—had come from France. There were emperors, kings, princes, princesses, ambassadors, military dignitaries, industrialists, bankers, pashas, sheiks, thousands of guests, but Ismail had bought enough

The celebration banquet of the opening of the Suez Canal. *Édouard Riou, Album /
TopFoto*

to make sure every one of them could eat each of the twenty-four
dishes served as though they were in France.

Even so, after ten o'clock, it hardly mattered. No one paid
the least attention to the silverware, the china or even the food,
because that was when Empress Eugénie, covered in diamonds,
made her grand entrance. From that moment on, the party was
all about her.

Eugénie played her final role the next day when she left behind Ismail's elaborate trappings and made an official visit to Suez
City. Alongside her was the man who had made the canal a reality: her cousin, Ferdinand de Lesseps. In that old city of little
streets and long shadows, she distributed medals bearing his image to workers and thanked them. Then, with a last, longing
look at Egypt, she boarded *l'Aigle* and set its nose toward France,
sending up a prayer that God would help her with what lay ahead.

It was the last time the empress would look to the future with
any kind of optimism . . . the last time she would see "a wonderful future for my son" . . . the last time she would be truly happy.

CHAPTER THIRTEEN

LAST DAYS

FIVE DAYS OF SAILING FROM CAIRO WERE NOT ENOUGH TO PREPARE EUGÉNIE FOR THE SHOCK when she landed in Toulon on December 5, 1869. The brilliant sunshine and cocooning heat of Egypt were replaced by the wintery skies and penetrating chill that had settled on France. And the chill was not just from the temperature.

Politics had turned a cold shoulder to the Second Empire. The early economic successes had cooled, and foreign policy failures, such as the Mexican incursion, had embarrassed and angered many of the French. Eugénie had hoped positive results would come from Napoléon's speech to parliament a few days earlier when he outlined a more liberal direction of his reign. He had already relaxed controls on the press and given workers the right to organize and strike. Now he said he would yield more power to government ministers and the Corps Législatif, France's parliamentary body.

It wasn't enough, and opposition only increased. It came from an assortment of factions: republicans, royalists who favored the *ancien régime* of the Bourbons, monarchists who preferred the Orléans claimants to the throne, Catholics angered by what was seen as antipapal policy under the emperor, and even from farmers and business people who had been Napoléon's main supporters but who now were up in arms over his free-trade treaties.

It would require a master politician to pull all those together, and no matter what he had been in the past, Napoléon III clearly was not that now. He was exhausted, sick and often lethargic, thanks to the opium doctors had begun giving him that year to counteract his increasing pain. His health problems had begun during his six years of imprisonment in Ham, which left him with chronic pain in his legs and feet which became more intense in the cold. He used a cane and walked slowly. He kept his rooms overheated to ease his discomfort, and he smoked cigarettes incessantly in the closed confines. Distrustful of physicians who had told him he had "stone disease," he maintained it was "just rheumatism" and spent time at warm water spas like Vichy in an effort to deal with his problems.

The empress was shocked by the change she saw in him after her two months away. Although he'd complained about his physical problems in his telegrams to her, the reality was much worse than she had imagined. He was noticeably weaker and had severe abdominal pains; he was urinating blood and could not sit down or ride a horse for more than a few minutes. His normally soft voice was now little more than a whisper, and his handwriting had become almost illegible.

Doctor after doctor was called to the royal palace. They all agreed that what had been suspected was true: the emperor had a stone in his bladder. And they agreed on another thing: no surgery.

Although the French doctor Jean Civale had developed lithotripsy forty-five years earlier when he devised a small forceps that could be inserted into the urethra to grab the stone so it could be crushed into fragments that would easily pass with the urine, the practice carried risks. Infection could set in, especially because sterilizing of equipment was still not regularly practiced, and repeat procedures might be necessary if all the fragments were not passed. Leftover fragments could block the urethra leading to greater pain, internal bleeding and erectile dysfunction.

There was also the possibility of rendering the emperor incapacitated while under anesthesia because there was not yet a method of monitoring an anesthetized patient. Verifying pulse rate and breathing were a decade away. Nonetheless, the use of ether and chloroform was by then widespread, especially for childbirth. Queen Victoria, for instance, had accepted chloroform for the delivery of her eighth child in 1852.

How much of the doctors' decision to avoid surgery was based on fear is uncertain. Sir Henry Thompson, who had been summoned to remove bladder stones from Belgian's King Leopold I in 1862, expressed his worries about undertaking a royal procedure in a letter to his wife. "I slept only one and a half hours last night . . . I got thinking about my case and I got horribly anxious about it in the night. No one knows how anxious except those who are placed in like circumstances."

If Napoléon should die during surgery, surgeons knew they would be blamed and their careers would be over. Yes, Napoléon's physicians reasoned, without treatment the emperor would be in discomfort for a while, but most stones, they said, were small and passed naturally. Once that happened, the sixty-one-year-old emperor would be fine, they told each other hopefully.

Eugénie was not told what the problem was. The doctors maintained they wanted "to avoid frightening her," and Napoléon himself agreed. It was his "rheumatism and a cystitis," they told the empress. Granted, it was acute, but, no, they couldn't suggest anything that would help him or make him more comfortable. He'll get better, they said.

That left the empress with even more worry. She knew Napoléon had earned his reputation as "the Sphinx" with his reluctance to share things, even with her. He'd nearly destroyed their marriage when he kept Paca's illness and death from her, but now what was he keeping from her? He was dismissive of her concerns. The doctors would tell her nothing. She felt as though she were being treated like a child. What she didn't know at the time was that the physicians had written out their diagnosis and sealed it in an envelope she would find, unopened, in Napoléon's desk only after his death.

His worsening condition was apparent to all who saw him, however, and he took to dyeing his thinning hair and using cosmetics to conceal his pallor when in public. Even family dinners, which usually delighted the emperor because of the time with the prince impérial, didn't cheer him. Now he could hardly sit through a meal. And if he had to travel, even a short distance, Napoléon, who loved all things equestrian and believed riding horseback in public showed his authority, now called for a carriage and had it padded with cushions.

The government, afraid that news of Napoléon's health problems would lead to more unrest and even calls for his abdication, kept silent and warned newspapers against spreading "alarms about the health of the emperor." The international press was not constrained: a British journalist wrote how the smiling and pleasant Eugénie looked on while Napoléon had "a careworn expression" when the imperial couple appeared together at Longchamp for the Grand Prix de Paris in the spring of 1870.

Eugénie's usual way of helping Napoléon—attending ministerial meetings and advising him—seemed beyond her now. The ministers he'd brought in during her absence were new to her. She didn't know them as she did the previous ones, hadn't worked with them or learned their interests. The new prime minister was Emile Ollivier, whom she *had* worked with on prison reform. However, he had succeeded in getting her excluded from the council meetings, officially "in order that opinions may not be attributed to her which she does not entertain, and that she may not be suspected of an influence which she does not desire to exercise." She complied, but being sidelined and excluded from important affairs of state was demoralizing.

Eugénie paced the halls of the Tuileries Palace trailed by whispers that had become nearly a steady drone. Some said the empress was "troubled and irritated by the parliamentary and liberal movement" her husband had initiated. They conveniently ignored the change of mind she'd had during her Suez Canal trip, even though she'd let everyone know she agreed the government had to be liberalized to prepare the way for their son to govern. The opposition press accused her of taking advantage of the emperor's visibly weakened condition, manipulating him like a puppet on strings. Often they distorted her comments and quoted them out of context. They dug up all the old slanderous cartoons and gleefully returned to their favorite way of vilifying her as "that Spanish woman."

As empress, Eugénie had determinedly ignored slurs and insults printed in the press and gossip in government hallways, but now, tired, disillusioned and consumed with worry about Napoléon's health and her son's future, she became hypersensitive to even implied criticism. When one of her favorite authors, George Sand, wrote a novel, *Malgrétout*, about an ambitious Spanish woman, Eugénie saw it as an attack on her and was deeply hurt. How could one woman slander another in fiction? she questioned. She had backed Sand's work, even trying to put her in the Académie Française and awarding her a 20,000-franc grant when the author was in financial trouble. Sand, a committed republican, had rejected both, but now when she learned of Eugénie's hurt feelings, she was quick to deny that the portrait of her Spanish heroine had anything to do with the empress. But the wound remained.

At the same time, Queen Isabella II of Spain moved in across the street from the Tuileries. She had been forced off her throne in a military uprising and fled straight to France with her husband, her children and her lover. Eugénie knew the queen was spoiled and promiscuous, but she was a fellow monarch, so the empress made her welcome.

Unfortunately, Isabella's flight would be the spark that ignited another crisis, a major one that would wipe all thoughts of George Sand, *Malgrétout* and every other slight from Eugénie's mind. The queen left a throne empty, and the Spanish offered it to the Prussian prince, Leopold of Hohenzollern. He wasn't eager to accept, but Otto von Bismarck, Prussia's chancellor and master of *realpolitik*, had other ideas. He saw the open throne as the opportunity he'd been waiting for to prod France into a war. If Leopold accepted, France would be surrounded by countries ruled by Prussians, a situation he knew Napoléon could not accept.

Bismarck was confident he could defeat Napoléon after seeing at the World's Fair in 1867 how badly out-of-date French military equipment was. He'd also taken note of Napoléon's declining physical condition and was aware that France would have few allies if it stood against Prussia. Too many other countries feared and resented France's power in Europe, but no one just then was worried about "little" Prussia. In addition, war with France was a rallying call Bismarck knew he could use as a catalyst to bring about German unity, so he encouraged Leopold's father to accept on his son's behalf.

Eugénie had been circumspect about the Iron Chancellor ever since her first regency in 1859 when, as she read diplomatic documents, she saw signs of growing militarism in Prussia. She had warned Napoléon then and urged him to place French troops on the Prussian border as a warning. He declined and opted to move cautiously. The emperor was already concerned about France's loss of prestige in Europe and he, like Bismarck, recognized the weaknesses of France's army—yet he had been unable to convince his own generals to accept conscription or a change in general staffing procedures. Napoléon did not want to take unnecessary risks, especially after the debacle in Mexico.

The emperor still took comfort in believing he had the country's support. A large majority had approved the liberal changes he proposed in a plebiscite in May 1870. He rejoiced to see that the people's approval rating of his government had returned to the level it had been in 1851 when he staged the coup d'état that led to his takeover of the government. Eugénie and Napoléon euphorically told their teenage son, the prince impérial, about the results after the plebiscite. "It is *your* throne that is rising on seven million votes," his tutor Filon remembered them saying. "France is with us." The seven million votes represented more than 85 percent of those cast. But the election had been a referendum on Napoléon's liberalized domestic policy, not on the Second Empire's foreign relations. The French population was less than pleased with those.

The préfets, or provincial governors, reported to Paris that criticism of the government was increasing in the provinces, areas that were usually staunchly Bonapartist. The French public had also begun grumbling that Prussia was disparaging France by trying to thrust a German princeling onto the Spanish throne. In the press and on the streets, the people made their rancor clear. How can we let Prussia dictate who sits on the throne of a sister Latin country? After all, the Spanish royal house has been connected to France since the time of Louis XIV when the Sun King put his second son on the Spanish throne, and if we now let the Germans take control of Spain, we'll be surrounded by Teutonic rulers.

The French found Bismarck's move particularly galling because it had echoes of a previous battle for the Spanish succession and struggles among European royal houses for power. Plus, there was still the festering wound from France's own misguided venture of trying to impose a foreign ruler on Mexico. Prussia should not succeed in getting control of another throne when France had failed. National pride was at stake.

Bismarck sat back and gloated: things were moving just as he thought they would.

Napoléon, despite his misgivings, felt pressure to act and decided to send a mild rebuke to Prussia. He suggested a European conference to settle the issue, a proposal met with disdain. He also sent his ambassador to talk to the Prussian King Wilhelm I, who was on vacation at the spa of Bad Ems. Although the German prince had by then withdrawn as a candidate for the Spanish throne, the French ambassador was to seek the king's assurance that he would never propose another German candidate. *Never* was a long time, the cautious Wilhelm said; he couldn't make promises about the indeterminate future.

In the end, no one was happy with Napoléon's hesitant approach, not his own ministers and certainly not his wife. Eugénie believed Bismarck was taunting France; this was not about the dynasty, she said, it was about the nation. Something must be done, though the empress wasn't entirely convinced at that moment that that *something* meant taking up arms.

The bellicose press, on the other hand, bayed for war. Napoléon, recognizing the country's feelings, had installed a new foreign minister after the May elections, replacing the pacifist Count Napoléon Daru with the Duc de Gramont, who was violently opposed to Prussia and who had long been the French ambassador to Austria. Gramont and fellow ministers told the emperor that war was the only way to save the honor of France. Eugénie disagreed: "May God grant that there be no war" but then added "But peace bought at the price of dishonor would be as great a misfortune, and France should never put up with it."

Bismarck watched and waited. He needed something stronger than Napoléon's mild rebuke to rouse his countrymen's sense of nationalism so he could draw them together under one flag. When King Wilhelm I prepared a conciliatory response to the emperor, Bismarck surreptitiously grabbed the dispatch before it was sent and removed a few phrases to make what would become known as the Ems Telegram sound as though Prussia was insulting France. "That," said the self-satisfied Bismarck, "should have the effect of a red rag on the Gallic [French] bull."

It had been a bitterly cold winter and a long one. Snow and ice persisted in some areas and it seemed as if summer would never arrive, but in July, just as the Council of Ministers gathered to discuss the Ems Telegram, it finally turned hot—and brutally so. Temperatures soared to over 100 degrees Fahrenheit, and the stifling heat smothered the country for days. Ministers in their court attire were dripping with sweat as they crowded into the council chambers to decide whether to send their country into war against Prussia. Eugénie, in one of her lightest gowns, went to the meeting.

It was July 14, not yet a national holiday, but people poured into the Place de la Bastille and onto the streets carrying flags and banners with patriotic slogans and calling for war. Ministers could hear their cries as they filed into the scorching council chambers. Over the noise, the leader of the monarchist party called for calm. France had won the diplomatic war, he said, so nothing more needed to be done. He was shouted down, accused of being a traitor and pro-Prussia.

Prime Minister Ollivier had originally seen little need for the army and had long opposed increasing or modernizing it, but even he was caught up in the atmosphere. Yes, he concurred, France had done everything it could diplomatically, so war was the only remaining option for defending its honor. He accepted the responsibility of sending the country into battle "with a light heart."

The empress sat through the meeting without speaking. She felt the affront to France, the "slap in the face" as the foreign minister described it. She believed Prussia had to be made to answer for its behavior. But she also felt the pain of sending men into war, toward their own deaths. Just a few months earlier she had felt compelled to visit the graves of other French soldiers who had died fighting for their country in a foreign land. She had placed flowers there and mourned them in her letter home to her son. Now, she feared, France was sending more young men to graves, men whose families would never see them again. Hopefully it would be a short war, she told herself, and the men would be home quickly. France would prevail and regain its honor, and families would be reunited.

On July 15, 1870, France mobilized, and Prussia immediately followed suit. They were at war.

The Duc de Gramont, the virulently anti-Prussian foreign minister, claimed that Eugénie had spoken strongly in favor of the war at the council meeting. Gramont, however, had not been at the meeting, but Prime Minister Ollivier had. He was the presiding officer, and he maintained the empress sat quietly throughout the proceedings.

When she left the meeting to return to her private quarters, Eugénie could hear the crowds celebrating, singing "La Marseillaise" and chanting "To Berlin! To Berlin!"

She saw nothing to celebrate: France was doing its duty, doing what it must for its honor. And she, too, would do her duty.

CHAPTER FOURTEEN

SHADOW OF THE GUILLOTINE

ONCE MORE, EMPRESS EUGÉNIE STOOD AT THE PRIVATE TRAIN STATION OF THE CHÂTEAU DE Saint-Cloud saying her goodbyes and holding her tears in check, keeping her face calm and her veneer of confidence and courage in place. This time, however, it was not a departure for a glamorous event like opening of the Suez Canal. This time she was sending her husband and son off to war.

Events had unfolded with alarming speed. France began mobilizing troops on July 15, 1870. Prussia did the same that afternoon. The following day, France declared war. Less than two weeks later, Napoléon, despite his limited military experience and poor health, and against all advice to the contrary, announced he would take personal command of the army. He named Eugénie as regent once again to govern in his absence: France was in her hands.

The public was delirious with war fever and excitement. It was the moment everyone had waited for. Here was the opportunity to put the Prussians in their place once and for all and show them who the real power in Europe was.

But in Saint-Cloud, 10 miles outside Paris, the mood was anything but euphoric. There, on July 28, Napoléon and Loulou, the fourteen-year-old prince impérial, prepared to board a private train that would take them to the front. With them were a physician and numerous aides. The emperor had donned the uniform of a general while Loulou was dressed as a sublieutenant complete with a sword at his side. "Do your duty," his mother told him, as she made the sign of the cross on his forehead and struggled for composure. As soon as the train vanished from view, she broke down in tears.

She had deep reservations about the war, but in the end, Eugénie also believed there was no alternative. After Prussia had insulted France over who should take over the Spanish throne, the Prussians had to be taught a lesson. It was a duty and matter of honor.

Duty and honor. Duty and honor. She had heard those words so many times, all her life in fact, from her father glorifying the campaigns of Napoléon Bonaparte; from Stendhal who made Bonaparte's wars seem like adventure stories when he related them to her and her sister; and from her husband as he talked of realizing his uncle's dreams. Her own family motto, A Free Homeland Is of Greater Importance than the Death of a Kinsman, meant duty and honor, too. Eugénie could feel those words in her heart, but not until she watched her husband and son go off to war did she realize how painful it would be to actually live them.

It was excruciating for Napoléon as well. He was weak and in pain from the debilitating bladder stone episodes. Normally the emperor would have ridden, as tradition demanded, on horseback at the head of the army through the streets of Paris, cheered on by adoring crowds. His bladder stones made that impossible. At the same time, for a commander-in-chief to be seen taking a train to the front would be humiliating. As a result, the emperor's train had been rerouted around Paris and out of sight from crowds.

To project confidence to the nation, Eugénie remained at the imperial family's summer residence in Saint-Cloud rather than rushing back to Paris.

Not that the public or military needed additional confidence under the sunshine of that hot, dry summer. "We'll be home by Christmas," soldiers bragged, a cry that would be echoed by their descendants forty-four years later when they left for the First World War. The men and boys of 1870, armed with their new Chassepot rifles, the most up-to-date gun available, and sporting their handsome uniforms with bright red trousers, marched off happily. Crowds cheering "*À Berlin*" were so thick that Paris omnibuses had to find alternative routes to get to destinations. At train stations, well-wishers chanted "Rout the German blockheads!" and held out bottles of wine to the departing troops, reminding them that "the German hates the Frenchman but loves his wine."

Stores stocked up with French–German dictionaries people could use themselves or hand to the passing troops, as well as maps of Germany to help the French follow the victorious route of their army. "La Marseillaise," now permitted again after years of being banned because it had been composed during the French Revolution and was seen as a call to rise up against tyranny, could be heard throughout the city sung joyfully and almost nonstop.

Thomas Evans was not among those cheering. He'd been at Saint-Cloud to say goodbye to Napoléon the day before the emperor and his son had left for the front. Evans had arrived expecting to see the emperor as usual, standing on a balcony of the château smoking a cigarette. Instead he found him closeted in his overheated office looking worried and exhausted.

"The future of France looks dark and uncertain," Evans wrote in his journal after the farewells. He was convinced Napoléon was getting bad counsel from his advisers, especially Gramont, the foreign minister, who was widely considered "vain and impetuous" and eager to cross swords with Prussia. "This man will bring war," one observer had warned Evans. Even Gramont's cousin, the British diplomat Lord Malmesbury, who was a close friend of Napoléon's, had counseled that Gramont did not have "the diplomatic genius he credited himself with."

Unfortunately, Napoléon, distracted by his health and exhaustion, was more worried about France's ebbing power in Europe and declining public support for the Second Empire at home. Yet, he was also facing increasing public pressure to punish Prussia for insulting France. Making the well-known Gramont foreign minister, he hoped, would appease the public.

Lillie Moulton also visited Saint-Cloud just before Napoléon's departure. Like Evans, she found the atmosphere deeply depressing. She and her husband had been invited to a party that was abruptly canceled, but the two of them were asked to stay for dinner. "I never regretted anything so much in my life," Moulton wrote. "No one spoke. Every now and again the emperor would look across the table to the empress with such a distressed look it made me think something terrible was happening."

Doubts plagued Eugénie, too, as she waited in Saint-Cloud. As July turned into August, telegrams from her husband at the front chipped away at the illusion that France's army was invincible. Although nominally in charge, Napoléon had delegated responsibility for leadership of the two field armies to Marshal François Achille Bazaine and Marshal Patrice de MacMahon. What the emperor saw when he arrived at army headquarters disturbed him. "Nothing is ready here," he complained to Eugénie. "There is nothing anywhere but muddle, incoherence, delays, quarrels and confusion."

On August 2, in a more positive dispatch, Napoléon told her how proud he was of their son after he had behaved calmly during a recent skirmish with the enemy, even picking up a spent shell in the aftermath of the fighting. "He might just as well have been strolling in the Bois de Boulogne."

The skirmish in question was hardly a major victory, but the French press portrayed it as such. The engagement was brief and the Prussians put up little resistance, but the fourteen-year-old prince came in for criticism. He was ridiculed by reporters saying he had been "playing like a child on the battlefield, playing as men were being killed." For Eugénie, herself a frequent target of the press, such reports were profoundly distressing.

On the day Eugénie received the message about their son, Napoléon was at the head of the army marching toward the German town of Saarbrücken. He was hoping to win a key battle before the Germans had fully mobilized, but neither he nor the rest of the French high command realized how quickly the Germans had put their troops into the field. In one battle after another, German bombardments began cutting down the French. Their new breech-loading rifles were no defense against heavy artillery of the Prussian's six-pounder. It did the French soldiers no good to attempt to conceal themselves from the enemy: their bright red trousers gave them away.

The Prussians further dismayed the French by attacking in a radically new fashion: small groups dispersed through the area rather than a long line formation that had historically been the staple of warfare. The French commanders were, as generals before and after them have done, still fighting the previous war.

History weighed heavily on Eugénie. She could feel it in every hallway, every corner of Saint-Cloud as she walked the corridors of the château and strolled the pathways of its park. It was here that Marie-Antoinette brought her children for "healthy air," where the first Napoléon declared himself emperor of France in 1804, and where forty-eight years later her husband did the same. But it was also here, during the Wars of Religion in 1589, where Henri III was assassinated by a Catholic fanatic. Ancient history, to be sure, but those memories only added to her anxiety and fears for what lay ahead.

Eugénie, becoming more tense as the battles continued, asked the priest at Saint-Cloud to join her for dinner on August 4 to celebrate the feast day of St. Dominic de Guzman, the thirteenth-century founder of the Dominican order of monks who was a distant connection of the empress's family. The priest noticed that even though there had been encouraging news from the front that day, Eugénie frequently leaned her hand on the table, as if seeking

support. She asked him to pray for her and the country at the ba-
silica of Notre-Dame-des-Victoires.

Our Lady of Victory turned a deaf ear. On that very day,
more than 325,000 Prussian troops poured across the border with
thousands of reservists quickly following. They overran Alsace
and Lorraine and chalked up victories almost faster than they
could be located on a map. One thing finally slowed them down:
"wretched Champagne." Temperatures suddenly plunged in that
northeastern region and torrents of rain turned Champagne's
chalky landscape into a morass of sticky gray muck that caked
on soldiers' boots and seeped inside. French soldiers were rattled
by the startling change in the weather. There's something weird,
even creepy, about this, they whispered to each other. It's a por-
tent, they said, as their losses mounted almost by the minute.

Even though supply wagons sank up to their axels in the
waterlogged terrain, the Prussians kept advancing while French
losses mounted. New weapons had made killing faster and easier
for both sides. The French wielded their Chassepot rifles and the
mitrailleuse, the world's first machine gun, nicknamed "the coffee grinder." The Prussians, however, had something even dead-
lier: long-range artillery.

Damage inflicted by both sides shook even the most battled-
hardened soldiers. "It was senseless butchery," recalled a Prussian
sergeant after one battle. "There were bodies heaped up everywhere, yet one looked in vain for a single intact corpse. I spotted
a beautiful pair of cavalry boots lying on the ground and picked
them up; there were legs and feet still inside." The carnage was so
terrible, said another witness, that even victories felt like defeats.

In Saint-Cloud, Eugénie's depression deepened. "I am good
for nothing," she wailed to her ladies-in-waiting after learning
of France's defeat in one battle. "A bad dispatch reaches me and I
completely collapse. I am more of a wife and mother than regent."

She had good reason to question her role as regent because
ministers in the newly liberalized government were undercutting
her. They met without her knowledge and did not bother to send

her reports. Even Prime Minister Emile Ollivier was withholding information and important decisions from her, intimating a woman had no place in government. "The Empress," he said, "is too vocal and opinionated."

Nevertheless, because of Napoléon's regular telegrams from the front, Eugénie was probably more informed about the true state of the war than anyone else in government. The emperor wrote to her not only as his wife but also as his regent.

Meanwhile, despite her problems with Ollivier and other ministers, the empress struggled to continue to present the government as a united front to the public, vowing not to interfere with military decisions and refraining from attacking political ones. She visited the fleet in Cherbourg in Normandy where a French squadron was preparing to sail to the Baltic. "We are accustomed to seeing our empress come forward whenever there is danger to be faced," the admiral welcoming her said. The visit was a wise choice as Eugénie always felt at home among sailors. She delivered a warmhearted message and ended by reading the emperor's proclamation to the army.

The situation with Ollivier and the ministerial council, however, had become intolerable, and Eugénie knew something had to be done. It didn't help that each day brought news of defeats and retreats. Nearly everyone had been convinced of the strength and competence of the army; it looked so handsome and brave, and when lined up for reviews, it appeared massive to the public. It had no way of judging how low the numbers were compared to what was needed. What it did see was that, in just days, everything was unraveling. Parisians grew restive.

Then, on August 6, after days of depressing reports, some good news: French troops numbering 70,000 had defeated a Prussian force nearly twice as large and had taken 25,000 prisoners, including the crown prince of Prussia. "Paris," said one observer, "gave itself up to an orgy of joy."

It didn't last long. News of the supposed victory turned out to be a hoax, perpetrated to prop up the Bourse. It was good news falsely manufactured to send prices higher on the stock market, giving the wealthy the chance to profit. Joy turned to rage, and angry mobs poured into the streets as the real news spread. How could this be happening? Who's responsible? Fury and a desire for vengeance spilled out. "We're in for a warm night tonight," the Paris police chief warned.

Watching the war in Europe progress were two American women, the novelist Louisa May Alcott and her sister May, an artist. Louisa had just published *Little Women* to critical acclaim and was touring the Continent with May when the conflict broke out, stranding them in Switzerland and preventing them from moving on to Italy.

"It seems such a silly war," May wrote to their mother. "It's all the more provoking to have our plans upset just because one man [Bismarck] wants a little more territory. Just now everything looks rather black for the French for the Emperor has underrated the strength of the Prussians." From the distance she could see things more clearly than the French themselves.

With the situation in Paris rapidly deteriorating, Prime Minister Ollivier sent an urgent message to Eugénie in Saint-Cloud, warning that revolution was imminent and that she should sign a decree putting Paris under martial law. He begged her to leave Saint-Cloud and come to Paris immediately to help calm things. Eugénie signed the decree and said she would leave for Paris first thing in the morning. Then she went to bed. It was nine thirty.

Two hours later, she was awakened by her chamberlain bearing a telegram from her husband. "Our troops are in full retreat," he said. "We must concentrate on defending the capital." A few minutes later another telegram came in announcing two more defeats, the towns of Forbach and Froeschwiller in Alsace lost to the Germans and hundreds more Frenchmen lost, as well.

Eugénie was staggered by the news. Within fifteen minutes, she was dressed and in the drawing room of the château where her ladies-in-waiting had already assembled. "The dynasty is lost," she said. "We must think only of France." One of her ladies-in-waiting burst into tears. Eugénie, struggling to hold herself together, quickly pleaded, "No emotion, please. I'm going to need all my courage."

Feeling alarm and terror growing inside herself, she climbed into her carriage for the ten-mile trip back to Paris. Along the way, however, she felt a change come over her. She became, as she remembered, "a completely different woman, no longer agonized, no longer weak. I felt calm and strong, lucid and resolved."

At one in the morning, Eugénie stepped out of her carriage and strode swiftly into the darkened halls of the Tuileries Palace. With the furniture draped under dustcovers put on when the imperial family had left for its summer stay in Saint-Cloud, the palace appeared haunted by ghostly shapes. Servants, caught by surprise at the empress's arrival, ran ahead, pulling the sheets off furniture. "Leave them on," Eugénie said as she raced through the hallways to her office. She hoped desperately that the war could be ended quickly and she could return to Saint-Cloud to await her son and husband.

The empress wasted no time in taking charge. Sleeping ministers were roused and told to be at an emergency council meeting with the regent at three thirty. A nearly panic-stricken Ollivier urged Eugénie to issue orders for the arrest of opposition figures and the shutting down of opposition newspapers, a move which would essentially give the empress dictatorial powers. She refused. "Then call the emperor back to Paris!" he pleaded. Again, Eugénie refused, saying she did not want her husband to return "with the shadow of defeat hanging over him."

When the meeting ended, Ollivier realized he had overstepped his bounds and scrambled to redeem himself. "She was wonderful, we were all deeply impressed," he told the empress's secretary as he exited the council chambers. In a telegram to Napoléon, he raved about Eugénie's inspired leadership. "We are all united and discuss policy in the Council in complete agreement. The empress shows us a magnificent example of strength, courage and nobility of soul." His ploy came too late, for by then, the empress was ready to dismiss him, along with the rest of the cabinet.

With her decision made, Eugénie relaxed enough to be able to write a note to her nieces in Madrid. "Everything remains quiet here, although we can't be sure it'll continue. A state of emergency has been declared and the war continues, but be brave and don't worry about us. I'm in no way downcast despite the unpleasant moments of last night."

The following day, August 8, only brought more "unpleasant moments." The stock market crashed, and the government collapsed. Under the constitution, Eugénie legally could not dismiss the cabinet without a vote of the parliament. She hurriedly recalled the legislators and won their backing. She then followed through and fired the entire cabinet, including Prime Minister Ollivier, and brought in people she could trust. It was the first time a female French ruler had done such a thing. She named Count Palikao the new prime minister, a move that won support in both Paris and the countryside.

Filon, her son's tutor, however, was stunned and told her she had overstepped her authority and warned she was behaving in a "revolutionary manner." Eugénie was not deterred. The empress brushed him aside. "I must," she said. "I have no choice."

She then issued a proclamation that was published throughout the country. "People of France, the war has begun unfavorably for us, but remain steadfast. I am with you, faithful to my mission and to my duty. You will see me foremost as your leader defending the flag of France."

They were not empty words. Fearing a siege after reading Napoléon's telegram calling for the defense of Paris, Eugénie immediately commanded her new ministers to increase the National Guard, reinforce city fortifications with naval guns, blow up bridges and block tunnels. To ensure an adequate food supply, the empress arranged for thousands of sheep and cattle to be brought into the city and set them grazing in public parks, such as the Bois de Boulogne and the Luxembourg Gardens. She also sent major works of art to safety in Brest on the coast of Brittany.

Eugénie then moved to increase her visibility, appearing regularly in public to reassure people and keep morale up. She visited Paris's military hospitals every day and established two more. She also organized a redoubt for the government in Tours should the Prussians occupy Paris and made a diplomatic move trying to convince Austria to join France in an alliance against Germany. Vienna refused, leaving its ambassador in Paris, Prince von Metternich, downhearted. "What a future for us, this omnipotence of Bismarck," he lamented.

Still, Eugénie worked nonstop, not bothering to change her gown or eat more than a morsel at her desk. Coffee and her own nerves kept her going, and chloral hydrate (knockout drops) forced the small amount of rest she took. Chloral hydrate produced drowsiness rapidly and, in its liquid form, dropped into someone's drink surreptitiously became known as "slipping the mickey" and led to date rape. It was removed from the United States market in 2012 and is now available only by prescription. It is considered mildly addictive.

As Paris then anxiously awaited news from the front, Eugénie's secretary wrote, "The Empress has become the center of everything, the soul of the defense and the government's real head." Her friend Mérimée agreed. "She is firm as a rock, although she does not hide the horror of the situation. She has admirable courage and her calmness is truly heroic."

One of her ladies-in-waiting, however, had a different, more intimate view of the empress: "Her face was ravaged by worry and disappointment. Every trace of beauty had vanished from that pale countenance, which seemed as though furrowed with sorrow. I really thought that she would never smile again."

"Poor Eugénie," lamented Louisa May Alcott in a letter as she followed the events from Switzerland. "She's doing her best to keep things quiet in Paris but the papers tell us that the French have lost two big battles and that the city [is preparing] for a state of siege. I side with the Prussians, for they sympathized with us in our war [the US Civil War] and old Nap didn't. I guess he's going to get a good thrashing and he deserves it. The French here say he's on his last legs, that he's sick and so nervous he can't command the army. Poor old man! He's a troll and one can't help pitying him when all his plans fail."

Every attempt by French forces to regroup and advance was crushed, leaving commanders increasingly disheartened, none more so than the emperor himself. "Growths on his eyelids sealed his eyes," said one soldier. "His face was ashen, his back bent double . . . He could only sit a horse at the cost of agonizing stabs of pain . . . During meals, his ADCs [aides-de-camp] saw him suddenly shaken by intense shivering, tears running down his hollow cheeks." Another witness remembered how the emperor was so wracked by pain that he was knocking his head against a tree and sobbing.

Napoléon realized he'd become a burden to the army and turned command over to Marshal Bazaine, announcing that he would return to Paris. Eugénie was horrified when she heard the news. In a hastily written telegram to her husband, she warned that "If you return as a beaten man, you will be stoned, not only with stones but with dung!" Eugénie's secretary was alarmed by her strong words, but the empress was adamant: "Don't you realize he's doomed if we don't stop him?"

Napoléon, the man who had been the all-powerful emperor of France, yielded to his wife. It was another indignity following on the heels of renouncing his command. "I seem to have abdicated," he said to Bazaine. He stayed put, however, wandering idly around army headquarters with no role to play. But the jobless emperor, even with his swollen eyes, was seeing events more clearly than the generals. Aware the army was edging ever closer to defeat, he sent his son away to safety. Then he prepared for his own end: he would die on the battlefield as befitted a Bonaparte. Against all advice, he went to Sedan, near the Belgian border, where the army was then encamped and said he would join the pivotal battle ahead as a common soldier.

With high bluffs surrounding it, Sedan was probably the worst place the French could have chosen to camp. "We've caught them in a mousetrap," said one gleeful Prussian officer as he looked down on the French. Quickly, the Prussians began moving up their long-range artillery.

A French general put it more graphically: "Here we are in a chamber pot, about to be shitted upon."

On September 1 at four in the morning, Prussian forces charged over the Meuse River. By noon, the French were surrounded. Bismarck ordered "a circle of fire" sent down on the 130,000 Frenchmen trapped below.

The emperor, realizing this was the end, had dressed to make sure he stood out. He dyed his hair to cover the gray and waxed his mustaches so he would look like his pictures and be recognized by the Prussian troops. He polished the gold braid on his kepi and uniform to a brilliant shine and put on the glittering grand star of the Legion of Honor. Then he rode out, staying on horseback by making a Herculean effort to ignore the searing pain from his bladder stone.

For five hours, Napoléon did his best to get himself killed, riding from place to place, wherever the fighting was fiercest. All around him men and horses fell and died, shots rang in his ears, blood splattered him, his own guards were slaughtered, yet he seemed to be in an invisible bubble. No matter where he rode in the ferocious battle, not a single shell or blade touched him. "I was unlucky," Napoléon said to his aide-de-camp later.

By the end of the afternoon, more than 104,000 French soldiers, nearly all of his army at Sedan, had been killed, wounded or taken prisoner. Unwilling to let the slaughter continue, Napoléon ordered a white flag raised and a message of surrender sent to King Wilhelm of Prussia. "Not being able to die among my troops, it only remains for me to surrender my sword," he said.

The emperor was then hauled off to prison in Germany. In one short month, the bloodiest war of the century had finally come to an end—and the Second Empire was dead.

When word of Napoléon's defeat and surrender reached Eugénie the following day, she fainted. When she was revived, she erupted in a torrent of words that flabbergasted her listeners. "A Bonaparte would never have surrendered!" she shouted. "He must be dead, you're keeping his death from me, oh, why didn't he kill himself?" On and on she went in a wild, uncontrolled mixture of disbelief, rage and grief, finally running from the room and slamming the door behind her. "We remained there speechless and stunned," said her secretary, "like men who had just survived an earthquake."

A few minutes later, the empress reappeared. She was now calm and composed and immediately called a council meeting, but there was little to be done except wait for further news, to find out what had happened to the emperor after his surrender. It came: Napoléon had been taken to prison in Germany, but the prince impérial had escaped. To where, no one knew.

What next? Would the Prussians now advance on Paris? Rumors were flying everywhere, the uncertainty keeping everyone on edge.

As the evening wore on, crowds that had begun to grasp the magnitude of the disaster sought an outlet for their anger and someone to blame for the debacle. They began gathering in the Place de la Concorde and outside the Tuileries Palace, shouting for the monarchy to be overthrown and the Bonapartes chased out.

The next morning, Sunday, September 4, Eugénie attended early mass in the Tuileries chapel as usual, but she was so distracted that she pulled on a gold shawl rather than the black one she'd been wearing every day. One by one and then in groups, ministers and friends came to plead with her. "Call up the National Guard," some said. "Leave this inferno," others begged. Eugénie refused. "I won't move," she said, "but I will not allow a shot to be fired."

Thomas Evans, who was already setting up hospital tents to treat the wounded, tried to get through the crowds and offer his help to the empress. When he was turned away, he parked his carriage nearby in readiness to hustle her away if worse came to worst.

Inside the palace, aides were frantic. "Our situation [is] becoming worse every hour," her secretary warned. "Place de la Concorde is full of armed National Guardsmen and they are not there to defend you. What they have in mind, in fact, is the reverse." Eugénie was unmoved.

Then a delegation of former ministers arrived, arguing that she would not be deserting her duty but rather sacrificing herself to save France "from the horrors of a revolution" if she relinquished her crown.

Eugénie was finally persuaded. She agreed to abdicate but only if they would find her a house where she could stay in Paris and "share our besieged capital's sufferings to the very end." She said she believed in the gallantry of the French and that they would not harm her. The ministers could only shake their heads at her refusal to face reality.

But the scene outside was grim. Unruly mobs, hunting for a scapegoat, began baying for *l'espagnole*, that Spanish woman. Guards at the palace asked permission to open fire or, at least, beat back the crowds with rifle butts. "No, no bloodshed," Eugénie ordered. "I won't allow it at any price."

The mob, however, had begun surging from Place de la Concorde into the courtyard of the Tuileries, their cries of *À la guillotine!*—To the guillotine!—reverberating through the palace. As Eugénie would recall, "No one who has not heard it can realize the horror of the roar of a crowd that has only one desire—to tear you to pieces."

With nightmares she'd had about sharing the fate of Marie-Antoinette now about to become a reality, she finally yielded to the entreaties of two ambassadors who had become friends, Prince von Metternich of Austria and Count Nigra of Italy, and agreed to leave the Tuileries. Refusing to let anyone accompany her but her widowed reader, Madame LeBreton, Eugénie followed the two men toward a side door of the palace, where they had left a carriage nearby. They were shocked to discover it was no longer there.

They dashed to a different exit, but crowds were ahead of them, so they turned toward another one connected to the Louvre—only to find it locked. No one knew where the key was, until an old retainer appeared with it and opened the door. Past the paintings and sculptures, Eugénie and her men raced toward an exit from the museum.

Prince von Metternich stayed with the two women in the doorway while Count Nigra stepped out to hail a *fiacre*, a horse-drawn cab. That's when nearly everything fell apart. A youth recognized the empress and began shouting. Fortunately his cries were lost in the uproar of the mob as Metternich and Nigra hurried the women into the cab. "Are you nervous?" Nigra asked the empress. "No, you don't feel my hand trembling on your arm, do you?" she replied. "One must be bold." Then, mindful of the ambassadors' duties to their own governments, which would soon have to deal with France's new rulers, she sent the two men away and directed the cab to the home of a friend.

Along the way, she saw storekeepers pulling down warrants boasting that they supplied goods to the imperial family. "Ah, so soon," Eugénie said. When they reached Eugénie's intended destination, however, no one was there. They tried another home, but an alarmed servant refused them entry. "Just be glad I don't denounce you," the servant shouted as she slammed the door.

Where to next? The streets were now jammed, and things had happened so quickly that Eugénie realized she had no idea where to go and almost no money to pay for transportation. *The American Legation? Perhaps the American ambassador could help.* But Eugénie couldn't remember the address.

That's when she remembered another American, her dentist Thomas Evans.

His address came easily to mind: it was on the Avenue de l'Impératrice, the Avenue of the Empress. Eugénie directed the cab there, paid off the driver and knocked on the door, hoping desperately someone would let them in. Evans's housekeeper, unaware of who they were, explained that Evans was at the American Ambulance helping set up facilities for wounded soldiers but that he should be home soon because he had a dinner party tonight. She then invited the two women to wait in the library. The American Ambulance, its name based on the French for *field hospital*, would remain on the western edge of Paris and evolve to become today's American Hospital. It would play a distinguished role in treatment of the wounded in both world wars.

When Evans accompanied by his nephew, Edward Crane, arrived, the housekeeper warned him about "two mysterious ladies anxious to see you." One of them is wearing a bowler hat, she told him in dismay. When he realized the woman in a bowler hat was the empress, he was more than a little dismayed himself. Eugénie had grabbed the hat as she ran from the palace, and both she and Madame LeBreton looked bedraggled, not like women of the imperial court.

Eugénie rose and greeted him. "Vile days have come, and I have come to you for protection and assistance," she said.

Evans was a clever and ambitious man who loved being center stage. Now, upon hearing of Eugénie's plight, he realized he was being given the chance to take on the biggest role of his life: a knight in shining armor rescuing a damsel in distress, perhaps the most famous damsel in the world.

Evans had known and admired her since her youth when he first began treating her, and he considered her a friend. He'd grown increasingly concerned about the empress's safety for several days as he traveled back and forth across the city. He'd felt the change in the public's attitude and seen how its anger had grown, hence his preparation of a getaway carriage for Eugénie and the message that he was willing to help. Now, as Eugénie told him she feared for her life, Evans called on his formidable organizational skills and his years of experience in international travel to put them at her service.

Eugénie asked Evans to get her out of Paris so that she could catch a train to the Normandy coast and then a boat to England. That's far too dangerous, he insisted, you'd be recognized and dragged back to Paris. Instead, Evans proposed traveling by private carriage to Deauville on the English Channel where his wife Agnes was already on vacation. She could rest there while he searched for a boat to England. Seeing no other option, Eugénie agreed.

First, however, they had to get out of Paris, which seemed ready to explode at any moment.

Evans hurriedly made up a bed for the empress and her companion. "Stay quiet," he told the women explaining about the dinner party in the house that evening. "Get some sleep. We'll leave early."

Leaving Crane to host the party alone, Evans went to search for a way out of Paris. Skirting Place de la Concorde, he saw how the menacing crowds surrounding the Tuileries Palace had grown, their cries of *To the guillotine!* reverberating with deafening intensity. Guards were stationed at the exits from the city, but there did not seem to be wholesale searching of vehicles or people. He thought he could talk his way past them.

By the time the dinner party was over, Evans was ready to finalize plans for their escape with Crane. For reasons unknown, the empress had a passport issued by the British embassy with an exit visa from the Préfecture de Police. The passport, which had never been collected, was issued for a physician returning to England with his patient. *This is perfect,* Evans realized, and he began assigning roles. Dr. Crane would become Dr. C. W. Campbell, and the empress, his sick patient, Mrs. Burslem. Evans took on the role of Mrs. Burslem's brother, with Madame LeBreton as the patient's nurse. He found one of his wife's hats with a veil that shadowed the face and an old raincoat and gave them to the empress as a rudimentary disguise. He then began stuffing a bag with money. He knew there would be necessary bribes and other expenses ahead.

At five in the morning, Evans hurried the group into his carriage, and they headed west before most of Paris was awake. Eugénie was amused to discover that Evans's carriage had a large letter *E* on the door. Just like mine, she said, but without the crown.

At the exit from Paris, guards peered into the carriage. Eugénie felt a moment of panic, remembering how Louis XVI and Marie-Antoinette had been stopped and arrested in Varennes in their attempt to escape from Paris. Evans leaned out the window, holding his newspaper to obscure the face of the empress. "We're on our way for a few days in the country," he said, and the guards nodded. At the customs check farther on, officers merely waved them on. They didn't even need the passport and the carefully prepared story. All of them breathed a sigh of relief.

They had escaped Paris, but 200 kilometers, or 125 miles, of uncertainty lay ahead.

After several miles of travel, Evans found a country inn where he purchased bread, sausage and cheese and then another carriage with fresh horses. "You'll have to picnic inside the carriage," he told the women. "We're still close enough to Paris that you could be easily recognized." He bought a fresh newspaper and was relieved to see there was no mention that the empress had fled.

Evans maneuvered the new carriage, facing west, alongside his own, now pointed east back to Paris. Opening doors on each carriage, the women stepped from one directly to the other hidden from view; not even the coachmen could see them. Their relief at getting underway again unseen was tempered by the new driver's announcement that he could take them only as far as Pacy-sur-Eure, which was 16 miles away and far short of their destination.

Don't worry, Evans told the women. With luck and the well-filled purse, he would find a way.

But it wasn't easy. No one in Pacy was willing to give up a

day of work or a conveyance to haul strangers. While Eugénie and Madame LeBreton sat in the carriage and worried, Evans roamed the streets of the village until he found a broken-down rig that had not been used since the railroad had arrived twenty years earlier. Finally, he was able to buy two horses to pull it—not a team, but one old plow horse and a "nice gray mare." He and Crane pieced together a broken harness with rope and string. The empress had a new chariot.

It got them another 11 miles, to Evreux, and after that to another village where they were able to buy some lunch and obtain fresh horses. But they were startled when they suddenly heard cries of *Vive la république!* and "La Marseillaise" being sung. The empress blanched, and Madame LeBreton began to shake. Evans climbed down to ask the innkeeper about the noise. "Some of the *gardes mobiles* on their way home from a review," he was told. The *gardes* were essentially conscripted reservists given little or no training and told to protect the home front. They had apparently made frequent stops for refreshment along their route and were feeling happily tipsy.

Fresh horses, however, could not make up for the dilapidated carriage the party was riding in. It broke down repeatedly, forcing Evans and Crane to invent creative repairs on the roadside as daylight faded. Not until ten that night did they manage to reach La Rivière-Thibouville, where a gloating innkeeper looked at the nattily dressed Evans and told him her rooms were full and there were no available horses. A pile of francs induced the innkeeper to remember another room, and the two women were escorted to a tiny chamber with two hard beds and a washstand. "It's really too funny," said the empress, but her laughter was nervous, Evans remembered. The stress of the day and her worries about her son and husband had taken a toll.

In the middle of the night, a clattering of hooves and loud shouting jolted them awake. "It's nothing," the landlady said when Evans questioned her. "It's just game wardens chasing poachers."

Evans arose early and began canvasing the countryside for horses, but to no avail. They would have to risk the train.

It was nearly disastrous. When she boarded the train and took her seat, the empress pulled back the veil of her to wipe her face. At the same moment the stationmaster walked by. He stopped and stared at her, and Eugénie held her breath until he moved on. It's unclear whether he was simply staring at an attractive woman or if he had recognized her but let her go, perhaps still a supporter of the empire. Either way, she was temporarily safe once more.

By the time they reached Lisieux in Normandy, the beautiful fall weather which had accompanied them from Paris had disappeared. An unrelenting downpour had turned streets to mud. Evans left the empress and Madame LeBreton shivering in a doorway as he and Crane splashed through puddles to find a carriage. They were still about 18 miles from their destination of Deauville. The mud, rain and cold would slow them down, and so would the dark.

The relief they felt when they finally reached Deauville was tempered by the need to still remain out of sight yet get to the hotel where Mrs. Evans was staying and, following that, find some way of getting to England. They crept through the garden in the dark to the back door of the hotel. If Mrs. Evans was shocked to find a disheveled empress and her lady-in-waiting on her doorstep, she took it all in stride. Within minutes, she had them in dry clothes and fed then tucked into her own bed while her husband and his colleague walked to the port.

Evans and Crane surveyed the array of boats and finally spotted what they were looking for: a large, sleek yacht with an English registration. It was christened the *Gazelle*. The two boarded and expressed their curiosity about the craft to its owner, Sir John Burgoyne, who proudly showed them around and said he would soon be returning to England. Evans carefully broached the subject: Would he take passengers, one very special passenger? And could he leave with the morning tide? Sir John shook his head. The weather forecast was bad.

Evans then explained who the special passenger was. Sir John was stunned and promptly refused. Spies were probably on her trail, he said, "and I am not about to take any chances!"

Evans became angry. "Where I come from," he said, "a gentleman would do anything in his power to help a lady in danger." Sir John hesitated, then said he would talk it over with his wife, who was below in a cabin. Unlike her husband, Lady Burgoyne *didn't* hesitate. "Well, of course! Bring the empress aboard," she said.

Evans hadn't realized that Sir John's reluctance may have been influenced by his long military career, most of which was spent fighting Napoléon Bonaparte. He had served with the Duke of Wellington, seen action in Spain and been the chief engineer of the British occupation army in France. To rescue a Bonaparte— even one by marriage—must have left him conflicted.

The decision, however, was now out of his hands: his wife had spoken.

It was agreed that Eugénie and her companion would board at midnight and the yacht would leave on the morning tide. As Evans and Crane disembarked, a French police agent suddenly appeared and asked to see the yacht. He gave no explanation. A nervous Sir John conducted a tour while the two Americans made a quick exit. The agent left without giving an explanation for his unannounced visit.

A few hours later, Eugénie and Madame LeBreton slipped aboard in the dark. Lady Burgoyne was ready with food and beds.

The next morning, seas were initially calm as the yacht pulled out of the port of Deauville and made its way into the English Channel. Eugénie rejoiced in being back at sea, on her way to safety. The worst apparently was over.

But several hours later, as they neared the Isle of Wight, a ferocious storm blew up, hammering the yacht with violent waves which threatened to capsize the craft. Lightning flashed, and rain fell in torrents. Madame LeBreton screamed, convinced they were about to die, and dropped to her knees praying. Nearly everyone was terrified and seasick as the storm raged. Sir John and his crew struggled through the hours of the tempest to keep the yacht afloat. Even the empress, who loved storms at sea, admitted to concern.

"The little boat was jumping on the waves like a cork," she said. "I really thought we were lost." Afterward, she confided to Evans that she was struck by how, if they had sunk, no one would ever know what happened to her. "There could not have been a more fitting and welcome grave."

On September 7, 1870, what was left of the weather-beaten yacht limped into the harbor at Ryde on the Isle of Wight. It was four o'clock in the morning. Shaken but relieved, Evans took the empress and her companion to a hotel, the best on the island. They were refused rooms. Only a better class of clients were accepted, they were told, not unkempt people like you—words Eugénie probably never thought she'd hear.

Evans eventually found another hotel. It was a step or two down in quality from the first one they visited, but it was welcoming. When Evans went to the empress's room to check on her, she had in her hands the English Bible that had been placed in the room.

She was reading the Twenty-third Psalm. "The Lord is my shepherd . . . Yea, though I walk through the valley of the shadow of death, I will fear no evil . . ."

CHAPTER FIFTEEN

LAND OF HOPE, DREAMS OF GLORY

SAFETY ONLY BROUGHT MORE WORRIES, AND THEY CAME FLOODING IN AS EVANS FERRIED Eugénie from the Isle of Wight to the British mainland port of Hyde. "Where's my son? Where is the prince?" she asked repeatedly. "Is the emperor all right?"

Evans scurried to get news, buying up English newspapers and talking with sailors at the port. The prince impérial had been located. The emperor had sent him with an escort to Belgium and from there on to Hastings on the southern coast of England. But Loulou was reported to be unwell.

With rumors and false alarms floating everywhere, Evans knew he would have to verify the information before he told the empress her son was only miles away. "It's a cold, just a cold," the prince told him when the American arrived in Hastings and saw that the youngster was indeed sick. His cold, however, did not prevent the prince from peppering Evans with questions. "How is my mother? What about my father? Where are they? What's happening in France? Are the Germans still there?"

Evans returned to the empress with the news. Before he could finish, she was running out the door, not even stopping to put on a coat. "Loulou's here? Take me to him right away!"

The reunion was tearful and joyful, made more so when Eugénie received word that her husband was being held in the elegant and comfortable Wilhelmshöhe Palace near Kassel in Germany. France, however, was in disarray with German troops marching toward Paris and the hastily empowered Government of National Defense fleeing the city and now working from the city of Tours in the Loire Valley. Léon Gambetta, named provisional president, had escaped from Paris by hot-air balloon.

Eugénie's impulsive rush to see her son had the result Evans feared: she caught his cold, which made her more impatient. Napoléon had already written to her: "When I am free, it is to England I wish to go and live with you and Louis in a little cottage with bow windows and climbing plants." Eugénie clamored to find a house, and Evans agreed to help.

He settled on Camden Place outside Chislehurst in Kent. It was a large manor house, not the little cottage Napoléon fantasized about, but it was easily reached from London and not far

Napoléon III and Eugénie's home in exile in Chislehurst, England. *Alfred Young Nutt, 1847–1924, Royal Collection Trust, 1876*

from Windsor where Eugénie's friend, the widowed Queen Victoria, was living. Thanks to its previous owner, who happened to be a Francophile, Camden Place resembled a French château and was furnished in French style. It was also on a direct line to Charing Cross station in London.

"It will do," Eugénie told Evans when she saw it. Evans did not tell her it had been the home of one of Napoléon's former mistresses.

Within weeks of fleeing France, the empress found herself surrounded by her court again. One by one, her staff from the Tuileries Palace appeared at her door and asked to resume the duties they had had in Paris—the maître d'hôtel, the grand chamberlain, her secretary, her son's tutor, the palace butler, some of her ladies-in-waiting and several others all came. Camden Place began to feel cramped. With so many people and the future uncertain, Eugénie tried to discourage them, but they refused to leave. Then her chef from Tuileries arrived, prompting a sigh of relief from Eugénie. "No more English seaside resort food," she said and quickly found room for him.

Evans, meanwhile, found a place for himself and his wife in London while continuing to look after the empress and the prince impérial as they settled in. He also went to work on the teeth of the British royal family who lavished gifts on him and invited him and his wife to gala events. He was back on center stage.

Eugénie, however, was restless and worried about her husband. Queen Victoria, who visited her at Camden Place on November 30, 1870, was appalled by Eugénie's appearance: "very thin and pale, but still very handsome." But there is a "deep sadness on her face" and often "she has tears in her eyes."

The empress's sadness had grown following news of the death of her close friend Prosper Mérimée. He had died September 23 just days after she fled Paris. His passing left her without the one person who had known her nearly her entire life and who had been close to her family. Mérimée was nearly sixty-seven when he died, about the same age as Napoléon. His death left Eugénie more anxious than ever about the fate of her husband.

Although Evans had made a private trip to see the emperor in prison and told Eugénie he was doing well, the empress felt she must see for herself and reassure Napoléon about their son. They also needed to talk about their future. There were things that could not be said in letters.

Dressing simply in black and traveling incognita in an unmarked carriage, she left England via ferry to Ostend in Belgium and traveled the 300 miles east to Kassel in Germany, managing to stay out of public view the entire time.

The autumn weather was picture-book perfect, and temperatures were mild when she arrived at Wilhelmshöhe. Napoléon was on the steps to greet her, but his greeting was far from warm, and it stunned her. Then he led her inside and gave her the welcome she had been hoping for.

And she found that Evans was right: Napoléon's health had improved in the plush surroundings of Wilhelmshöhe Palace. When he arrived there, he was delighted to see a portrait of his mother. It had been placed there in 1807 by his uncle Jérôme when he was made king of Westphalia by the first Napoléon. During his reign of only six years, Jérôme emptied Westphalia's treasury for his own pleasures and had turned the palace into a showplace, filling it with portraits of the Bonaparte family.

Eugénie remained with Napoléon for four days, during which time they talked about their future. They knew that if tradition were followed, the emperor would be freed once the war officially ended. The imperial couple began to regain some of the warmth and comfort they'd once felt as the supercharged emotions of their last days in France drained away. "From our past grandeurs, nothing remains of what once separated us," Eugénie told him. "You and Louis mean everything to me . . . yet not for one moment do I miss the brilliance of our past life. Simply to be together again, that is all I wish for."

Napoléon's "jailer" was an old Prussian general, Karl von

Monts, who originally saw the emperor as the personification of evil and Eugénie as nothing but a frivolous, extravagant woman. His views began to soften during the empress's visit. "When I think of her I see a woman possessing maturity of mind, acquired late, perhaps; sure of herself, sagacious, combining agreeable manners with the intelligence of the woman who has made the interests of the public her own," he said in his memoirs. "My feelings concerning the poor woman were those of deep compassion, increased by the thought that she must be conscious of having been the cause of the punishment."

But for all her good qualities, Monts wrote that the empress was too forceful for his taste, that she had imposed her political opinions on Napoléon. As for the emperor, "He was a humane man who had unfortunately given way to political pressures which he should have resisted," the general wrote with a conspicuous jab at Eugénie.

Eugénie left Wilhelmshöhe reassured about her husband's health and his affection for her. He had explained how upset he was when he had not heard from her for three weeks, but then several letters arrived together. Shortly after she returned to England, he sent her flowers for the November 16 feast day of the saint whose name she bore. "I hope that you received, yesterday and today, my little flowers," Napoléon wrote. "They are not very beautiful, but I could not find any others. My thoughts are with you and I suffer from being far away from you on this day more than any other."

IF THE TWO DISCUSSED A POSSIBLE RESTORATION DURING THEIR TIME TOGETHER IN GERmany, neither of them spoke of it publicly. But the news from France was bad. The new Government of National Defense, put in place after the overthrow of the Second Empire, futilely battled on against the relentless Prussians who advanced steadily toward Paris. It was not always in a straight line according to General Philip Sheridan, the Civil War veteran President Ulysses S. Grant

had sent to France as an observer. The Prussians' route from Sedan took them through Champagne where, as Sheridan recalled,
"Almost every foot of the way was strewn with fragments of glass
from champagne bottles, emptied and broken by the troops who
had looted the cellars of the champagne houses. The road was literally paved with glass, and the amount of wine consumed (none
was wasted) must have been enormous."

On September 19, the Prussian army reached Paris and
promptly surrounded it, determined to squeeze the city's defiant residents into submission. In less than a month, supplies of
nearly everything Parisians needed to survive were exhausted.
Without heating or cooking oil, residents cut down trees for fire-
wood, more than 600,000 of them, trees Eugénie and Napoléon
had planted along boulevards and in the city's parks and squares.
Those in the vast Bois de Boulogne which the couple had opened
as a public park were chopped down as well. Thousands of sheep
and cattle that Eugénie, in anticipation of the siege, had moved
into the city and set grazing in parks as a source of food, were
slaughtered. So, too, were animals in the zoo: yaks, zebras, bears,
monkeys, kangaroos . . . not even two beloved elephants, Castor
and Pollux, were spared.

By December, Paris was on the brink of starvation. What
bread there was contained increasing amounts of sawdust and
straw (a sample of the bread can be seen at the Carnavalet Museum in Paris!). Horses, donkeys, dogs, cats and rats "were eaten
grudgingly at first," said one historian, but soon became familiar
staples. One woman, Victorine Brocher-Roudy, spotted a ven-
dor unloading some canned goods and bought one for her baby.
When she got home and opened it, she discovered "it was a paste
of mouse meat and they hadn't even removed the skins!"

Christmas 1870 was grim indeed, but it would have been
worse had it not been for a few of the city's gastronomic palaces that put together holiday menus aimed at flaunting their
resistance to the Germans and celebrating the holiday. Included
were such epicurean fancies as consommé of horse, dog liver

brochettes, fillet of dog shoulder and salmis of rat. Café Voisin, with a menu headed *99th Day of the Siege*, featured elephant consommé, bear chops, stuffed donkey's head and marinated kangaroo. The pièce de résistance, however, had an uncertain provenance: it was *le chat flanqué de rats*, cat garnished with rats. Happily, wine cellars, like Voisin's, were still well-stocked, so diners had memorable wines like the 1846 Château Mouton

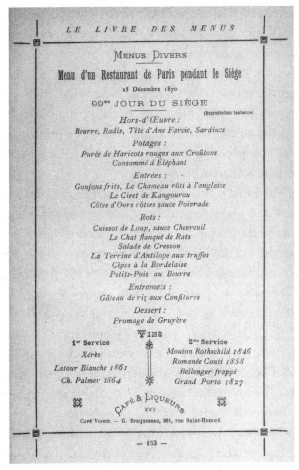

The gastronomic restaurant Voisin in Paris served zoo animals as main courses for Christmas 1870 with the best wines from their cellar. *Gallica-BNF, in Le Livre des Menus: complément indispensable du "Guide Culinaire" by Auguste Escoffier, with Philéas Gilbert and Émile Fétu, 1912, p. 153*

Rothschild and 1858 Romanée Conti to wash down such an unconventional meal.

Their revelry didn't last long, however. In early January, the Prussians lost patience and began shelling the city with heavy artillery. Bismarck, however, having accomplished his goal of uniting the German states and ensuring France was no longer Europe's major power, sought an end to the war. He could feel international opinion turning against him as the siege went on, but he was unable to find a credible government to negotiate with. Eugénie, still officially the regent, was in exile, and he would not consider the newly formed government of France legitimate because it had not been elected by the people.

Recognizing Bismarck's quandary, representatives of all sides, including royalists, who were squabbling over what the French flag should be, flocked to England and made approaches to the empress, hoping to use her for their own ends. Eugénie refused to deal with their bickering.

Even Plon-Plon, who had once accused Eugénie of being nothing but a fashion plate, came calling. He said he was now a republican but wanted the empress's support. Unfortunately, he couldn't resist lecturing her on how terrible her governing as regent had been. Eugénie was not about to put up with his supercilious rant.

"No doubt had you been in Paris on September 4 . . . presumably you could have told us just what we ought to have done," she snapped. "But you were not there, as you never were at any really dangerous moment, on all too many occasions." Plon-Plon left in a huff, as did others who found they could not manipulate her.

Eugénie believed her personal acquaintance with both the king and Bismarck could serve to gain better terms for France from the Germans. She wrote the Prussian king asking him to leave France's territory intact. He refused. Germany would always fear an attack from France, he wrote. It needed the French provinces of Alsace and Lorraine as a buffer, a layer of protection. But he expressed regret that she had not joined the negotiations in person to keep France from "the anarchy which threatens a nation whose prosperity the emperor has successfully promoted for twenty years."

Eugénie was disappointed and frustrated but when Bismarck sent her a telegram proposing a coup that would reinstate her as empress, she was appalled and rejected it out of hand. A coup? That would lead to the very revolution she had been determined to prevent by leaving France.

Napoléon congratulated her for refusing the offer. "I am in complete agreement with you, and the letters I have written, which crossed with your last one to me, will show how well we understand each other, body and soul."

Still, Eugénie wondered: If she returned to France and called parliament back, would they be able to achieve a more advantageous peace settlement? No, Napoléon replied sharply. "We cannot take such risks which might end in ridicule and being arrested . . . After the position we have held in Europe, all our actions must bear the hallmark of dignity and grandeur." The empress stood down. Any plans for a future role would have to wait until the emperor was released from prison.

Finally a new government, the Third Republic, emerged to replace the Government of National Defense. The new government passed a bill formally removing the emperor from power and laid the blame for the Franco–Prussian War squarely on his shoulders. It signed an armistice with Germany in February 1871, but the terms were onerous. Alsace and Lorraine were ceded to Germany, and, to rub salt in the wound, Bismarck chose the fabled Hall of Mirrors in the Château of Versailles as the site where King Wilhelm of Prussia was declared emperor of the newly united Germany.

Germany then released Napoléon and, as a parting blow, sent France a bill for the cost of his imprisonment.

Napoléon joined Eugénie at Camden Place in England on March 20, 1871, just four days after their son's fifteenth birthday. His health had continued to improve, and he was free from governmental worries; he said he was ready to settle down with Eugénie and be "a country gentleman." Napoléon sold off property he owned in Europe, and Eugénie disposed of part of her jewelry collection to make their new lives comfortable. They were to say it was the happiest period of their married lives. They took long walks in the countryside and traveled the byways and lanes in a little carriage. They spent hours every day as a family, reading and talking with their son.

Eugénie knew that Napoléon would want contact with the wider world, and remembering what her mother once had done, she organized social and intellectual events that added a "welcome distinction to the rural neighborhood." Scientists, writers, journalists and even some members of parliament trekked to Camden Place to converse with the exiles.

Behind the image of domestic bliss, however, pro-Bonapartist politicians were scheming and dreaming of the empire's return. So many came to Camden Place that the government of France's new Third Republic under President Adolphe Thiers became worried and sent spies to watch visitors and the "country gentleman and his wife." The spies camped in a nearby windmill, which amused Napoléon and Eugénie for they could clearly see light reflected off the lens of the telescope the French had installed.

Such skulduggery did not curtail plans being formulated inside Camden Place. Those gained momentum when an agent for the Rothschilds, whose banking interests covered much of Europe, told them that more French would vote for Napoléon than any other candidate for leadership of the country. The British ambassador in Paris seconded the report.

Such news boosted the emperor's spirits and may have been one of the reasons he agreed to surgery for his bladder stone, even though such an operation was risky. He'd had a recent attack but remained stronger and healthier since his release. The future beckoned again, and he was ready to take the risk. He also, for the first time, told doctors to disclose all details of his health problems to Eugénie. She was relieved when she learned the full story and supported his decision to have the delicate operation. "I profoundly hope that having undergone so much awful pain," she wrote to her mother on the eve of his surgery, "he will get better and eventually be completely cured. I am praying for this and am sick with worry."

Leading experts and surgeons were summoned to Camden Place for the surgery in January of 1873. Heading the medical team was Sir Henry Thompson who had successfully treated Belgium's King Leopold I for a similar problem a decade earlier. Since then there had continued to be improvements in the procedure, and the success rate had improved as well. Whereas 20 percent of those who underwent such an operation two decades earlier died, the mortality rate was now only 2 percent.

Napoléon was anesthetized with chloroform. Doctors performing the operation were shocked by the size of his stone. When it was grasped by forceps, they could tell it was as large as a pigeon's egg. "How did this man ever sit a horse?" one doctor exclaimed. But Napoléon did well during the surgery in which the stone was crushed into fragments so they could be removed; a second procedure took place four days later to clear additional pieces. There were so many fragments, however, that a third surgery

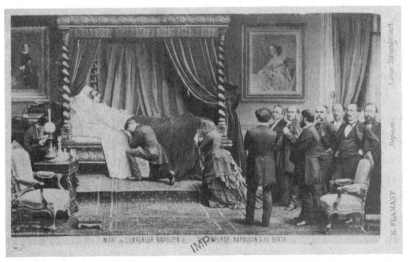

Napoléon III on his deathbed. *Emmanuel Flamant, Musées de Compiègne, GrandPalaisRMN (Domaine de Compiègne) / Gérard Blot*

was scheduled. But before it could take place, the emperor became seriously ill from a buildup of waste products in his blood. He became delirious and began failing. A priest was called, and the prince impérial was summoned home from school. Eugénie, kneeling at Napoléon's bedside, held his hand as the last rites were administered. Within minutes, Napoléon was dead. It was January 9, 1873.

Eugénie threw herself across his body, sobbing, "It's not possible." At that moment, the prince came through the door and realized he was too late to say goodbye. He dropped to his knees beside his father's bed. His tutor Augustin Filon was to write, "He knelt down as a boy, but he rose up as a man."

More than 17,000 people came to Napoléon's funeral at the Catholic church in Chislehurst, but Eugénie was too distraught to attend. The emperor's death represented for her not only the loss of the partner she'd grown to love and respect but also the end of dreams and hopes she'd cherished since childhood.

The teenage prince impérial led the cortege behind the coffin after the funeral. As he left the church, he was met by shouts of *Vive Napoléon IV!* and *Vive l'empereur!*

THE TRAINING AND EDUCATION OF THE HEIR TO THE NAPOLEONIC DYNASTY NOW RESTED solely with Eugénie. It would be more than a year before Loulou reached his legal adulthood, and Napoléon's will had made it clear that until then she would be in charge.

Camden Place had been a dull bivouac for a teenager, especially one who had been in a front row seat for major events and who had gone to war at age fourteen. Loulou had been excited then and convinced that France would win, that they would return in triumph. Instead he was angered and depressed when Napoléon sent him away before the final battles. He felt he was being treated as a child again. Filon, his tutor, understood and saw he had become more withdrawn and serious. I'm no longer going to be called *the Little Prince*, the prince said, or even Loulou; I am now Louis. He is ready for something different, Filon told

Eugénie, and she agreed. Louis needed both more independence and more formal education.

He was sent to King's College in London where he loved being anonymous. Even though he was a Bonaparte, no one recognized him on the streets of the city. He could go about unknown, unrecognized, blending in. He thought it was hilarious, a great joke when a pedestrian bumped into him accidently and didn't apologize. "Real life," he called it. He could happily sit at cafés, flirt and attend plays and sporting events with friends, but the studies? They weren't what he was interested in. They bored him—and he couldn't sit still in class.

His mother, herself a fidgety child who still preferred action and physical activities, sympathized and understood. She made sure hunting parties and hikes were added to his life, and she bought the prince a small boat. It was christened *Le Dauphin*, the traditional title given to the heir to the French throne as well as being the French word for *dolphin*. The prince took to the water like the *dauphin* he was.

Eugénie also organized trips to Italy, Spain and Switzerland. Arenenberg in Switzerland was a particular favorite because it was where Napoléon had spent his childhood. The emperor had been devastated when he was forced to sell the estate to finance his political campaigns, but Eugénie had surprised him by buying it back as a birthday present. After his death, she felt her son should get to know the place where his father had been raised and where he had done his own training to become emperor, so she took him there for extended stays.

Wherever Eugénie and Louis traveled, they found themselves at the center of rumors. "They're looking over the princesses for a possible bride," newspapers said. The rumors grew in strength as Louis approached his eighteenth birthday and would become head of the Bonaparte family.

Already there was talk of a liaison with Queen Victoria's youngest daughter, Princess Beatrice, but religion was seen as a problem. The Protestant princess would not be allowed to marry a Catholic prince. Louis visited Scandinavia. Was he there to sail the fjords or to see the daughters of the royal houses? Louis brushed off questions of matrimony; he was young and "thirsty for powder," he said. Gunpowder.

Pressure was growing on Eugénie, meanwhile, to organize a celebration of his eighteenth birthday, but she was reluctant. Louis had already made it clear he would not assume any political role until he had proven himself as a leader and as a soldier to earn the respect of the French people. Only then, and only if they called on him, would he return to his native country. "But," said Bonapartists to Eugénie, "you are still recognized as the regent, so this [birthday celebration] will make it clear that the prince impérial is now Napoléon IV."

She and Louis finally agreed. In front of the crowd that gathered at Camden Place on March 16, 1874, Louis, now to be formally known as Napoléon IV, acknowledged that, should France call him to rule, he would answer positively despite his youth. "United to my mother by the most tender and most grateful affection," said the prince, "I shall labor without remission to outstrip the march of years." At the mention of Eugénie, all eyes turned to her, and she was enthusiastically applauded. By the end of the speech, the audience was enthralled. "How well he speaks, the Little Prince," people at the ceremony remarked to the empress. "Would anyone have believed it?" Even *The Times* wrote the next day, "Napoléon IV is holding in his hands the Second Empire, and only awaiting an opportunity to turn it into a Third."

Predictably, the ceremony also sparked renewed anti-Bonaparte tirades. One newspaper accused Eugénie of having manipulated the ailing emperor and of bragging "This is my war" about the Franco–Prussian War. The accusation was picked up and repeated through the years, even though the first mention of it only came three years after the end of the war and a year after the death of Napoléon III.

Louis was able to ignore the calumny because his focus at the

The coming-of-age of the prince impérial on March 16, 1874. *Ernest Appert, Musées de Compiègne, GrandPalaisRMN (Domaine de Compiègne) / Franck Raux*

moment was absorbed by his new school: the Royal Military Academy at Woolwich, a place that seemed made for him. It trained its "gentlemen cadets" to become commissioned officers in the British Regiment of Artillery and Corps of Engineers. The cadets studied mathematics, sciences, French, the Classics, drawing, fencing and dancing as well as "military science," which was gleaned from accounts of past battles. Woolwich had recently expanded to include sports facilities and gunnery practice ranges, which added to Louis's pleasure in the school. But the military academy's most important role was to break the tradition of letting officers' commissions be purchased by those who could afford them rather than having those positions assigned to men who were trained for them. The students at "the Shop"—the original building of the Royal Military Academy had been the workshop of the arsenal—were readied to be the new skilled, professional army officers.

Louis thrived at the Shop, picking up the English slang the school was noted for to match the French jargon his mother deplored. The phrase *talking shop*, for instance, came from there and moved into general parlance.

Louis finished seventh overall in his class, but he was ranked first in riding and fencing. He said he wanted to become proficient in artillery as his great-uncle Bonaparte had done and, as a result, was assigned as a commissioned lieutenant to the Royal Horse Artillery at the nearby Aldershot Garrison after his graduation in January of 1875. As a witness remarked, Louis loved "its discipline, its discomforts and hardships, its opportunities for self-reliance, its nights under canvas."

His time at the Shop was seen merely as training by his mother and British authorities, but he had other ideas. Louis avidly followed news about conflicts throughout the world, but reading about them was not enough. He wanted action. He still had his thirst "for powder" and wanted to be fighting in a war. "I wish he was a girl," Eugénie lamented in a letter to her mother, fretting that her son's audaciousness and "strong sense of duty" when combined "might succeed in making him commit some imprudence or folly."

When Great Britain became entangled in a war against the Zulu Kingdom in South Africa in 1879, Louis was desperate to join in, but Eugénie refused. The prince persisted. "Do you want me to fade away," he asked, "[or play] the part of princely commercial traveler like the fairy tale princes, [out] to view all the princesses and boast of my political elixir?" In any case, he said, he wasn't ready to let his "wings be clipped by marriage." He was only twenty-three.

Eugénie relented but expressed her fears to Filon. "The justice of my son's remarks will explain to you why, although I still argued with him, I resigned myself at last to the inevitable." Queen Victoria, who also had been against Louis going to South Africa, capitulated as well but stipulated the prince impérial should have a full-time escort and be confined to a desk job. Prime Minister Benjamin Disraeli was furious about interfering with the army by ordering special treatment for one soldier, but he gave in. "How could I resist two old stubborn ladies," he said. The prime minister was seventy-five; the "old stubborn ladies" were in their fifties.

Although Louis got his way, his mother was subjected to pressure from the Bonapartist party to change her son's mind. The party protested that the prince should not be fighting in a foreign uniform for a cause that was not France's. Besides, party representatives said, all hopes of restoring the empire would disappear without the heir. Eugénie replied that her son's mind had been made up.

On February 27, 1879, Eugénie and Louis boarded a private train sent by Queen Victoria to take them to the port of Southampton on the English Channel. There the prince embarked on a ship that would take him to Durban in South Africa and the battleground he had been longing for. His mother told him she was "sad but resigned and very proud." As she stood on the dock, a forlorn Eugénie was handed a telegram from Queen Victoria. The monarch wished Louis luck and to Eugénie she said, "May God protect your beloved son." Victoria worried about his fate but was also aware that a firestorm of bad publicity would result if anything should happen to the pretender to the French throne while he was on assignment with the British. The recriminations would be overwhelming.

Although he was assigned to headquarters with the army in South Africa, Louis talked himself into a position with the quartermaster and joined scouting parties. A French reporter interviewed him and came away impressed. "This was not some little princeling, but an impressive and commanding personality gifted with enormous charm, and a complete Frenchman."

Louis had told him, "I should hate to be killed in an obscure skirmish. Dying in a big battle would be all right, the hand of Providence."

Eugénie knew her son well, and positive interviews and cheery letters he wrote her did not fool her. She was aware of his impulsiveness and impetuousness. She knew the boy who had walked on the railing of the palace would never be content with a desk job. She could guess he would be in the midst of skirmishes and that he would probably take too many risks. When he left he had told her, "It's not enough [for me] to leave; [I] have to come back with honor." His words kept the empress in a nervous state. "I expect only bad news," she wrote to her mother. "I shall end up mad if this awful uneasiness goes on torturing me."

Her intuition was right: Louis had been involved in a skirmish in May against a band of Zulus. Sword in hand, he charged them screaming ferociously. The surprised *impis*, or warriors, ran off.

Eugénie's anxiety only increased when she learned what happened and told Queen Victoria she was going to South Africa. The queen, sympathizing with her friend's concern, contacted the commander-in-chief of the British forces and asked him to urge the prince to return at once.

On June 1, Eugénie wrote Louis that he should consider coming home. "I will never advise you to leave the battlefield," she said. "You know my heart is not capable of such cowardice. But if the British win, your presence would not be necessary." On the same day, Louis had written her a short note saying he was leaving on a reconnaissance mission in advance of what could be a major battle.

While scouting the terrain, the prince's group stopped for a rest in a deserted *kraal*, a temporary camp and holding pen for cattle. Without warning, more than three dozen Zulu warriors brandishing *assegais*, short spears with sharpened iron tips, leaped from the tall grasses and descended on the British contingent. The soldiers, caught by surprise, struggled to remount and escape. A strap broke on the prince's horse's saddle, and as he fell, his foot caught and his horse bolted. Two other of his fleeing comrades were killed. Louis, finally freed from the strap, was left to face the impis alone.

"He fought like a lion," one of the Zulus said later. The prince's body was recovered the following day.

When news of his death was telegraphed to Queen Victoria on June 19, she said, "Poor woman! Poor young man!"

The Duke of Bassano was sent to tell Eugénie. Seeing his face, she exclaimed: "Is he wounded? I will leave for Africa at once." When tears filled the duke's eyes and he struggled to say something more, she realized the truth and fainted. Her doctor was called and revived her. She sat unmoving and mute in her armchair, a shell of a

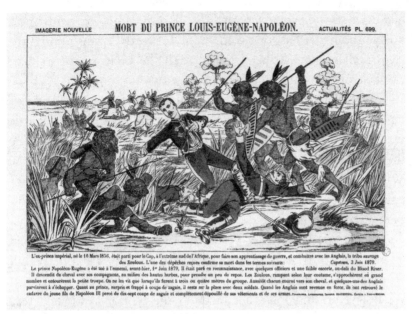

The prince impérial fighting alone against Zulu warriors. *GrandPalaisRMN (MuCEM) / Franck Raux*

woman, her grief too profound for tears. A lady-in-waiting guided her to bed, but she lay there, motionless. She didn't sleep—couldn't sleep—and said not a word. She refused to leave her room, eating only when food was forced on her, sleeping only as if by accident. The empress was waiting for her son's coffin.

Louis's body arrived aboard the steamer *Enchantress* a month later. When it was delivered to her home, Eugénie, for the first time in weeks, rose voluntarily and rushed down the stairs. She threw herself on the coffin, trying to embrace it, knowing the long travel time and poor embalming meant she would not have a final look at her beloved son. But she refused to leave the side of the coffin and knelt beside it in prayer until dawn.

The following day, she asked Dr. Evans to make the official identification of the body, a formality that had not been possible in South Africa. The dentist pulled a notebook from his pocket and told the other medical men in attendance the location of fillings he had done to the prince's teeth. The identification was confirmed, one of the first ever done using dental records. Evans pinned the two medals that had been found with the body to the prince's chest before closing the coffin.

Eugénie by then was so weak and overcome she could not attend the military funeral her son was given. Queen Victoria, who was fond of the young prince, sent three of her sons, including the Prince of Wales, as pallbearers. She even left her solitude at Windsor to attend the Catholic mass at Chislehurst with the Princess of Wales and Princess Beatrice. As the titular head of a Protestant sect, she sat outside the sanctuary for the service. Prince Napoléon, the fifty-seven-year-old Plon-Plon, and his two sons, Victor and Louis, led the procession. An estimated 40,000 people attended the funeral.

For them and for others around the world, Louis had represented that fairy-tale prince he did not want to be—young and handsome and dashing in his uniform in the pictures in the newspapers, always smiling, hopping from one glamorous place to another in the company of the beautiful people of the world. Thousands had poured their own dreams and desires into him. That the fairy tale had a tragic ending only made it more than perfect for them, one more thing they could vicariously project onto him, grief without personal pain.

For Eugénie, it was a story all too real, as was the pain. She felt her own culpability in it, a sense of fatality she always carried. When Queen Victoria came to see her after the ceremony, she could barely whisper. "Because of my race [Spanish]," Eugénie told her, "I bestowed the quixotic gift, that readiness to sacrifice everything for an ideal, while the emperor bequeathed the traditions of his family."

Her losses were unbearable: her country, her husband, her son, all gone, all vanished in less than a decade.

"For her," Dr. Evans said when he saw the empress, "there is no tomorrow."

CHAPTER SIXTEEN

ON HER OWN

THE TOMORROWS DID COME, BUT THEY CAME OF THEIR OWN ACCORD, FILLING EUGÉNIE WITH sorrow and disquiet. How was she to carry on living with everything she loved taken from her? The tapestry of her life was threadbare. She knew she had to do something, something more than sit and grieve. Perhaps if she saw where her son was killed she could say a meaningful farewell to him and fill in some of those holes she felt.

She began planning a trip to Zululand where he had died. She hoped to escape the memories that haunted her and put to rest the rumors and finger-pointing that had come in the wake of the prince impérial's death. Newspapers were filled with speculation and conspiracy theories. Had his killing been orchestrated by Queen Victoria to prevent a potential Bonaparte restoration? Had French politicians or Freemasons been behind his death to circumvent a return to the empire? Or, worst of all, had Eugénie herself played a part so that she could remain unchallenged as regent?

Eugénie disregarded the rumors and innuendos as the lies she knew them to be, but she craved the whole truth about her son's death.

Queen Victoria knew her friend well enough to not try dissuading her from making the trip, and she even agreed to finance it. The six-month war had ended shortly after the prince's death.

Nonetheless the queen remained concerned about the reputation her country was acquiring for having let the prince fight in one of *its* wars, one that led to his death.

At the same time, Victoria was determined to make sure Eugénie would be well-protected. Her concerns were well-founded because what is now known as South Africa was then a collection of small colonial settlements—some Dutch, some British—and independent tribal states and an area where conflicts could flare up unexpectedly. Summoning General Sir Evelyn Wood, a veteran of the Anglo–Zulu War to her quarters, the queen informed him that he was to be the empress's escort.

In March 1880, the beginning of the Southern Hemisphere's fall, Eugénie started what she saw as a pilgrimage. With General Wood, his wife and two of the prince impérial's closest friends from his regiment, as well as several others, she set sail from Southampton, bound first for Cape Town where she would stay at the residence of the high commissioner for Southern Africa, Sir Bartle Frere.

Her arrival on April 16 brought home to her the reality of her son's last months of life as Frere had welcomed the prince impérial almost exactly a year earlier. In a letter to Queen Victoria two days later, Eugénie wrote, "I need not tell you, what cruel emotions I felt when I saw the places from where my poor child started, full of hope and believing he had found the opportunity for showing that he was worthy of his name."

What Eugénie may not have known is that Frere had been responsible for provoking the war which took her son's life. Frere had been sent to Cape Town to impose an unpopular system of confederation on Southern Africa to unite the whole region under British control and provide cheap labor for United Kingdom mines and sugar cane plantations in Africa. By the time Eugénie arrived, Frere had already been censured by the British government for his reckless behavior and, within three months, would be recalled to London and removed from office for the actions that led to the Anglo–Zulu and Boer Wars. Frere had acted much as Bismarck had when he tricked Napoléon III into the Franco–Prussian War but with less success. He had angered the Zulus, calling them "a bunch of savages armed with sticks" and then exaggerated recent incidents. He went on to issue an ultimatum that proclaimed the Zulus to be liars and prone to "treachery to an extent that [we] could not have believed even savages are capable of." Zulu king Cetshwayo responded as Napoléon III had responded to Bismarck: he declared war, the war that would claim the life of Napoléon's son.

After a brief stay in Cape Town, Eugénie and her party sailed around the Cape of Good Hope north to Durban on the Indian Ocean and then traveled on to Pietermaritzburg, where it began the nearly 200-mile trek northeast to Nqutu where the prince impérial had been killed.

"I'll ride," Eugénie said. She was fifty-three and still an outstanding equestrian, but General Wood said no. You don't know the land with its uneven terrain and steep slopes, he insisted, and there are hostile, unpredictable tribes in the area. Instead of her riding horseback, Wood said he would personally drive her in a "spider," a light carriage pulled by four horses.

Eugénie acquiesced and was pleased they would camp along the way, remembering her son's pleasure in sleeping under the stars and constellations of the Southern Hemisphere. The days were still warm, but the nights could be chilly with temperatures dropping to the forties or even as low as thirty, especially as they climbed toward Ulundi, "the high place," in Zulu, and the capital of the Zululand. From Ulundi, they would make the last few miles of their journey to Nqutu and the kraal where Eugénie's son had been killed.

Along the way, however, Eugénie would get her first glimpse of Zulus. One of her son's friends traveling with her reported to Queen Victoria, "Suddenly the well-known cry of respectful greeting 'Inkose' was heard and a body of about 50 natives carrying assegais and sticks appeared. Poor Empress, as we who know her best anticipated, the first sight of the assegai caused her great emotion and it was truly a sad scene, she overwhelmed with grief with these almost naked natives sitting in a semi circle before her ignorant of the sorrow caused by their presence."

Eugénie recovered her composure and was, as ever, eager for activity, finding the travel too slow, even though she realized her desire to visit every place her son had stopped was contributing to the slow pace. But on May 25, more than a month after arriving in Cape Town, the empress's tent finally was pitched in front of the Nqutu kraal. The kraal was surrounded by tall grasses and *mealies*, the maize or corn that was the local dietary staple. There were still remnants of thatch from the deserted huts in the kraal, but the site was dominated by the marble cross Queen Victoria had sent as a memorial to the prince, and the graves of the two soldiers who were killed in the same skirmish. With an iron fence and concrete blocks around the cross, Eugénie thought it looked more like an English cemetery than an African village. It was frustrating for she had wanted to see the place exactly as her son had seen it. Sensing her disappointment, one of her party snuck out in the middle of the night and cleared it all away.

When she saw what had been done, Eugénie was moved and, the following morning, asked to visit the site of her son's last camp alone. She walked the area for more than three hours, according to one of the prince's friends who was with her. "She ate nothing all day," he said. "Her wonderful energy alone sustained her, and she walked with an almost feverish strength."

Eugénie, although nervous about meeting them, had asked about the Zulus her son fought and learned they all agreed he fought well, "like a lion," as they said. She also learned that the prince, in death, had been given the highest honor Zulus could render an opponent, a ritual called *hlomula*, when warriors in a battle each stab the corpse of a particularly fierce opponent as a sign of respect. For the Zulus, there was no higher calling than fighting valiantly and passionately. The eighteen wounds on the prince's body proved he had indeed been awarded hlomula. There was also a slight incision in his abdomen which the Zulus said had released his soul. Although his clothes were taken to "purge the pollution of his blood," the prince's medals were seen as his personal talismans and left behind. These were the medals Dr. Evans would pin on his body before closing the coffin for a final time.

It was a wrenching moment for the empress, but at the same time a comfort knowing that the prince had been given a form of last rites by enemies in recognition of his bravery. She also was gratified to learn that the Zulu who threw the first spear at her son was a king in his own right, Langalibalele, the king of the amaHlubi tribe of Zulus and one of the most famous warriors and resistance fighters in the country. Eugénie had, at first, been upset to learn that her son had not died fighting with his sword, but she became even more impressed when witnesses said the prince impérial had grabbed the spear Langalibalele threw at him and used it as a weapon against the Zulus even as, wounded, he managed to draw his revolver with his left hand and fire at them. The impis recognized a fellow warrior.

On the night of June 1, 1880, the anniversary of her son's death, Eugénie knelt in prayer before the cross Queen Victoria had sent. Candles were lit, and the stars the prince loved shone brightly overhead. As the night wore on, Eugénie saw shapes in the long grasses around the kraal—they did not feel like a threatening presence—Zulus were watching over her, she thought. The night was perfectly still, but as morning approached, the candles suddenly flickered. "Is that you?" the empress called out. "Do you want me to go home now?" She felt her son's presence and a final farewell from him that told her he was at peace.

When the morning sun arose, Eugénie walked to the place where she sensed the prince had fallen. Her instinct was confirmed by his friends: it was the exact spot. She collected plants and grasses from there to take back to England. In their place, she planted a willow cutting that was brought to her from St. Helena, where Napoléon Bonaparte had spent his last years in exile.

She added ivy she had carried with her from Camden Place, then asked that the railing around the spot where her son was killed be replaced and that some sod from the area be dug up for her to take home.

She was leaving South Africa with the sad knowledge that his death might well have been avoided, for even the Zulus said he might have been saved if Lieutenant Carey, his commander, had turned back to face the impis instead of ordering his men to retreat. Though angry and upset, rancor was not part of Eugénie's makeup. She understood actions in battle were governed by many unknown forces. When Carey later was court-martialed for his cowardice in the skirmish, she joined in his appeal and wrote authorities, "Let there be no recriminations. Let the memory of [the prince impérial's] death draw together in common sorrow all those of us who loved him, and let no man suffer either in his good name or in his career." Lieutenant Carey was reinstated.

Eugénie departed South Africa on June 26 aboard the steamer *Trojan* and crossed the Atlantic to St. Helena, site of Napoléon Bonaparte's final exile and death. There, she paid her respects and collected Parma violets, that symbolic flower of the Bonaparte family. They had been brought there for Bonaparte and now some would be transplanted again along with willow cuttings from Bonaparte's garden to be joined with the grasses and mealies of South Africa in England. Once again, Eugénie would bring the family together.

ONE MORE TASK REMAINED, HOWEVER: THE CREATION OF A FINAL RESTING PLACE FOR HER husband, her son and herself. Land around Camden Place was not for sale, and Camden Place itself was crowded, both with life and memories. When, shortly after returning from South Africa, she learned Farnborough Hill was being sold, she welcomed the idea of a new home where she could start over. The moment she saw the property with its vast grounds and majestic trees, she knew this was the place and bought it for £50,000.

Farnborough Hill, where Eugénie spent her last fifty years and is buried between her husband and her son. *Farnborough_Hill_summer, Wikimedia Commons, Thundering Typhoons!, CC BY-SA 4.0 https://creativecommons.org/licenses/by-sa/4.0*

Its location appealed to her: it was near Aldershot where her son had been based before going to South Africa and not far from the Windsor home of her friend, Queen Victoria. Plus, connection to London was easy. Eugénie began to feel excited: she could now do something for her son and for her husband. Her old pleasure in building reemerged and gave her a new goal. She contacted Hippolyte Destailleur, the French architect who had built Waddesdon Manor in England for Baron Ferdinand de Rothschild. Legend has it that Eugénie sketched her ideas for the estate in the sand with her cane for Destailleur. The odds of this are slim: Eugénie was only fifty-four then and still very active; she wasn't using a cane, and there was no sand around Farnborough. Nevertheless, in whatever manner he learned about the empress's plans, Destailleur must have been intrigued and immediately agreed to join her in turning the new property into the home and memorial she envisioned.

The project would be massive and extremely expensive, but, in some ways, financing it would be the easiest aspect. Eugénie had already proved herself a good businesswoman, and when the imperial family went into exile, her income was the key to their livelihood. Napoléon III's fortune was, by comparison, much smaller—approximately 160,000 francs or $779,000 today. Rumors that he had stashed millions of pounds in British banks were untrue. His wealth was concentrated in property he owned throughout Europe.

Eugénie, on the other hand, had purchased jewelry as investments throughout her reign, and it paid a handsome return. The sale of 123 pieces in June of 1872 by Christie, Manson and Woods auction house—about half of her collection—brought in 1,125,000 gold-francs, $540 million today, and a private sale of several other pieces to the Rothschilds brought £150,000, or nearly $6 million in today's money.

Yet there were still pieces of jewelry she kept for herself: the emerald-and-diamond brooch in the shape of a clover leaf that was Napoléon's first gift to her and her wedding ring. She was wearing both when she fled from the Tuileries, and they were the only jewelry she ever wore after Napoléon's death.

Eugénie also added to the family finances during their exile by indulging her love of technology and invention to modernize vineyards she owned in Spain with her mother. Manuela, then nearing eighty, was incensed, as were local farmers who complained bitterly about Eugénie's importing French engineers and soil experts. The empress quickly changed tactics and hired a Spanish manager. The new manager, following Eugénie's guidelines, switched the varietals in the vineyards and built a new press and cellars. The result was an award-winning wine, one that captured a medal at the World's Fair in 1878 which, in turn, garnered a truce not only in the vineyards but also in the usually contentious mother–daughter relationship.

When Manuela died shortly after the prince impérial's death, Eugénie inherited not only the vineyards but also her mother's extensive properties and wealth, which included forests, farms, mills, foundries and houses in Castille, Navarra, Rioja, Andalusia,

Aragon, Extremadura and Biscayne. The income from the Spanish properties amounted to approximately $47 million (today's value) annually. After the prince's death, Eugénie also became the owner of all the property that had been left to him by his father.

All these sources of income made financing her Farnborough renovation easy, and she told Destailleur to proceed.

Destailleur had the largest collection of architectural books and materials at the time and a healthy respect for the past that appealed to the history-minded empress. Her goal, she said, was to build on what existed and not obliterate it. "It is the great vice of France," she told her friend, the writer Lucien Daudet, "to have destroyed everything with each change of regime."

During the Second Empire, Eugénie had worked hard with Prosper Mérimée to preserve some of France's great buildings. With Farnborough as her canvas, she now sought to paint "a proxy history of France" showing how Bonapartism had effected gradual changes for the betterment of the country. "The present has no right to abolish the past," she told Daudet. "It must sustain it while improving it."

What existed at Farnborough was a large manor house said to be "in the old English style." She knew Napoléon would have loved it with its bow windows and cottagelike feeling. In addition, the woods around resembled those at the Château de Compiègne which they both adored. She named the woods on the western side of Farnborough, with its lake and large field for sports, Parc Compiègne.

The house itself was on a hill, but even better, Eugénie saw, was another hill called Coombs that was visible from Farnborough. It was the ideal spot for the church and memorial she envisioned. She would be able to see it every day from Farnborough; it was close but separate so that monks she hoped to establish there would have their own farm and means to sustain themselves.

Her excitement in planning the church and house was obvious in the letter she wrote to Queen Victoria soon after the purchase: "I believe that my dear child, if he could see it, would like it. It's near to the Camp [Aldershot] where he spent time which he loved to recall, and it's not too far from Windsor." Being close to Windsor also meant Eugénie would be able to see the queen frequently. The friendship between the two women had grown and become important to both.

Victoria wrote in her diary that she had received "a dear letter from the Empress, full of the purchase of land she has made, & the building of a house & Mausoleum." The queen also noted that there was "a good new house" on the property.

The good new house had been built twenty years earlier by Thomas Norton Longman, then Britain's leading publisher, for his family of eight children. What the empress needed, however, was far different, and she set about enlarging and modifying it. She knew she would have many visitors, for she was already dealing with a small "court" of those who had come with her from France. Plus, she had her own specific requirements: she wanted to reproduce the prince impérial's study exactly as it had been at Camden Place; she wanted a private salon where she could house her collection of Marie-Antoinette items; she needed to accommodate the furnishings from the Villa Eugénie, especially the seven large tapestries of the Don Quixote story, and all the other memorabilia she had collected through the years.

She also had one special request: the door to the dining room should be extra wide. She and Queen Victoria, in their full-skirted formal dinner dresses, would stand at a door politely saying "After you" over and over again whenever they dined together. Who should take precedence? A deposed empress or a reigning queen? No more: Eugénie ordered a door wide enough for the two of them to go through together.

The latest technology, still a fascination, was also an important feature. She ordered the most-up-to-date central heating and had a mechanized shutter made to rise from the floor of the dining room to block out glare from the setting sun. She added greenhouses, stables, private rooms for regular guests like her brother-in-law, the Duke of Alba, and a "winter garden" room of glass where she could look directly onto the statue of her son with his favorite dog, Nero. She also made sure her own suite of rooms looked directly at the site of the church and mausoleum.

Learning what all the empress intended, Queen Victoria wrote, "She will have to build many servants rooms." And she did.

As work got underway, Eugénie settled first into a cottage owned by her bankers and then into a home in London. Within a few months, however, she received word the Duke of Alba was dying, and she left for Spain to spend time with her sister's family, now her only remaining relatives. The duke, whom she once thought she loved, had become not only her brother-in-law, but also her friend. He was the one person with whom she could share memories of her sister, and she had relied on his kindness and had valued his advice. His death brought back the sadness she had tried to run from with her building projects.

It also brought home to her that her pilgrimage, begun with her trip to South Africa, was not yet complete. She needed to re-visit the places where her son had grown up, places that had been important in his young life, and say a farewell to them. She would continue the pilgrimage after her time in Spain, she decided, and the trip would also give her a chance to view a statue to her husband being raised in Milan. The French government, which had banned Eugénie from entering France, unbent enough to give her permission to travel across the country. Traveling incognita after Alba's funeral, she went from Milan to Arenenberg, Napoléon's childhood home in Switzerland, before going to France and Compiègne.

At the château where she had once lived, she joined those in line for general admission and began her tour. She was saddened to find that her son's garden there looked like "an overgrown village cemetery," but she continued on, no one paying attention to her until the curator recognized the woman in the heavy black veil walking down a hallway and was struck dumb. On reaching her son's apartments, Eugénie broke down in tears, and the curator rushed to close the doors and give her privacy to regain her composure. A few minutes later, a dignified empress but heart-broken mother quietly left the château for the last time.

Fontainebleau proved difficult as well when an old guardian who had known the imperial family spotted her and, crying, knelt before her.

The Tuileries, set on fire at the end of the Franco–Prussian War, was in shambles, but she walked the garden and stopped to pick a flower. A guard rushed to tell her that was not permitted, but he was stopped by another who said, "Don't you know who that is? That's the empress. Let her be."

One last flower to add to her memories. Her pilgrimage was complete.

WHEN EUGÉNIE RETURNED TO ENGLAND, SHE WAS IRRITATED TO DISCOVER THERE HAD BEEN little progress at Farnborough since her departure. It was all in an "appalling disorder," she said. Ready or not, the impatient empress moved into the house to oversee and, as far as the architect was concerned, interfere with the work, changing her mind and demanding improvements as the project progressed. But the house was done to her specifications.

In 1881, the empress sold Villa Eugénie, the house Napoléon III had built for her in Biarritz, to the Banque Parisienne. She had the furniture sent to Farnborough. The furniture was a disappointment; she lamented, "it is as worn as if I had used it forever." She plunged into interior decoration for Farnborough, restoring some of the Villa Eugénie furniture, replacing other pieces, using the objects and paintings the French government sent after agreeing they were her personal property. One visitor said the house was "populated by so many glories, splendors, all the silent portraits, all the relics, furniture, objects that have been associated with those glories and splendors, and which are now only mementos."

For Eugénie, surrounding herself with such mementos meant she was now recognizing she would spend her life in England, "the only place she could live with dignity." In gratitude to Victoria who had allowed her to settle there, who had extended her friendship, Eugénie was determined to retreat from all politics and anything that might offend the queen or her host country.

Politics, however, followed her into exile. Her longtime nemesis Plon-Plon was disgruntled that, in his will, the prince impérial had skipped over him and instead named his son, Prince Victor, the official heir of the Bonaparte dynasty. Plon-Plon reacted by trying to seize power in a poorly organized coup in January 1883. The government of France's Third Republic arrested him and tossed him in jail. It fell to Eugénie to try to reconcile the family and get Plon-Plon released. In an attempt to avoid a political incident between France and England, she slipped out of England without telling the queen and called the two sides of the family—those who supported Plon-Plon and those who backed Victor—to a meeting in Paris, hoping to unify the Bonapartist party under the name of Napoléon. They refused, and the exasperated empress returned to Farnborough two days later.

When Queen Victoria learned of the expedition, she expressed relief that there had been no incident. Plon-Plon went so far as to admit he had been touched by Eugénie's initiative and thanked her in a long letter from prison. The French government, realizing it had nothing to fear from Plon-Plon, released him. But when Eugénie asked him to reconcile with his son Victor, Plon-Plon refused. The refusal, coupled with Eugénie's granting an allowance to Victor as the heir, killed any hopes of peace between him and the empress.

In a strange way, it was the French government that finally brought calm to the family feud. In 1886, it banned all members of royal and imperial families who had ruled France from entering or living in France. Plon-Plon settled on an estate in Switzerland, and Victor moved to Brussels.

This left Eugénie in peace to finish the work on the memorial church which was paramount to her. Its main function was to serve as a final resting place for the remains of Napoléon and the prince impérial.

Destailleur gleaned architectural references from French history and Eugénie's own life to design a mausoleum replete with Gothic references and Spanish inspirations. It included an impression in miniature of the dome of the Invalides in Paris where Bonaparte was entombed. The marble sarcophagi for Napoléon and the prince impérial were donated by Queen Victoria, and an area behind the altar was left for the coffin that would one day hold the remains of the empress. She set up a trust to guarantee the future of the monks who were to oversee the church and say memorial masses. The church was dedicated to St. Michael, the patron saint of France, and monks from the Benedictine monastery at Solesmes in France were brought to the church. They were famed for their scholarship, and Eugénie was enchanted by the beauty of their liturgy. She visited the church every day she was in Farnborough.

When the building was completed, Eugénie went to her garden and dug up shoots she had brought from St. Helena. Bonaparte's weeping willows draped the entrance to the crypt.

CHAPTER SEVENTEEN

THE MATRIARCH
OF EUROPE

THE GIRLS WERE DIRTY, THEIR HAIR WAS HANGING DOWN, AND THEIR HANDS WERE FULL OF mud pies. "It could be Paca and me," Eugénie thought as she watched the students from Hillside School laughing and playing at the lake on that Pentecost holiday. She called out, "Come up to the house for tea!"

The stunned girls rushed to clean up as their teachers hurriedly dusted them down and reminded them of their manners, and then all of them, nervous and in awe, appeared at the door of Farnborough Hall to be greeted by an empress.

They knew about her, of course; everyone in Farnborough did. They saw her bicycling on the streets and pathways around her estate. They knew she gave wonderful tea parties every year on the birthday of Queen Victoria. And they knew she was coming to their school to hand out prizes at the end of the year.

Until now, though, they'd never seen her up close. She looked regal and intimidating in her beautiful black gown. Her posture was perfect, and people said her back never touched a chair when she sat. She entertained the most famous people in the world. Even the queen came to call and so did the Prince of Wales.

They were just students—whatever would they say to an empress? Could they remember how to curtsy? Would they even be able to stammer out a *merci beaucoup*?

Within a few minutes, however, all their worries were forgotten: they were enchanted, and so was Eugénie. Having children around her made her feel young again, even as they brought back memories of her own childhood and her son, the prince impérial.

Those memories now were bittersweet, constant companions that ebbed and flowed through her consciousness, sometimes overwhelming, sometimes a background hum as Eugénie worked to recompose her life. She had said her goodbyes to all the places of her old life and those she had shared with her son. Now she could begin to get to know the new place she found and would call home for the rest of her life.

Farnborough in Hampshire was an old English country village, first mentioned in the Domesday Book in 1086. Now, eight centuries later, it was growing, changing and readying itself to meet the twentieth century head-on. How much of its history Eugénie was aware of is unclear, but given her rebellious nature and her love of sports and rigorous physical activity, she surely would have been intrigued by the fact that Farnborough in 1860, the year Paca had died, had been the site of the last illegal bareknuckle prizefight.

Billed as *The Fight of the Century*, it pitted one of Eugénie's cherished Romanis, Tom Sayers, dubbed "the Champion of England," against an Irish-American fighter, John Camel Heenan, "the Champion of America." Farnborough was chosen for the fight for much the same reason Eugénie chose it: it was close to London and had good railway connections. Such was the excitement that extra trains, "specials," had to be put on to transport the crowds to Farnborough. Train tickets for the specials were marked *To Nowhere*, a move aimed at avoiding the police.

Nowhere was thronged with tens of thousands of people on April 17, the day of the fight. Rules were simple: a round lasted until one man was knocked or thrown down, so rounds could last a few seconds or go on indefinitely. The fight was over when one man couldn't get up again.

As the two fighters entered the ring at seven thirty in the morning, betting was wild and nonstop. It was a gruesome affair. By the forty-second round, Heenan was blind from the pummeling his face had taken, and Sayers was fighting with a broken right arm. Then, after two hours and twenty-seven minutes of ferocious brawling, the police suddenly arrived, charging into the fight and flashing warrants for arrests. Spectators fled in every direction, disappearing from Nowhere to somewhere faster than snowflakes on a hot oven. Among them were the Prince of Wales, authors Charles Dickens and William Makepeace Thackeray as well as the prime minister himself, Lord Palmerston.

The bloody spectacle led to the adoption of rules for modern boxing known as the Marquess of Queensberry Rules, mandating, among other things, the use of gloves for fighters and outlawing biting, kicking and gouging.

It was the sort of scene Eugénie could easily have imagined herself and her sister Paca being caught up in when they were girls—not the fight because she abhorred violence—but running and hiding from the police. If the Prince of Wales, still a teenager at the time, ever told her about visiting her hometown for the match, he would probably have found an amused listener.

His mother, Queen Victoria, and the rest of her family, including the now grown-up Prince of Wales, were regular visitors to Farnborough, sometimes coming as often as once a week. Despite their many differences in background and personality, Eugénie had grown to love the queen. In their widowhood and solitary positions, they had become extremely close. They could talk to each other as equals and gossip about family and friends with no fear of their conversations being leaked to the press.

Eugénie had not had a close friend since the death of Paca, and the queen had never had a girlfriend, so when Victoria suggested they drop the titles they used to address each other and instead call each other Sister, Eugénie felt a sense of comfort. She valued the warmth and understanding the queen had shown her at the death of the prince impérial, and she was deeply grateful for the monarch's allowing her to live in England.

That didn't stop her from pursuing other interests, however. New technology continued to fascinate her, especially "moving pictures." When motion pictures first appeared in England in 1888, she became a fan and fell in love with Charlie Chaplin films. Cars? Not so much. She was not convinced automobiles were the future of transportation after having to be pulled out of a ditch several times. (It was only later she learned her chauffeur had been spending more time in a bar than in the garage.)

Although France was no longer Eugénie's home, its progress, particularly in the field of science, was never far from her mind. She followed Pasteur's accomplishments, especially his development of vaccines, and treasured the time she had spent with him in his lab, carrying equipment for him and watching him work. She was also fascinated with the pioneering work of Marie and Pierre Curie in radioactivity. As a fierce opponent of sex prejudice, Eugénie took enormous satisfaction when Marie became the first woman to win a Nobel Prize in 1903, which she shared with her husband, and a second one in 1911 for discoveries involving elements of polonium and radium.

A few years earlier, the empress came to the rescue of a frustrated Guglielmo Marconi, who had left Italy for Great Britain in hopes of gaining more support for his work in developing the wireless telegraph. Eugénie gave him her yacht to conduct his experiments. Marconi was so grateful that when he finally succeeded in sending a message from North America to England in 1896—the message going to King Edward VII—the next message he sent was to Eugénie, thanking her for her help.

Not long afterward, the empress heard news that must have thrilled her to the bone. The British military announced that Farnborough would be the home of an airship shed for building its first dirigible. According to local gossip, soon there would be "flying machines," that is, airplanes. Flying captured Eugénie's imagination, and she went immediately to meet the man at the center of it all, Colonel Sam Franklin Cody.

Cody, an American, was half genius and half con man. He happily led people to believe he was the son of "Buffalo Bill" Cody. He dressed like the famous showman, wore his hair long like the sharpshooter, cultivated a similar goatee and even ran a similar Wild West show for a time. In fact, his real name was Samuel Franklin *Cowdery*, no relation at all to Buffalo Bill.

Somewhere along the way, Cody, as Cowdery now called himself, became interested in kites and began mechanizing them. His story was that a Chinese cook on a cattle drive in the Old West had taught him how to fly kites. Whatever the truth, Cody soon developed a "war kite" which the British military was able to use for observation in the Boer War. He was then called in to develop a dirigible, a "large balloon" as Eugénie referred to it, and take it on its first flight from Farnborough to London. He also would pilot the first airplane flight in Great Britain, which also lifted off from Farnborough and landed in London in 1908. Before all that, however, Cody found himself enmeshed in a story even better than the ones he spun about himself: he was to teach an empress to fly. Or, at least, that was what Eugénie evidently told him when they met. She was already in her seventies, and Cody realized this was a story that absolutely had to have a happy ending. There was no way he could risk an accident in the air with such an august personality beside him. It took all of Cody's slick talking to keep the determined empress on the ground, but she finally accepted his decision. But she then surprised him by peppering him with detailed and knowledgeable questions about every aspect of aeronautics. From that day on, she became an avid spectator at air shows which followed.

Eugénie was equally tenacious when it came to causes she believed in, among them women's suffrage. She was eager to see women gain the right to vote and complained that France lagged far behind Britain on that front. But rather than actively joining the movement as she would have liked, she kept a low profile which, in turn, kept the British relaxed about her presence in their country. Instead, she made her support clear by inviting Britain's leading suffragists, such as the activist Emmeline Pankhurst, to Farnborough and helping them financially.

Another visitor was a young musician and composer named Ethel Smyth who spent three months in jail for her suffragist activity. Smyth was attracted to Eugénie's beauty and may very well have been in love with her. She wrote of "the perfection of [Eugénie's] proportions," her pale face with gray hair and her "gliding" walk, "the most graceful style of progression imaginable." Eugénie might have been flattered, but her only interest in Ethel, who had intimate partners of both sexes, was one of friendship. The two shared a love of sports, and both were outstanding riders. Eugénie, always supporting sex equality, was eager for her friend's compositions to find success in the male-dominated world of music, and she broke her self-imposed rule of not appearing publicly to attend the premiere of Smyth's *Mass in D* at Albert Hall in London.

Eugénie, however, lacked an ear for music. When she and Ethel were invited to visit the County Lunatic Asylum for Women near Farnborough, the institute's orchestra serenaded them. Afterward, Ethel remarked to Eugénie that it must have been very difficult for the orchestra to learn "En partant pour la Syrie," the anthem Napoléon's mother had composed and which they played to honor the empress. Eugénie was surprised. "Really? Is that what it was? I thought it was 'God Save the Queen.'" She was hugely embarrassed and promptly wrote a thank-you letter to the orchestra members.

The empress was embarrassed again when she took Ethel to meet Queen Victoria at Balmoral. Ethel, unaware of the strict protocol, spotted the queen and empress in conversation and wandered up to introduce herself. "How do you do, Queen?" As Ethel later recalled, the queen "looked at me as if I were some strange insect."

Such incidents, however, did not thwart the friendship between Ethel and Eugénie. Ethel was a frequent guest on Eugénie's yacht, *The Thistle*, although not always a happy one. Unlike the empress, she was subject to seasickness and not enthusiastic about storms as was her host. When they sailed into a gale along the west coast of Africa, Ethel remembered seeing Eugénie "lashed, chair and all, to the mast" so she could watch the storm as it raged.

Nor did the empress avoid other kinds of storms. Growing up in Granada with its vibrant Jewish and Muslim populations had inculcated Eugénie with a lifelong hatred and intolerance of racism and anti-Semitism. When the French Jew, Captain Alfred Dreyfus, was convicted of treason for supposedly spying for Germany in 1894, she was horrified. Although mindful of her promise to Victoria not to engage in politics, Eugénie didn't hesitate to let those close to her know how she felt. "France should be ashamed," she said. Her belief in Dreyfus's innocence and confidence that anti-Semitism was the cause of the case cost her friends, including one who ran out of the room when the conversation revealed the empress was ardently pro-Dreyfus. "And she didn't even curtsy as she left," the aggrieved Eugénie said. Like Victoria, she had her own sense of protocol.

The Dreyfus Affair, as it became known, did, however, bring her closer to others like Prince Albert I of Monaco. The prince was not only a vocal Dreyfus supporter but also an avid oceanographer, which appealed to the sailor in Eugénie. She spent long stretches of time on her yacht, visiting ports throughout the Mediterranean basin, venturing north to the fjords near the Arctic Circle and skirting the west coast of Africa. She also joined world-famous yachtsman Sir Thomas Lipton, founder of Lipton tea, in sea racing and even returned to Egypt to sail through the Suez Canal again, this time without fanfare and the elaborate agenda. She might even have made a stop at the Cairo Zoo to visit her pet turtle Reine.

Travel, Eugénie said, was the only thing that lifted the "terrible depression" that was her constant companion.

She decided to fulfill the childhood dream that had been denied her when a teacher pulled her from a ship she had stowed away on. Eugénie would sail to India, and this time there would be no teacher to stop her. She nearly made it, but when she reached Ceylon, today's Sri Lanka, she fell ill and had to disembark. A young civil servant was sent to look after her. He was Leonard Woolf, whose liberal views and international outlook, as well as his youthful vigor, were the tonic the empress needed to regain her health and return to Europe. Woolf would go on to become an author and publisher, as well as the husband of Virginia Woolf.

The sea never lost its attraction for Eugénie, nor did warm climes. Each year she found English winters more miserable and longed for sun and warmth, knowing they would also bring relief from her rheumatism.

But she was also missing France where key years of her life had been spent and where she had become an empress and mother. She appreciated its more relaxed Latin attitudes and took pride in its achievements, knowing she'd played a part in creating many of them. Though now in exile, she still loved France and felt she was part of the country, and that the country was part of her. When visitors criticized it, she defended it. "What do you mean French decadence? I don't see any trace of it," she told one guest. "France is a great country and respected everywhere!"

France's Third Republic had found its feet after years of uncertainty and fears of anything named Bonaparte. At the time it was established after the Franco–Prussian War, there had been some talk of reinstating a form of monarchy, but that was ultimately rejected. As one of its early presidents said, "Republicanism seems to be the form of government that divides France least."

By the 1880s, the republic was riding a wave of prosperity, one known as la belle epoque, or the Gay Nineties, which reflected a remarkable comeback after the country's soul-crushing defeat in the Franco–Prussian War. For Eugénie, it was a validation. She saw in the new France all the plans, advances and policy seeds planted in the Second Empire coming to maturity and delivering the benefits she and Napoléon III had envisioned.

Although the government had banned former ruling families

from living in France, it had granted Eugénie permission to pass through the country. As time passed, it relaxed its rules further and allowed the deposed empress to build a house as a winter residence on the Mediterranean coast near Monaco. A childless, aging widow—the relic of an almost-forgotten time—did not seem to be a threat to the youthful vigor of the country.

Eugénie was pleased but couldn't resist teasing the authorities who, in her opinion, were too self-satisfied and assured. She named her new house Villa Cyrnos. It was the Greek name for Corsica, birthplace of the Bonapartes, the family that had made French governments shudder. Yet, she remained cautious and wary of the government, remembering how her husband once told her (prophetically, as it turned out) that they had to do things quickly because no French government survived more than twenty years.

Building a new house and developing a garden helped Eugénie push aside those concerns and begin pursuing other interests. She envisioned a large house surrounded by beautiful flowers, trees and walking paths to take advantage of the magnificent views from the rocky promontory poking out into the Mediterranean and to give her space for challenging exercise. Having learned her lesson in Spanish vineyards, she made sure to hire local architects and landscape designers to do the work.

While that may have avoided conflicts with workers, it did nothing to speed up the work. It was abominably slow and driving Eugénie mad. In desperation, she sent her secretary, Jean-Baptiste Franceschini-Pietri, to crack the whip and get things moving. He, too, was frustrated and traveled back and forth incessantly between Farnborough and Cyrnos to try to complete the project. It took three years, but he was finally able to tell the empress the house was ready.

Eager for the warmth of a Mediterranean sun, Eugénie arrived in January 1895 . . . and was stunned to find Cyrnos buried under snow. It was one of the coldest winters ever in the south of France, and the new heating system which the empress had ordered barely made a difference in the icy interior.

To her immense relief, temperatures improved by the end of the month and visitors—old friends and new—began pouring in. Queen Victoria would come over from Nice in a cart drawn by her donkey Jacquot, sometimes with her beloved servant (and probably lover) John Brown in his kilt and topee.

The Prince of Wales was also a frequent visitor, as was the Austrian empress, Elisabeth, or "Sissi," who visited so often she was given a key to the garden door. Frequently she would slip in to walk before seven in the morning and stay silent behind a bush or tree, then jump out suddenly and frighten Eugénie. Although Sissi was thirteen years younger than Eugénie, the two had their love of exercise and unconventional childhoods in common. Unfortunately, it was a friendship that would come to a tragic end when Sissi was fatally stabbed by an Italian anarchist in 1898. Eugénie was devastated. To lose a friend so much younger was almost unbearable.

In 1901, her grief became raw again when she received news of the death of the eighty-one-year-old Queen Victoria, the woman to whom she owed so much, the only person with whom she had been able to share some of the most intimate thoughts of her life. "I feel even more than ever a foreigner, alone in this land," Eugénie said.

And yet, she wasn't alone. Far from it. Eugénie's memory was so precise and her library and files so comprehensive that nearly everyone in politics and power still came to seek advice or information from her, some clandestinely. Two presidents of the Third Republic which had banned her from France and still refused to officially recognize her—Félix Faure and Raymond Poincaré—were spotted in unannounced meetings with her. The French foreign minister was in contact as well. British politicians like David Lloyd George and Winston Churchill also consulted Eugénie, as did the Spanish diplomat and humanitarian Rodrigo de Saavedra y Vinent, Marquès de Villalobar, who would try to save the nurse Edith Cavell from execution during World War I.

Her friend, the writer Lucien Daudet, was impressed with her continued interest in and knowledge of world affairs even as she grew older. "The Empress talks almost exclusively about politics these days," he wrote in 1912 when Eugénie was eighty-eight. "Every incident reminds her of something analogous in the past, and her incomparable memory, her unique experience reminds one of that splendid ruined city in *The Jungle Book*, from where a persistent voice rises: 'I am the guardian of the treasure of the city of Kings.' Really, she is the last to guard the treasure of tradition, experience, foreign policy . . ."

But much as Eugénie enjoyed discussing the past and spending time with old friends, it was the new friends, the young friends like Daudet (most of them were at least fifty years younger than Eugénie), who stimulated her and kept her feeling young. She had become a touchstone for them, to learn firsthand from her about the past and to connect directly to pivotal events of the nineteenth century. Many, like Daudet, were gay and appreciated her welcome and lack of bias. She built a dormitory at Farnborough where many of them stayed for extended periods. Her "lack of sensibilities," as one described it, was something that had always been with her and which was clear during her time on the throne. She had not only pinned the cross of the Legion of Honor on the lesbian artist Rosa Bonheur, she had helped her and other women get the police permits necessary to wear trousers, and she regularly included gay artists and writers in her parties. Spending time with her was like making the pilgrimage to Mecca, they said, or perhaps to Olympus.

Among those who made the pilgrimage to see her was a young fashion designer named Coco Chanel, who would become famous for her "little black dress." Chanel was eager to meet the woman in a black dress who had created haute couture.

When the writer and artist Jean Cocteau, then a mere nineteen-year-old, was introduced to the empress, Eugénie, in her usual manner, took his arm and dragged him at top speed through the garden, talking nonstop all the while. He was taken aback, but at one point, she bent over, picked a flower and put it in his buttonhole. "I can no longer decorate poets with honors, but I can give you this," she said. Cocteau was captured. Her eyes were a "heavenly blue, although their keenness had been diluted," he recalled. "It was like a whole sea of blue water looked into you." Cocteau heard in her "raucous" voice "a memory of the bullring, the laughter and chatter of the young Eugénie de Montijo which were to frighten and fascinate the shy Napoléon III."

But among the many who came to pay homage to the empress, one young man stood out: Arthur Hugenschmidt. Everyone, including Eugénie, knew that Napoléon III had fathered Hugenschmidt, but who his mother was remained unclear. The Comtesse de Castiglione, one of Napoléon's last mistresses? Or was it Mrs. Hugenschmidt who, like her husband, had been a servant at the Tuileries Palace?

Arthur was born six years after the prince impérial, and his birth was a painful affront to Eugénie. She refused to see the child. Napoléon's three other illegitimate sons had been born during his bachelor years, long before Eugénie came into the picture, so she could ignore them. Napoléon had already made arrangements for them, and they were out of sight. But a child born right under her nose was hurtful and humiliating, a flagrant flaunting of his affairs that showed no concern for her feelings. Her feelings were hurt even more when she discovered that Napoléon had asked Dr. Thomas Evans, her friend and rescuer, to care for the boy when the Franco–Prussian War erupted.

Evans, however, was also the emperor's friend and shared his nineteenth-century chauvinistic attitude that a man had the right to indulge his desires wherever those desires took him. He accepted Napoléon's commission and took Arthur, then about eight years old, back to Philadelphia and raised him. Like Evans, Arthur studied medicine and dentistry and joined Evans in his practice in Paris before setting off on his own.

After the prince impérial's death, Eugénie grew curious about this other son of Napoléon's and, using Evans as an intermediary, asked Arthur to come to Farnborough. She was shocked when

Hugenschmidt walked in. "You look so much like him!" she exclaimed. Arthur was nearly a perfect double of the prince impérial, and he was almost the same age as her son was when he
died.

From that point on, Arthur was a permanent fixture in Eugénie's life, a surrogate son who shared private "family" moments
with her and whom she indulged, even letting Arthur, a talented
amateur photographer, take pictures of her. He was loyal and
modest, and the empress happily found she could discuss nearly
anything with him, even politics, because so many of his dental clients were prominent figures. Among them were Raymond
Poincaré and Georges Clemenceau, both men who would become presidents of France.

IN THE BEAUTIFUL SPRING OF 1914, EUGÉNIE, CARRYING SILVER CUPS AS PRIZES, AGAIN
made the trip down to Hillside School, whose students she had
invited to tea and which would later move into Farnborough itself. The girls were in a feverish state. They had memorized their
speeches in French for her and styled their hair with a pouf in
front hoping to hold in place the crown of white roses and ferns
the empress would place on their heads. They practiced their
curtsies over and over again to make sure the crowns would not
fall over their eyes as they stepped back.

Eugénie smiled at them, proudly but almost sadly. She was
eighty-eight and feeling some aches and pains, but that was not all
that was bothering her. Something else was unnerving . . . like a
constant buzzing in her head. "I feel an electricity in the air," she
told friends. "Another war is coming."

That seemed almost absurd as she boarded *The Thistle* a few
weeks later with her cousin and companion, Madame Antonia de
Vejerano d'Attainville. They planned to sail along the Dalmatian
coast. They had spent time in Venice, site of Eugénie's triumphal visit before her opening of the Suez Canal, and Ravenna,
a city whose mosaics recalled the Moorish heritage of her native

Granada. Now they planned to see the breathtaking coastline on the other side of the Adriatic Sea. It had been a calm, warm trip after a year that had already seen dramatic storms. The empress had been glad to be back on her yacht and seek warmth, sun and new distractions.

As they skirted the pebbly beaches of Croatia, Marconi's new wireless telegraph on the yacht suddenly clicked into life. The message was staggering: Austria had issued an ultimatum to Serbia saying it had no intention of granting it independence . . . this following the assassination a month earlier of Austrian Archduke Franz Ferdinand by a Serbian nationalist.

Eugénie had been right about electricity in the air and began running through the current political alliances and entanglements in her head. Austro–Hungary could count on support from Germany and its truculent kaiser, and maybe Italy; they'd formed the Triple Alliance three decades earlier, but it was set to expire in 1915. The more informal Triple Entente of Great Britain, France and Russia would probably back Serbia, but she was convinced "something is rotten in Russia," as she had told the French ambassador in January of 1914. She believed its nobility was corrupt; the Russian people knew it and would not stand for it.

She fretted about Great Britain, too. Would the largest empire in the world join in a fight against other empires? Would it fight with France to defeat the Germans? She wanted to be sure. She turned *The Thistle* back toward England and Farnborough.

THE ELECTRICITY EUGÉNIE HAD SENSED WAS DUE IN LARGE PART TO KAISER WILHELM II. She'd already had several perplexing encounters with Wilhem II, but still held some affection for him as she had been fond of his mother, Princess Victoria, the eldest daughter of Queen Victoria who had youthfully wished that Eugénie had been her mother.

Years earlier, in 1902, the young kaiser had sent the empress a "very respectful letter" in which he asked her to accept a bracelet with a portrait of his mother, hoping she would accept it "as a memento of a faithful friend." It was an odd gesture from a man who had grown to detest his mother and seemed determined to eradicate the English half of his heritage.

During Eugénie's trip to the Norwegian fjords five years later, she had arrived in Bergen and was surprised to find the fjord full of German cruisers. They were awaiting the arrival of the kaiser, she was told. Worried that Wilhelm would think she was avoiding him if she left, Eugénie decided to anchor *The Thistle* between two of the cruisers, "like a miserable little prisoner of war in their midst," she said. At eleven thirty that night, booming guns announced the kaiser's arrival. Eugénie had already gone to bed, but one of his aides came onboard at midnight to ask if Wilhelm could visit. "Yes, but at 11:00 a.m. tomorrow," she said, "and he should come in civilian dress."

Despite the kaiser disparaging *The Thistle*, saying it "could easily be fitted into one of the cabins of his yacht," they spent two hours together. Eugénie's friend, Isabel Constance Vesey, who was traveling with her, wrote home that "the Empress rather likes him and says he is always most agreeable and charming to her." Her own reaction was that the kaiser "wore too many rings, a bracelet and yellow shoes." Eugénie may have liked Wilhelm in a social setting but she was clear-eyed about him when it came to politics. He hated England.

On Eugénie's trip back to Farnborough, she heard that what she predicted had come to pass: war was declared. With Great Britain now fighting alongside France, she believed the loss in the Franco–Prussian War of 1870 would be avenged. Her only worry was how she could help.

Although she had no official role, she appealed for calm in letters to leaders and authorities with whom she remained in contact such as the czarina of Russia and King Carol I of Romania. She donated *The Thistle* to the British navy and offered Villa Cyrnos to the French government as a field hospital. Still diffident about the ex-empress, the government said *No, thank you*.

Undaunted, Eugénie decided the dormitory she had built

to house her young friends like Daudet and Cocteau could be turned into a hospital for wounded British officers. She spared no expense, bringing in the latest medical equipment and medicines. She was seen flying down the hallway as she tried out the newest wheelchairs, taking one or two falls as she experimented with the crutches she'd ordered. Getting patched up by the nurses she'd hired pleased her, she said, for it made her feel like a fellow patient.

Although Eugénie did everything she could to make the hospital comfortable and cheerful, she was on edge. She read every detail about the war in the newspapers but complained that her failing eyesight meant she had to use a magnifying glass. King George V, Victoria's grandson who was now on the throne, called her nearly every day with news. She charted troop movements on maps.

Eugénie had said, "God will punish me by giving me a long life," but now, for the first time, she prayed to the same God for a longer life. She was ninety years old and wanted to live long enough to see Germany defeated, to see the Allies victorious, to see Alsace and Lorraine reunited with France, to see 1870 avenged. When, at last, it became clear that victory was within reach, her staff was stunned to see her running around the house "almost like a girl of twenty," cheering and telling everyone the Allies could not be beaten.

As the Great War came to an end, the empress, now ninety-two, mentioned to Hugenschmidt a letter she had in her files, a letter from Kaiser Wilhelm I admitting that Alsace and Lorraine should be part of France. Hugenschmidt told his patient President Georges Clemenceau about the letter, and Clemenceau, then in the middle of treaty negotiations with Germany, told the dentist to bring it to him as quickly as possible. With the letter in hand, Clemenceau, a tenacious and fiercely aggressive politician known as the "Little Tiger," retrieved the two provinces for France.

The king of England, meanwhile, had dispatched his sons, the Prince of Wales and the Duke of York, to Farnborough to invest the empress with the Dame Grand Cross of the Empire for her work during the conflict. Eugénie was deeply touched.

She had accomplished what she wanted. Picking up her magnifying glass, she sat down and began reading the full text of the treaty that had been negotiated in Versailles. But with each word she read, she became more and more disturbed. *This is not what I wanted, not what I prayed for. A war to end all wars? No! Germany will never accept this.* The treaty, she realized, would only pave the way for more conflict. The Allies, the proud victors, needed to remember the thousands of "well-trained German officers" now left unemployed and the "millions of Russians who could supply them with men." The conditions of the treaty set the stage to "create a terrible force which some day could crush Europe" and "provide materials for a Holy War."

Eugénie put her magnifying glass down, picked up her cane and walked slowly down the hall, a tired and deflated old woman.

CHAPTER EIGHTEEN
CASTILIAN SUNSET

"NOWADAYS I AM A VERY OLD BAT," EUGÉNIE TOLD A FRIEND. "BUT, AS BUTTERFLIES DO, I still feel I must fly towards the sun. Before death takes me, I should like to see my Castilian sun one more time."

It was the fall of 1919 and another English winter was approaching. For the first time in five years, she could think of escaping it, of traveling, of her beloved sea.

Just three months earlier, she'd gone to a movie theater to see a newsreel. The images were jerky, the long line of cars moving like windup toys, and people jumping up like jack-in-the-boxes to see the "Big Four" at the Château de Versailles to sign the peace treaty ending World War I. Even without her magnifying glass, Eugénie had no trouble recognizing Georges Clemenceau and David Lloyd George. They'd both come to talk with her at Villa Cyrnos. And she saw Woodrow Wilson, too—everyone recognized him with his dour face and silk top hat. Even Vittorio Orlando, the Italian prime minister and smallest of the "Big Four" in more ways than one, was clear in the black-and-white film.

Five years had passed since the assassination of Archduke Franz Ferdinand and his wife and the start of World War I. Five years of seeing young men wounded and broken, many of them brought to the hospital Eugénie had created, some never to leave. It seemed impossible that there could be room for more grief in her life, yet more tears and heartache had come.

Eugénie had watched as the kingdoms and empires she knew were broken up, the rulers she'd talked with, dined with and vacationed with now in exile or dead. "King George will be the only one left," she wrote a friend, "for the nation loves him . . . But he will be very lonely, like a lighthouse in a stormy sea."

Eugénie understood and sympathized: her husband and her son were long gone, along with most of her friends. She had prayed that God would let her live to see the Allied victory, and He had done so . . . cushioning her, however briefly, from the waves of sadness that threatened to consume her. She tried to be sanguine. For the moment, there was a respite from tears and mourning. "Our epoch is a new beginning," she said. "Everything must be built on new foundations." A feminist through and through, she then added a troubled coda: "Do men know this?"

As the new epoch began, Eugénie longed for old friends, the places she loved and the opportunity to travel again. She knew her time was running out and she began planning her trip.

Arthur Bigge, who had been a close friend of the prince impérial and was now secretary to George V, came to say his good-byes and, on the behalf of the king, offer her the use of the royal yacht. Eugénie declined, concerned about possible political ramifications. She would travel as a normal tourist, she said. Then, surprising Bigge, she reached up and took down the portrait of her son that hung in the salon, a painting she had looked at every day since he was killed. She handed it to him. "It's yours," she said. Bigge, who had served in the military with the prince and had accompanied the empress to South Africa when she went to see where he was killed, was overwhelmed and moved by her gesture.

There was a finality in Eugénie's actions as she prepared to leave and one more task she said she was honor bound to complete. She had to find an appropriate home for the Talisman of Charlemagne which her husband had inherited from his mother. It was a locket-like piece, supposedly containing a fragment of the True Cross, that had been taken from the neck of the corpse of Charlemagne. Pictures of the bombardment of Reims Cathedral during the war were seared into her mind. If ever a place needed a talisman, that was it. She sent the relic off with hopes it could help restore the Gothic masterpiece to glory.

Accompanied once again by her cousin Antonia de Verajano d'Attainville and her maid Aline Pelletier, Eugénie arrived in Paris at the end of 1919 for the first time in years. She returned to the Continental Hotel which she knew well and where she had often stayed. It was across the street from the Tuileries Gardens where the palace that had been her home had stood. The burned-out hull of the structure had been cleared away, and she could see the trees and flower beds that replaced it from her room.

She was besieged by old friends, and, in spite of her limited vision, she recognized them and knew their voices. One was Lucien Daudet who remembered her sitting beside the marble fireplace, her profile as striking as ever, but he was saddened by her unseeing eyes. She welcomed him warmly and said, "I wanted to make the present journey in an airplane, but people would only have said that I was an old mad woman." The remark was out of character for someone who had flaunted convention her entire life. Perhaps she was feeling her frailty, knowing she would soon fly toward the sun in her own way.

Nonetheless, she seemed tireless talking about the past, the future and other friends. Only when Aline arrived to call her to dinner did she end the conversation. Eugénie rose and said, "Good-bye, little Lucien." It sounded like an ominous farewell, he thought.

The house she had built in Cap Martin, Villa Cyrnos, like so much of France, had suffered during the war. Only two towns out of the entire country had not lost young men in the conflict. Eugénie learned with sadness of the deaths of men who had worked for her at the villa. She began the necessary work and settled in to spend the Christmas holidays. She entertained Laetitia, Duchess of Aosta, the cousin who had been her proxy in purchasing the Cyrnos land, and the Cardinal Archbishop of Reims who came to thank her for the gift of the Talisman.

It was spring of 1920, and Eugénie set sail for her native land of Spain. As her ship arrived in the port of Gibraltar, British and Spanish warships docked there gave her a twenty-one gun salute. She was thrilled. The last time she had received such a welcome was a half century earlier in Egypt when she went to Suez for the opening of the canal.

Eugénie was now ninety-three, frail and nearly blind from cataracts, but she insisted on stopping in Jerez to see an old friend, the British Colonel Verner.

From there, the next stage of her journey was supposed to be by train to Seville. She refused and instead waited until her great-nephew, the duke of Alba, arrived in his car to drive her. There, the king and queen of Spain came to pay their respects. Afterwards, the duke drove Eugénie to Madrid. On her way, she asked him to stop in front of a house where she had lived as a young woman. The house and garden were abandoned, but an old man spotted them and came over to talk. Pointing at the house, he said, "Here, there once lived a beautiful countess who went away to marry a king." Eugénie smiled. It sounded like a fairy tale.

As in all good fairy tales, the beautiful countess was then carried off to a palace, the Liria Palace in Madrid, the duke of Alba's home. Liria Palace had also been the home of his grandmother, Eugénie's much-loved sister Paca. The duke installed her in Paca's room. Once again, the parade of family and friends began, and Eugénie called up memories of her childhood and shared them with the people she had known in her youth. She surprised them by recognizing many, even with her poor eyesight. When an aging dowager came to call, the empress said, "Ah, it's the Miraflorès girl."

Concerned about Eugénie's vision, the duke brought in an eye surgeon who said that, unlike his colleagues in England and France, he was willing to take the chance of removing the cataracts from the eyes of an empress. Eugénie agreed.

The operation was successful. With her sight restored, Eugénie recovered her energy and set about revisiting the places she loved as a child. She even went to a bullfight. She said she felt she was home, but how quickly the years had passed! All the people and places she had known. Had she really run off to the Romani camps, danced with a smuggler, climbed mountains, seen continents cut apart by an enormous canal? She could remember standing high atop the Pyrenees with both France and Spain at her feet. And the Exposition Universelle when it seemed the whole world was at her feet. Yet she also remembered a little girl in a plain linen dress dreaming of adventure and excitement. Oh, the stories that little girl could tell . . .

On July 10, 1920, Eugénie was overcome with exhaustion and sent to bed. She was coughing and running a high fever. As her condition worsened, a priest was called to administer the last sacrament. As he finished, Eugénie turned to him and her great-nephew and said, "It is time that I went on my way," then fell unconscious.

A few hours later, Eugénie died. It was the morning of July 11, and her Castilian sun was beginning to rise over the Spanish plain. She had just turned ninety-four.

Spain gave her a magnificent funeral with all the ceremony and honors due to a grandee of Spain and an empress. Afterward, her coffin was escorted to the railway station by a troop of halberdiers from the Royal Guard, a military unit used exclusively for the protection of the Spanish royal family. When the empress's train reached Paris on its way to Farnborough, her coffin was carried to a room set aside at the Gare d'Austerlitz.

Thousands of Parisians came to pass by the coffin and say farewell to a woman who had become the symbol of the past splendor and glory of France—and to whom many felt they owed an apology. Prince Murat, Napoléon's cousin, accompanied the coffin to England where Prince Victor Napoléon, her son's chosen heir, met it and escorted it to the empress's home at Farnborough. The British government announced that, on her arrival, Eugénie would be given a twenty-one gun salute.

On learning of the planned salute, the government of

France's Third Republic, perhaps alarmed by the popularity of a Bonaparte, reacted pettishly and lodged a formal protest. In a bit of royal tit for tat, King George V then ordered a battery of Royal Horse Artillery drawn up outside the abbey at Farnborough to remain there at attention during Eugénie's funeral. He also commanded that "La Marseillaise" be played at the end of the service. He and Queen Mary and other members of the British royal family, as well as the king and queen of Spain and representatives of all the European royal houses and descendants of the French imperial court, joined more than 60,000 ordinary French people who poured into Farnborough to witness the funeral of the last empress of France.

More striking, not a single representative of the French government was present.

Throughout the service, the doors of the abbey church were left open to allow the sun to shine in.

Eugénie now lies in foreign soil, far from the country she ruled, far from her Castilian sun, but forever settled between her husband and her son, just as she planned decades earlier. She remains a lasting symbol of personal liberty and independent strength, of a woman who adopted a country and made it her own.

And of a country who adopted her and made her their own.

★ ★ ★ ★ ★

ACKNOWLEDGMENTS

Twenty years of friendship, a few books written by each of us on various topics, a lot of time and wine shared, and then in 2022, the idea: Why don't we write a book together on Empress Eugénie? We had no idea how bumpy the road would be for two-plus years. Just the logistics were boggling. Imagine an agent in California and a publisher in New York, two authors splitting their time among Paris, Bordeaux and Périgord in France as well as shuttling back and forth to the US. Imagine tracking an empress born in Spain, raised in France and England, ruling France for twenty years, living in England for fifty years and traveling non-stop around the world. What a wonderful adventure!

We owe much to Andy Ross, our fantastic agent, for making it so. He liked the proposal and had the brilliant idea of taking it to Peter Joseph, who told us he had launched Hanover Square Press so that he could work more directly with authors on their books. We were the fortunate beneficiaries of that: a real editor who did real editing to help us make our story worthy of an empress. Our book got even better when Peter asked the Francophile Grace Towery to work on the manuscript as well. Thank you to all of you for believing in this book and helping us make it happen.

This adventure relied on a lot of technology, thanks to video conferences, emails, archives and books available online. It also led us to meet wonderful people in Europe and in the US: Dr. Christina Egli in Switzerland opened the doors of Arenenberg Castle and spent many hours sharing the story of Eugénie and

Napoléon. Farnborough Hill School in England and its acting headmistress, Zoe Ireland, welcomed us as royally as the empress herself might have. Ailsa West shared her love and knowledge of the school's direct connection to Eugénie, and the entire faculty and staff of the school adjusted schedules and classes so that we could appreciate the heritage they so carefully protect and so clearly treasure. Art historians Dr. Anthony Geraghty (UK), Dr. Alison McQueen (Australia) and Dr. Susan Taylor-Leduc (US) not only wrote groundbreaking books that we referenced extensively but also kindly answered questions and guided us to reconsider Eugénie's role as a builder. Dr. Elizabeth L. Block, senior editor in the Publications and Editorial Department at the Metropolitan Museum of Art in New York, had enlightening insights on fashion in her book *Dressing Up: The Women Who Influenced French Fashion.*

Let's not forget the archivists and curators we met and who were so helpful. Many thanks to Laurence Lynx, research librarian at the University of Toulouse; Jean-François Delmas at the Château de Compiègne; Chantal Prévôt at the Fondation Napoléon library; and Eric Diouris, curator at the Archives de Paris, whose patience and resourcefulness gave us access to precious documents. At the University of Pennsylvania the staff of the Kislak Center for Special Collections, Rare Books and Manuscripts made it easy for us to access the papers of Dr. Thomas Evans. Special thanks to Sean Quimby, the director of the Kislak Center, and archivist Holly Mengel, head of archives and manuscripts processing, who pulled innumerable boxes of Evans's papers for us multiple times. Thanks, too, to Eric Dillalogue, assistant director of operations; Sarah Heim, public services librarian; and the entire staff at the Kislak Center who made our research so easy—and gave us room to work. Our way there was paved by a happy bit of nepotism as Regan Kladstrup is in charge of incoming special collections, rare books and manuscripts.

Many friends from both sides of the pond came up with information or pictures we otherwise would have missed and opened doors we didn't know were there. Many thanks for their generosity to Isabelle Hossenlopp, expert in jewelry; Dr. Samia Spencer, whose deep knowledge of women's history and Egypt was incredibly helpful; Dr. Azza Heikal, whose passion for Egyptian art and knowledge of Egyptian history led us to discover artworks and paintings; and Françoise LaFon, whose work at universities in France and China means she can find treasures anywhere and shares them unstintingly.

Last but not least, we would like to thank our husbands, Don Kladstrup and Randy Resnick, who lived with Eugénie for two years, had to cope with ups and downs in her life as well as in theirs, and listen to long rants. Our marriages and friendship survived, and we are coming out better and stronger for it!

NOTES ON SOURCES

Although she was born 200 years ago, Empress Eugénie was a woman with today's ideas and attitudes, and she was always in a hurry. We think she would have approved of our gathering the notes about our research into this section rather than interrupting the story we were telling with footnotes or notes between chapters. That sort of notes would have slowed down her reading, which would have made her unhappy, so we didn't want to do that to you either.

Eugénie also wanted things to be correct and well-researched. We do, too, so we have probed archives in France, Spain, Switzerland and Great Britain to tell her story. We embraced her love of technology by extensively searching online materials as well as those in more traditional locations, remembering how she enjoyed the archives of Venice. We tried to put all our sources into perspective, particularly the new information we discovered. We share our sources with you here.

One thing we noticed as we worked on this book was that every previous biography of Eugénie—most done in the early and middle part of the twentieth century—was written by a man: we think the empress would have been pleased to see a couple of women peruse her life this time.

We have translated into English quotes and interviews we did in French and Spanish with journalists, historians and other experts, but have kept the original language for the titles of the various sources.

Eugénie is a fascinating woman and we hope these sources will encourage you to delve even further into her life.

CHAPTER 1: **Of Blood and Sun**

Much of the history of Spain came from by the book of Mark Lawrence, *Nineteenth-Century Spain*, 2020. Most details pertaining to Eugenia's family are from her letters to her mother and the letters exchanged by Mérimée and Eugenia's mother.

The details on the Kirkpatrick family and the brothers' feud (Cipriano and Eugenio) are from the work of Colin Carlin, *William Kirkpatrick of Málaga: Consul, Négociant and Entrepreneur, and Grandfather of the Empress Eugénie*, 2011, and *Captain James Carlin: Anglo-American Blockade Runner*.

The origin of the name Montijo is explained by Jean-Emmanuel Skovron in "De qui Montijo est-il le nom? Pour une meilleure connaissance de la famille espagnole de l'Impératrice Eugénie," *Napoleonica. La Revue* $20^{21}/_1$ (N° 39). Skovron also delved further into the history of Eugénie's family in "Les Montijo. Coup de projecteur sur la belle-famille de l'Empereur," in *Eugénie, impératrice des Français*.

France's female educational system was studied by Rebecca Rogers (*From the Salon to the Schoolroom: Educating Bourgeois Girls in Nineteenth-Century France*, 2005) and Françoise Mayeur (*L'Education des filles en France au 19ème siècle*). We also read numerous memoirs of young female students in France, such as George Sand (*Story of My Life*). The article by Gerald L. Gutek ("Johann Pestalozzi [1746–1827]. Career and Development of Educational Theory, Diffusion of Educational Ideas") explained the unconventional educational method of Johann Pestalozzi who inspired Colonel Amoros for the academy where Eugénie and Paca studied.

The song "Granada" was composed by the Mexican musician Agustin Lara in 1932 and the English lyrics were written by the Australian Dorothy Dodd in 1951.

Eugenia's grandmother, Maria Francesca de Sales Portocarrero y Guzman (1754–1808), Sixth Countess de Montijo, was one of the most important—and interesting—female figures of the Spanish eighteenth century. A liberal and a writer, she welcomed to her Madrid house the most politically advanced minds of her time, those who had been influenced by the French philosophers of the Enlightenment, particularly Rousseau, Montesquieu, Diderot and Voltaire. The countess was one of the founders of the feminine section of the Economical Society of the Friends of the Country and its secretary from 1787 to 1805. She was strongly opposed to the influence of Manuel Godoy on the monarchy and, hence, was exiled by the king to Logrono. Eugénie's father, Cipriano, was her favorite son, and she was a major influence on him. Her ideas, her love of freedom, her belief in women's independence were ingrained in Cipriano who would have passed them on to her granddaughter.

CHAPTER 2: **Marriage-Go-Round**

Eugenia exchanged numerous letters with her sister about her marriage, and they were published in the *Lettres familières* by the duke of Alba. Napoléon's passionate courtship of Eugénie is remarked on in many memoirs, letters and diaries of their contemporaries; they survive in various archives. Among them are Lady Augusta Bruce's letters, Count Viel-Castel (*Memoirs. A chronicle of the principal events, political and social, during the reign of Napoleon III, from 1851 to 1864*), Ambassador Hübner (*Neuf ans de souvenirs d'un ambassadeur d'Autriche à Paris sous le second Empire, 1851–1859*), Princess Mathilde (Philip Walsingham Sergeant, *The Princess Mathilde Bonaparte*, 2022, and Jérôme Picon, *Mathilde, Princesse Bonaparte*, 2000). The diplomats were, as they were expected to be, keen observers of the dynamics of the court of the new emperor. Contemporary paintings and engravings also show the pomp of the wedding.

CHAPTER 3: **Demands of Dynasty**

The discussion of Eugénie's sexuality relies on personal talks with contemporary psychologists and sociologists as well as readings of experts on female sexuality in the nineteenth century: Eleanor Janega, *The Once and Future Sex: Going Medieval on Women's Roles in Society*, 2023; Aïcha Limbada, *La Nuit de noces. Une histoire de l'intimité conjugale*, 2023; James F. McMillan, *France and Women 1789–1914: Gender, Society and Politics*, 2000. The dramatic birth of the prince and its consequences for the imperial couple's intimacy were contained in doctors' reports and articles. Accounts of Loulou's sumptuous baptism were in many newspapers, as well as in diplomats' dispatches.

Harriet Howard, born Elizabeth Ann Harryett (1823–1865), has long been considered the benefactor of Napoléon's coup. Although this is still accepted by many historians, in 2022 Ilmar Golicz published a long and detailed article, based on his research in archives and bank records, which established that Harriett Howard's financial situation would not have allowed her to support Napoléon's campaigns and coups.

Queen Elizabeth II ended the practice of royal public birth prior to the birth of her first child, Prince Charles (now King Charles III) in 1948.

CHAPTER 4: To Build a Dream

Eugénie and Napoléon's dream of Paris is well documented. Among the works we consulted are Nicolas Chaudun in *Haussmann, Georges Eugène, préfet baron de la Seine*; Eric Hazan in *The Invention of Paris: A History in Footsteps*; Bertrand Lemoine in *Les Halles de Paris*; and Luc Sante in *The Other Paris*.

The emperor was raised on the shores of Lake Constance in Switzerland where he learned to ice-skate proficiently. The day Lillie Moulton met him, he was suffering from a gout attack, which reduced his mobility.

One pavilion from Les Halles has survived. The Pavilion Baltard now is in Nogent-sur-Marne near Paris and featured often in historical movies.

The 1855 classification was established to promote French wines to visitors to the World's Fair. It applied to wines from the Médoc area of Bordeaux, with the exception of Château Haut-Brion, which is in the Graves. The wines were separated into five different classes based on quality and mostly price. The classification remains in effect, with only one change since the original rating was made: Château Mouton-Rothschild was promoted to Grand Cru in 1974.

CHAPTER 5: Sticks and Stones, Bricks and Mortar

Many historians and novelists wrote about Eugénie's love of building and decorating. The seminal book on Eugénie's building is by the Australian art historian Alison McQueen, *Empress Eugénie and the Arts: Politics and Visual Culture in the Nineteenth Century*. Eugénie's work with gardens was highlighted by Susan Taylor-Leduc in her *Marie-Antoinette's Legacy: The Politics of French Garden Patronage and Picturesque Design, 1775–1867*.

The fame of Biarritz and the preeminent role Eugénie played in its development as a summer resort for rich and powerful families has inspired novelists like Marie-France Lecat (*Villa Eugénie: ou les promenades d'une impératrice*) as well as diarists and historians. Among them is the entertaining—and gossip-filled—story of the imperial couple's life in Biarritz by Dr. Ernest Barthez (*La famille impériale à Saint-Cloud et à Biarritz*) and the academic history of Biarritz during the Second Empire by Philippe Cachau.

Many people walked in Eugénie's footsteps in the Basque country: Caroline Lampre (*Impératrice Eugénie, Madame de la Rhune*) is one example.

The British newspaper *The Guardian* noted in an article on May 27, 2024, "It was common for art dealers to scratch out women's names and replace it with a more commercial male's . . . In this male-dominated society, women were practically invisible, except in the home and not taken seriously as professionals." Katy Hessel was the reporter.

Marie Octavie Sturel Paigné (1819–1854) died from complications after the birth of her second child.

CHAPTER 6: The Empress's New Clothes

Eugénie's role in the creation of a new industry, haute couture and luxury, is often overlooked by historians. We made extensive use of information provided by experts of nineteenth-century fashion to understand and explain the image Eugénie wanted to project as empress, consort and regent of France. Much came from Elizabeth L. Block, *Dressing Up: The Women Who Influenced French Fashion*; Heidi Brevik-Zender, *Fashioning Spaces: Mode and Modernity in Late Nineteenth-Century Paris*; Kimberly Chrisman-Campbell, *Worn on This Day: The Clothes That Made History*; Bonnie English and Nazanin Hedayat Munroe, *A Cultural History of Western Fashion: From Haute Couture to Virtual Couture*.

One of the great admirers of Eugénie's elegance and sense of fashion was Queen Victoria, as Theo Aronson explained in *Queen Victoria and the Bonapartes*, London: Lume Books, 2021 (reprint edition). In her journal and letters to her uncle King Leopold of Belgium, Victoria frequently mentioned her admiration of Eugénie.

Details on Eugénie's jewels are available in the book by Emilie Bérard who worked with Laure-Isabelle Mellerio and Diane-Sophie Lanselle to write *Mellerio, le joaillier du Second Empire*. Eugénie's relations with Guerlain are discussed in Elisabeth de Feydeau's *Le Roman des Guerlain*. Joan DeJean charts the birth of the luxury industry in *The Essence of Style: How the French Invented High Fashion, Fine Food, Chic Cafes, Style, Sophistication, and Glamour*.

Pauline von Metternich (1836–1921) was a socialite in the courts of both Vienna and Paris. She was married to her uncle, Prince Richard von Metternich (1829–1895), the Austrian ambassador in Paris from 1859 to 1870. Pauline was close to Eugénie, who trusted her implicitly. Pauline's memoirs, however, painted a picture of Eugénie and her court that was less than flattering.

A romantic legend is attached to the emerald clover brooch beloved by Eugénie. Napoléon sent one of his aides-de-camp, Count Bacciochi, to order it, and the brooch supposedly was ready the next day and given to Eugénie, confirming the rumors of a marriage. In this case, the truth is even more romantic: Napoléon was constrained by royal protocol and could not give a jewel directly to his beloved because they were not yet officially engaged. Instead the lovelorn emperor organized a rigged drawing at Christmas. The first prize was an emerald and diamond brooch. Unsurprisingly, it was won by Eugénie.

CHAPTER 7: Readin', Writin' and Reignin'

Although the books by Desmond Seward (in English) and Guy des Cars (in French) are dated, they provided us with background information. The more recent book by Maxime Michelet on Eugénie and her relationship to power, although useful, is heavily weighted with his political views and had to be treated carefully. Archives in Paris and in England provided a balance.

Charlotte Corday believed Marat was responsible for the violence developing in France and hoped his death would lead to the creation of a peaceful republic. Her action had the opposite effect: it opened the doors to the worst era of terror in French history.

The fate of poor girls was dreadful. Their parents usually sent them to work at an early age to bring income to the family. They believed girls had no need to learn to write or read in order to work in a factory, on a farm or in a house as a servant.

The story we recount is one of the most famous stories about the origin of the bâchi and its red pom-pom. Another says there was an extra string left on the top of the hat so the maker made a knot of it. Whatever the origin of the pom-pom, touching the bâchi of a sailor with your left index brings luck—especially if the sailor does not see you!

CHAPTER 8: Ministry of Charity

Alison McQueen's book *Empress Eugénie and the Arts: Politics and Visual Culture in the Nineteenth Century* was a major resource for information on Eugénie's social work. We also used Eugénie's letters to family and friends. The French national archives on philanthropic associations (National Archives in Paris, cote F15, F16, F17) contain detailed information on their management by women and their relations with Eugénie. They gave us new insights into Eugénie's role.

Articles and books that revealed less-known facts include Jeroen Dekker's *Christian Carlier, La prison aux champs: les colonies d'enfants délinquants du Nord de la France au XIXe siècle* and Michel-Louis Lévy's "Garçons et filles à l'école" from *Population et sociétés*.

CHAPTER 9: Empressing

Two older books were important sources of information for this period of Eugénie's life: one was by the British historian William Smith which is available only in French, (*Eugénie, impératrice des Français*); the second by French historian Christophe Pincemaille (*L'impératrice Eugénie: De Suez à Sedan*). Both authors concentrate on the later part of Eugénie's reign. The memoirs of Dr. Thomas Evans, her dentist, were another key source of information. The archives of the University of Pennsylvania contain the only remaining copy of his full memoirs. Those subsequently published by his successor, Dr. Crane, were heavily redacted and contain numerous errors. We also relied on Eugénie's letters to her family and on Queen Victoria's journal and letters, now available online.

CHAPTER 10: Designing a Disaster

International politics and foreign policy of the Second Empire were authoritatively covered by Alain Plessis in *The Rise and Fall of the Second Empire, 1852–1871*. Additional details came from the unpublished memoirs of Dr. Evans, as well as those of diplomats. The Mexican incursion and Emperor Maximilian's death have been the topic of several articles, including Alain Gouttman's "Le martyr gênant de 'l'aventure mexicaine.' L'annonce de l'exécution de l'empereur Maximilien en France et en Autriche."

Raphaël Dargent provided some unusual insights into Eugénie and Napoléon's marital relations in the 1860s. He suggests that the decision to invade Mexico may have been made at a time when Napoléon was very ill and in pursuit of a failed actress named Marguerite Bellanger. Twice Napoléon fainted at Bellanger's apartment and had to be carried back to the Tuileries. When Eugénie discovered the liaison, she was furious. She charged into Bellanger's apartment shouting, "If you love the emperor, stop seeing him." It was to no avail. Eugénie believed the relationship was worsening his physical condition and affecting his mental capacity and, hence, endangering the country. At that point, she may even have told Napoléon he should abdicate in favor of their young son with her as regent, something he would have refused angrily. Although we have not been able to confirm Dargent's story about the timing of the Mexican decision, it is clear that Eugénie then left for the spa at Schwalbach in Switzerland. She stayed longer than scheduled. On her return, courtiers said the relationship between her and Napoléon was strained and Mérimée wrote, "There is no more Eugénie. There is only an empress. I pity and admire her."

Queen Isabella II of Spain (1830–1904) reigned from 1833 until her deposition in 1868. Her father King Ferdinand VII did not have a son and issued the *Pragmatic Sanction* which annulled the *Salic Law* to allow her to succeed him.

Rose O'Neal Greenhow (1813–1864) was a spy for the Confederacy during the US Civil War. In 1863 she was sent on a diplomatic mission to England and France. She published her memoirs in 1864 and shortly thereafter, she drowned off the coast of Wilmington, NC, while trying to escape a Union gunboat.

CHAPTER 11: "A Wave of Insanity"

The 1867 World Fair has been studied by a wide range of historians and recounted in numerous memoirs. We have taken advantage of several, including Lillie de Hegermann-Lindencrone's *In the Courts of Memory, 1858–1875*. Many of the books in our bibliography include chapters on the fair.

The Grand-Duchess of Gerolstein by Jacques Offenbach is an opéra bouffe that satirizes "unthinking militarism." Bismarck was said to leave the theater smirking because the French in attendance didn't grasp the real subject of the operetta.

CHAPTER 12 : Madame la Sultane de France

The Suez Canal inauguration is a well-known story but recent research sheds a new light on several events: Gilles Gauthier et al., *L'épopée du canal de Suez*, 2018; Azza Heikal, *L'orientalisme, un autre regard*. *L'Egypte illustrée*, 2020; Christophe Pincemaille, *L'impératrice Eugénie: De Suez à Sedan*, 2000; Edward W. Said, *Orientalism*, 2003; and David Todd, *A Velvet Empire: French Informal Imperialism in the Nineteenth Century*, 2023. Articles we utilized include Robert Solé's "Ismaïl Pacha. À l'heure européenne," published in *Ils ont fait l'Egypte moderne*, 2017; and Samia I. Spencer's "Un chapitre oublié de la glorieuse histoire de la francophonie. Langue et culture françaises en Egypte (1850–1950)," 2024.

Eugénie's fear of decay and also of relics was known to her entourage. Ethel Smyth explained that "she had a physical horror of relics which no sense of their sanctity had power to counteract." In one Italian cathedral she was, as a favor, "authorized" to kiss the shinbone of a local saint. Eugénie was repulsed. On another occasion, a nun learned she was suffering from rheumatism and told her that an application of the relic on the painful part would help. The empress kindly but firmly declined the offer.

CHAPTER 13: Last Days

The few months between Eugénie's return to France and the war declaration were at the core of Pincemaille's book *L'impératrice Eugénie: De Suez à Sedan* and Smith's *Eugénie, impératrice des Français*. Nancy Nichols Barker in *Distaff Diplomacy: The Empress Eugénie and the Foreign Policy of the Second Empire* provides useful but dated material. Charles-Eloi Vial discussed the fall of monarchies in *Le siècle des chutes. Abdications et déchéances en France, 1814–1870*. A more vivacious account can be found in *Crowns in Conflict: The Triumph and the Tragedy of European Monarchy, 1910–1918* by Theo Aronson.

CHAPTER 14: Shadow of the Guillotine

The human and political aspects of Eugénie's role in the Franco–Prussian War are gleaned from memoirs, personal letters and journals of her entourage or people close to her. One of them is by Augustin Filon, the prince impérial's tutor, in his *Recollections of the Empress Eugénie*.

The most important and reliable source on Eugénie's escape is the archives of the University of Pennsylvania in Philadelphia which has the personal papers of Dr. Thomas Evans. These gave us new information about Eugénie's dramatic escape from France.

The difficult negotiations of the last days of the Second Empire are fully described by Harold Kurtz in his *The Empress Eugénie* (1965); Christophe Pincemaille also provides insights.

Sir John and Lady Burgoyne could not appreciate the relief of having made it through the ferocious storm during Eugénie's escape because, within hours of their arrival, they were to learn that their only son, Hugh, had died when the ship he was captaining out of Finisterre in France capsized in the very storm they survived.

CHAPTER 15: Land of Hope, Dreams of Glory

We were able to add medical details to the treatment of Napoléon thanks to *The Cambridge History of Medicine* by Roy Porter and the book by Lindsay Fitzharris on Joseph Lister. Once again, the memoirs of Dr. Evans provided previously unpublished details.

CHAPTER 16: On Her Own

Sources of information on the prince impérial are sparse. Augustin Filon's *Memoirs of the Prince Imperial, 1856–1879* is the major record of his life. Although the short book by Suzanne Desternes and Henriette Chandet *Louis, prince impérial, 1856-1879* (1955) added some material, we were unable to verify parts of it. Thomas Pakenham's two books on southern Africa provided background, as did several others on the history of the region.

Anthony Geraghty's *The Empress Eugénie in England: Art, Architecture, Collecting* (2023) is an authoritative look at her work in Farnborough and a long and detailed interview with the author supplemented our understanding of her project.

The financing of Farnborough and evaluation of Eugénie's fortune was researched in numerous published and unpublished sources, including the archives of Barings Bank; the book by Denis Hannotin, *Enquête sur certains comptes privés de Napoléon III* (2022), which detailed some of the private financial transactions of the imperial couple; the sales catalogs of several different auctions of Eugénie's jewels; the article by P. Arrizoli-Clementel, "La Corbeille de l'impératrice" about Eugénie's finances as a bride; and an anonymous article titled "French Empress Eugénie: Patron and Collector." We also used Karine Huguenaud's article "Eugénie et la joaillerie avant et après l'Empire: une histoire de sentiments." ("Eugenia and Jewelry before and after the Empire: A Story of Feelings") (2020); and Pierre Ponsot's "Economie traditionnelle, techniciens étrangers, et poussée capitaliste dans les campagnes espagnoles au XIXe siècle. L'exemple de deux domaines d'Eugénie de Montijo." The latter explored Eugénie's wealth management strategy as an absentee landowner in Spain. William Smith in *The Empress Eugénie and Farnborough* detailed some of her ideas and goals for the building of Farnborough.

CHAPTER 17: The Matriarch of Europe

The information in this chapter came from a wide variety of sources, including Pierre Apraxine and Xavier Demange's *La Divine Comtesse: Photographs of the Countess of Castiglione*; Etienne Chilot's *Dans l'ombre d'Eugénie. La dernière impératrice en exil. (In the Shadow of Eugénie: The Last Empress in Exile)*, and Anna Klumpke's *Rosa Bonheur: The Artist's (Auto)biography*. We also relied on Sampiero Sanguinetti's *L'Enfant. La lingère, la comtesse et l'impératrice. Arthur Hugenschmidt (1862–1929)*, and Ethel Smyth's *Impressions That Remained*. Ferdinand Bac gave us background for Villa Cyrnos in "L'impératrice Eugénie au Cap Martin," in *La Revue Universelle*, March 15, 1927, as did Ernesta Stern in "Quelques souvenirs intimes sur l'impératrice Eugénie" published in *Revue Politique et Littéraire* for *Revue Bleue*.

From 1800, when the regulation was put in place by Napoléon Bonaparte, until 2013 (yes, 2013), French women were forbidden to wear trousers unless they had a permit from the police. Women in trousers were seen as cross-dressing which was considered a source of "social disruption." Eugénie disliked the lack of mobility fashion could impose on women. During her years as empress, she asked Worth to design shorter dresses for walking and helped many women get police authorization for trousers. Rosa Bonheur's original permit is now displayed on the walls of her studio in her Château de By near Fontainebleau. Copies are also displayed in the Rosa Bonheur restaurants.

Arthur Hugenschmidt's birthmother's identity remains a mystery. He was born September 22, 1862. Countess Castiglione was said to be his mother but her affair with the emperor had ended in 1857, five years before Arthur's birth. In that same year, her husband made their separation official. In explaining why, he said his wife refused to have sexual intercourse with him because she did not want to be pregnant again. However, in 1861 at a ball she and Napoléon disappeared for twenty minutes. When they returned, both were disheveled. Neither she nor her son Arthur denied the rumor that the countess was his mother, but doubts persisted: Why was Arthur put into the care of the Hugenschmidt couple? Why was Napoléon so attached to the boy? One possible answer is that Elisabeth Hauger, a laundry maid at the Tuileries who had married Christophe Hugenschmidt in 1855, was a mistress of Napoléon's and became pregnant by him. Her son was welcomed to the Hugenschmidt family because the couple had recently lost their two children. Another possibility is that Napoléon, knowing of the couple's recent loss of their own children, asked them to adopt the child assuring them he would pay for the baby's care. Both Elisabeth and Christophe Hugenschmidt remained in Napoléon's employ until his death, and Napoléon himself always kept a watchful eye on Arthur.

In a long interview Corsican journalist Sampiero Sanguinetti, author of the only book on Arthur, discussed the papers of his great-aunt, Léonie Cadiergues-Theus, which he had inherited. His great-aunt was a companion of Arthur Hugenschmidt in his travels. The papers, Sampiero said, imply that Castiglione was probably Arthur's mother. That possibility directly contradicts the work by Benedetta Craveri in *La Contessa*, in which it is stated that it was impossible for Castiglione to be Arthur's mother. The debate is still open.

CHAPTER 18: Castilian Sunset

Details of Eugénie's last voyage and her funeral were covered in international newspapers of the time.

SELECTED BIBLIOGRAPHY

Books

Alba, Duke of, with de Llanos y Torriglia, Felix and Josserand, Pierre. *Lettres familières de l'impératrice Eugénie*, 2 vol., Paris: Le Divan, 1935.

Anceau, Eric. *Napoléon III, l'impératrice Eugénie et Compiègne*. Paris: Fondation Napoléon, coll. "Conférences," dir. Eric Georgin, n.d.

Anceau, Eric. *Ils ont fait et défait le Second Empire*. Paris: Tallandier, 2019.

Anceau, Eric. *Napoléon III. Un Saint-Simon à cheval.* Tallandier, 2008.

Anceau, Eric. *Napoléon III, l'impératrice Eugénie et Compiègne*. Paris: Le Promeneur des Avenues, 2021.

Apraxine, Pierre and Demange, Xavier. *La Divine Comtesse: Photographs of the Countess of Castiglione*. New Haven: Yale University Press, 2000.

Aronson, Theo. *Crowns in Conflict: The Triumph and the Tragedy of European Monarchy, 1910–1918*. London: John Murray, 1986.

Aronson, Theo. *Queen Victoria and the Bonapartes*. London: Lume Books, 2021 (reprint).

Barker, Nancy Nichols. *Distaff Diplomacy: The Empress Eugénie and the Foreign Policy of the Second Empire*. Austin: The University of Texas Press, 1967.

Barthez, Dr. Ernest. *La famille impériale à Saint-Cloud et à Biarritz*. Paris: Calmann-Lévy, 1913.

Basch, Sophie. *Le Japonisme, un art français*. Dijon: Les Presses du Réel, 2023.

Bérard, Emilie with Mellerio, Laure-Isabelle and Lanselle, Diane-Sophie. *Mellerio, le joaillier du Second Empire*. Paris: éd. Réunion des musées nationaux, 2016.

Bizard, Dr. Léon and Chapon, Jane. *Histoire de la prison de Saint-Lazare du Moyen-Age à nos jours*. Paris: E. de Boccard, 1925.

Block, Elizabeth L. *Dressing Up: The Women Who Influenced French Fashion*. Cambridge, Massachusetts: MIT Press, 2021.

Bongrand, Caroline. *Louis Vuitton, l'audacieux*. Paris: Gallimard, 2021.

Brevik-Zender, Heidi. *Fashioning Spaces: Mode and Modernity in Late Nineteenth-Century Paris*. Toronto: University of Toronto Press, 2015.

Briot, Eugénie. *La Fabrique des parfums. Naissance d'une industrie de luxe*. Paris: Vendémiaire, 2015.

Brodsky, Alyn. *Imperial Charade*. Indianapolis: The Bobbs-Merrill Company, 1978.

Cachau, Philippe. *Biarritz sous le Second Empire*. Paris: Soteca, 2020.

Carette, Madame (née Bouvet). *My Mistress: The Empress Eugénie, or Court Life at the Tuileries*. London: Dean & Son, 1889.

Carlin, Colin. *William Kirkpatrick of Málaga: Consul, Négociant and Entrepreneur, and Grandfather of the Empress Eugénie*. Glasgow: The Grimsay Press, 2011.

Carlin, Colin. *Captain James Carlin: Anglo-American Blockade Runner*. Columbia: The University of South Carolina Press, 2017.

Carson, Gerald. *The Dentist and the Empress: The Adventures of Dr. Tom Evans in Gas-Lit Paris*. Graymalkin Media, 2023.

Chaudun, Nicolas. *Haussmann Georges Eugène, préfet baron de la Seine*. Arles: Actes Sud, 2019.

Chilot, Étienne. *La Dernière souveraine*. Montacher-Villegardin: Le Charmoiset, 2020.

Chilot, Étienne. *Dans l'ombre d'Eugénie. La dernière impératrice en exil. (In the Shadow of Eugénie: The Last Empress in Exile.)* Montacher-Villegardin: Le Charmoiset, 2019.

Chilot, Étienne. *Un Jardin pour Eugénie. La dernière impératrice au Cap Martin*. Blois: Le Charmoiset, 2022.

Chilot, Étienne. *L'entrevue de Palerme. L'impératrice Eugénie et le duc d'Aumale, 1896*. Blois: Le Charmoiset, 2022.

Cholet, Mona. *In Defence of Witches: Why Women Are Still on Trial*. London: Picador, 2022. (Translated by Sophie R. Lewis.)

Chrisman-Campbell, Kimberly. *Worn on This Day: The Clothes That Made History*. Philadelphia: Running Press, 2019.

Cogeval, Guy; Badetz, Yves; Perrin, Paul; and Vial Marie-Paule (dir.). *Spectaculaire Second Empire*. Paris: Skira, 2016.

Coll. *Napoléon III et Eugénie reçoivent à Fontainebleau*. Fontainebleau: Faton, 2012.

Cooney, Kara. *When Women Ruled the World: Six Queens of Egypt*. Washington: National Geographic, 2020.

Craveri, Benedetta. *La Contessa*. Paris: Flammarion, 2021.

Dargent, Raphaël. *L'impératrice Eugénie. L'obsession de l'honneur*. Paris: Belin, 2017.

Daudet, Lucien. *L'Inconnue, biographie historique*. Paris: Multimed Publishing SAS/ Jacques-Marie Laffont éd., 2010.

DeJean, Joan. *The Essence of Style: How the French Invented High Fashion, Fine Food, Chic Cafés, Style, Sophistication, and Glamour*. New York: Free Press, a division of Simon and Schuster, 2005.

DeJean, Joan. *How Paris Became Paris: The Invention of the Modern City*. New York: Bloomsbury US, 2014.

Des Cars, Jean. *Eugénie, la dernière impératrice*. Paris: Perrin, 2000.

Desternes, Suzanne and Henriette, Chandet. *Louis, prince impérial, 1856–1879*. Paris: Librairie Hachette, 1957.

Egli, Christina. *Napoléon III, l'empereur paysagiste*. Blois: éd. Le Charmoiset, 2024.

English, Bonnie and Munroe, Nazanin Hedayat. *A Cultural History of Western Fashion: From Haute Couture to Virtual Couture*. London: Bloomsbury Visual Arts, 2022.

Evans, Dr. Thomas W. *The Memoirs of Dr. Thomas W. Evans, Recollections of the Second French Empire*. Ed. Dr. Edward Crane. Wagram Press, 2015 (reprint).

de Feydeau, Elisabeth. *Le Roman des Guerlain. Parfumeurs de Paris*. Paris: Flammarion, 2017.

Filon, Augustin. *Recollections of the Empress Eugénie*. London: Cassell and Co., 1920.

Filon, Augustin. *Memoirs of the Prince Imperial, 1856–1879*. London: William Heinemann, 1913.

Fitzharris, Lindsey. *The Butchering Art: Joseph Lister's Quest to Transform the Grisly World of Victorian Medicine*. London: Penguin, 2017.

Gauthier, Gilles, et al. *L'épopée du canal de Suez*. Paris: Gallimard, 2018.

Geraghty, Anthony. *The Empress Eugénie in England: Art, Architecture, Collecting*. London: The Burlington Press, 2022.

Hannotin, Denis. *Enquête sur certains comptes privés de Napoléon III*. Paris: SPM, 2022.

Hazan, Eric. *The Invention of Paris: A History in Footsteps*. London: Verso, 2011.

Haussmann, G. E. *Mémoires*. Ed. Françoise Choay. Paris: Le Seuil, 2000.

Heikal, Azza. *L'orientalisme, un autre regard. L'Egypte illustrée*. Paris: L'Harmattan, 2020.

de Hegermann-Lindencrone, Lillie (Lillie Moulton). *In the Courts of Memory, 1858–1875*. NY: Harper & Brothers, 1912.

d'Hérisson, Maurice, le Comte. *Journal of a Staff-Officer in Paris during the Events of 1870–1871*. London: Remington & Co., 1885.

von Hübner, Joseph Alexander. *Neuf ans de souvenirs d'un ambassadeur d'Autriche à Paris sous le second Empire, 1851–1859*. Publ. Count Alexandre von Hübner. Paris: Plon-Nourrit, 1904.

Irving, Washington. *Tales of the Alhambra*. Philadelphia: Carey & Lea, 1832.

Janega, Eleanor. *The Once and Future Sex: Going Medieval on Women's Roles in Society*. New York: W. W. Norton and Company, 2023.

Jarry, François. *Hortense de Beauharnais*. Paris: Bernard Giovanangeli, 2009.

Jones, Colin. *The Smile Revolution in Eighteenth Century Paris*. Oxford: Oxford University Press, 2014.

Klumpke, Anna. *Rosa Bonheur: The Artist's (Auto)biography*. Michigan: Plunkett Lake Press, University of Michigan Press, 1997.

Kurtz, Harold. *The Empress Eugénie*. London: Readers Union Hamish Hamilton, 1965.

de La Cerda, Alexandre. *Napoléon III, Eugénie et la chapelle impériale de Biarritz*. Biarritz: CBR Éditions, 1998.

Lampre, Caroline. *Impératrice Eugénie, Madame de la Rhune*. Bayonne: Atlantica, 2020.

Lawrence, Mark. *Nineteenth-Century Spain: A New History*. London: Routledge, 2020.

Lecat, Marie-France. *Villa Eugénie: ou les promenades d'une impératrice*. France: Cairn, 2014.

Legge, Edward. *The Empress Eugénie 1870–1910*. New York: Charles Scribner's Sons, 1910.

Lemoine, Bertrand. *Les Halles de Paris*. Paris: éd. L'Equerre, 1980.

Limbada, Aïcha. *La Nuit de noces. Une histoire de l'intimité conjugale*. Paris: La Découverte, 2023.

Maneglier, Hervé. *Paris impérial. La vie quotidienne sous le Second Empire*. Paris: Armand Colin, 1990.

Mayeur, Françoise. *L'Education des filles en France au 19ème siècle*. Paris: Tempus Perrin, 2008.

McMillan, James F. *France and Women 1789–1914: Gender, Society and Politics*. London: Routledge, 2000.

McQueen, Alison. *Empress Eugénie and the Arts: Politics and Visual Culture in the Nineteenth Century*. London: Routledge, 2011.

Mérimée, Prosper. *Lettres à Madame de Montijo*. Ed. Claude Schopp, 2 vols, Paris: Mercure de France, 1995.

Merriman, John M. *The Red City: Limoges and the French Nineteenth Century*. London: Oxford University Press, 1985.

de Metternich-Sandor, Pauline. *Éclairs du passé (1859–1870)*. Zurich: Amalthea-Verlag, 1922.

Michelet, Maxime. *L'impératrice Eugénie. Une vie politique*. Paris: Editions du Cerf, 2020.

Morris, Donald. *The Washing of the Spears: The Rise and Fall of the Zulu Nation.* Pimlico, 1994.

Moses, Claire Goldberg. *French Feminism in the 19th Century.* Albany: State University of New York Press, 1984.

Mostyn, Dorothy A. *The Story of a House: Farnborough Hill.* Farnborough: St. Michael's Abbey Press, 1980.

Murray, Margaret Alice. *The Witch-Cult in Western Europe: A History of Scottish, French and British Witchcraft, with a Guide and Notes on the Spells and Familiars of Witches.* London: Adansonia Publishing, 2018.

Nimura, Janice P. *The Doctors Blackwell: How Two Pioneering Sisters Brought Medicine to Women—And Women to Medicine.* New York: W. W. Norton & Company, 2021.

Pakenham, Thomas. *The Scramble for Africa.* London: Abacus, 1992.

Pakenham, Thomas. *The Boer War.* London: Abacus, 1991.

Paléologue, Maurice. *The Tragic Empress: Intimate Conversations with the Empress Eugénie.* London: Thornton, Butterworth, n.d.

Papiers et Correspondance de la Famille impériale, vol. 1 & 2, 1870–1871. Paris: Garnier Frères, 1871.

Pincemaille, Christophe. *L'impératrice Eugénie: De Suez à Sedan.* Paris: Payot, 2000.

Picon, Jérôme. *Mathilde, Princesse Bonaparte.* Paris: Flammarion, 2005.

Plessis, Alain. *The Rise and Fall of the Second Empire, 1852–1871.* Cambridge: Cambridge University Press, 1985.

Porter, Roy (ed.). *The Cambridge History of Medicine.* Cambridge: Cambridge University Press, 1st ed., 2006.

Rainey, Henry. *Dr. Thomas W. Evans, America's Dentist to European Royalty.* Philadelphia: Evons Co., n.d.

Rogers, Rebecca. *A Critical Discourse Analysis of Family Literacy Practices: Power In and Out of Print.* London: Lawrence Erlbaum Associates, 2003.

Rogers, Rebecca. *From the Salon to the Schoolroom: Educating Bourgeois Girls in Nineteenth-Century France.* Pennsylvania: Penn State UP, 2005.

Said, Edward W. *Orientalism.* UK: Penguin Random House, 2003.

Samoyault-Vériet, Colombe. *Le Musée chinois de l'impératrice.* Paris: RMN, 1994.

Sand, George. *Story of My Life: The Autobiography of George Sand. A group translation.* Albany: State University Press of New York, 1991. https://archive.org/details/storyofmylifeaut0000sand.

Sanguinetti, Sampiero. *L'Enfant. La lingère, la comtesse et l'impératrice. Arthur Hugenschmidt (1862–1929).* Montachet-Villegardin: Le Charmoiset, 2017.

Sanguinetti, Sampiero et Elisabeth. *Tito Franceschini-Pietri. Les dernières braises de l'Empire.* France: Albiana, 2015.

Sante, Luc. *The Other Paris.* New York: Farrar, Strauss and Giroux, 2015.

Saunders, Edith. *The Age of Worth: Couturier to the Empress Eugénie.* London: Longmans, Green and Co. Ltd., 1954.

Schiffer, Lise. *Olympe. Être femme et féministe au temps de Napoléon III.* Paris: Vendémiaire, 2021.

Sergeant, Philip Walsingham. *The Princess Mathilde Bonaparte.* London: Legare Street Press, 2022.

Seward, Desmond. *Eugénie: The Empress and Her Empire.* London: Sutton, 2004.

Shealy, Daniel, Ed. *Little Women Abroad: The Alcott Sisters' Letters from Europe, 1870–1871.* Athens: University of Georgia Press, 2008.

Smith, William. *Eugénie, impératrice des Français.* Paris: Bartillat, 1998.

Smyth, Ethel. *Streaks of Life. Part 1: Recollections of the Empress Eugénie* (pp. 4–68), London: Longmans, Green and Co., 1921.

Smyth, Ethel. *Impressions That Remained*. New York: Alfred A. Knopf, 1946.

Smyth, Ethel. *As Time Went On*. London: Longmans, Green and Co., 1936.

Stefanini, Laurent (dir.). *À la table des diplomates. L'histoire de France racontée à travers ses grands repas, 1520–2015*. Paris: Iconoclaste Éditions, 2016.

Taylor-Leduc, Susan. *Marie-Antoinette's Legacy. The Politics of French Garden Patronage and Picturesque Design, 1775–1867*. Amsterdam University Press, 2022.

Todd, David. *A Velvet Empire: French Informal Imperialism in the Nineteenth Century*. Princeton & Oxford: Princeton University Press, 2021.

Vasseur, Édouard. *L'Exposition universelle de 1867. L'apogée du Second Empire*. Paris: Perrin, 2023.

Vial, Charles-Eloi. *Le siècle des chutes. Abdications et déchéances en France, 1814–1870*. Paris: Perrin, 2022.

de Viel-Castel, Count Horace. *Memoirs: A Chronicle of the Principal Events, Political and Social, during the Reign of Napoleon III, from 1851 to 1864*. Two volumes. London: Remington and Co., 1888.

Wallis, Keith. *Gemstones: Understanding, Identifying, Buying*. England: Antique Collectors' Club, 2012.

Watson, Joanne. *Empress Eugenie. A Footnote History (1826–1920)*. Tolworth: Grosvenor House Publishing, 2022.

Articles and Book Excerpts

Arrizoli-Clementel, P. *La Corbeille de l'impératrice*, CIETA, #70, 1992, pp. 163–167.

Bac, Ferdinand. "L'impératrice Eugénie au Cap Martin." *La Revue Universelle*, March 15, 1927 (Part 1), pp. 680–695, and April 1, 1927 (Part 2), pp. 50–67.

Block, E. L. "Maison Felix and the Body Types of Its Clients, 1875–1900." *West 86th*, vol. 26, no. 1, 2019, pp. 80–103.

Brunet, François and Talley, Jessica. "Exhibiting the West at the Paris Exposition of 1867: Towards a New American Aesthetic Identity?" *Transatlantica. Revue d'études américaines. American Studies Journal* [online], February 2017.

Carson, Gerald. "The Dentist and the Empress." *American Heritage*, June/July 1980, vol. 31, issue 4.

Courteaux, Olivier. "Charles Frederick Worth, the Empress Eugénie and the Invention of Haute-Couture." *Napoleon Organization Bulletin*, n.d., pp. 1–6. Accessed October 16, 2024, at www.napoleon.org/en/history-of-the-two-empires/articles/charles-frederick-worth-the-empress-eugenie-and-the-invention-of-haute-couture/.

Dekker, Jeroen. "Christian Carlier, La prison aux champs: les colonies d'enfants délinquants du Nord de la France au XIXe siècle." Paris: Les Éditions de l'Atelier; Editions Ouvrières, 1994.

Gambiez, Fernand. "Variation sur l'esprit de défense d'une revue de Longchamp à l'autre, 6 Juin 1867–29 Juin 1871." Armand Colin, Paris: *Histoire, économie et société*, vol. 7, no. 3 (3e trimestre 1988), pp. 381–397.

Glikman, Juliette. "The Myth of the Fourth Dynasty during the Second Empire." *Napoleonica the Journal*, vol. 5, issue 1, 2023, pp. 67–89.

Golicz, Ilmar. "Romancing the Throne: Louis-Napoléon Bonaparte, Francis Mountjoy Martyn, and Miss Howard." *Napoleonica the Journal*, vol. 2, issue 2, December 2022, pp. 117–153.

Gouttman, Alain. "Le martyr gênant de 'l'aventure mexicaine.' L'annonce de l'exécution de l'empereur Maximilien en France et en Autriche." *Le Sang des princes: cultes et mémoires des souverains suppliciés (XVIe–XXIe siècles).* Rennes: Presses universitaires de Rennes, 2014, pp. 63–74.

Gutek, Gerald L. "Johann Pestalozzi (1746–1827): Career and Development of Educational Theory, Diffusion of Educational Ideas." n.d. https://education .stateuniversity.com/pages/2319/Pestalozzi-Johann-1746-1827.html.

Huguenaud, Karine. "Eugénie et la joaillerie avant et après l'empire: une histoire de sentiments." ("Eugenia and Jewelry before and after the Empire: A Story of Feelings.") *Cuadernos de Investigacion Historica,* no. 37, 2020.

Lange, Olivia. "A Vacancy for the Throne." *The World of Interiors,* 2022.

Lévy, Michel-Louis. "Garçons et filles à l'école." *Population et sociétés. Bulletin mensuel d'informations démographiques, économiques, sociales,* October 1981, no. 151.

McQueen, Alison. "Les hôtels de l'Impératrice Eugénie à Paris: des lieux où s'exprimer." *Revue de l'art,* vol. 213, no. 3, 2021, pp. 32–51.

Morris, Thomas. "The Extraction of the Excruciating Bladder Stones." *Wellcome Collection,* September 19, 2019. https://wellcomecollection.org/articles/.

Ponsot, Pierre. "Economie traditionnelle, techniciens étrangers, et poussée capitaliste dans les campagnes espagnoles au XIXe siècle. L'exemple de deux domaines d'Eugénie de Montijo." *Instituto de Historia de Andalucia Cordoba,* 1981.

Rollet, Henri. "Le féminisme de l'impératrice Eugénie." *Revue du Souvenir Napoléonien,* April 1988, no. 358, pp. 49–56.

Skovron, Jean-Emmanuel. "De qui Montijo est-il le nom? Pour une meilleure connaissance de la famille espagnole de l'Impératrice Eugénie." *Napoleonica. La Revue,* vol. 39, no. 1, 2021.

Skovron, Jean-Emmanuel. "Les Montijo. Coup de projecteur sur la belle-famille de l'Empereur." *Eugénie, impératrice des Français.* Actes du colloque du Centenaire de la disparition d'Eugénie de Montijo, dir. Maxime Michelet, Paris: Éditions du Cerf, 2024, pp. 23–40.

Smith, William. "The Empress Eugénie and Farnborough." *Hampshire Papers,* no. 22, Hampshire Country Council, 2001.

Solé, Robert. "Ismaïl Pacha. À l'heure européenne." *Ils ont fait l'Egypte moderne,* Paris: Perrin, 2017, pp. 77–93.

Spencer, Samia I. "Un chapitre oublié de la glorieuse histoire de la francophonie. Langue et culture françaises en Egypte (1850–1950)." *Bilinguisme, plurilinguisme et francophonie. Mythes et réalités.* Dir. Toman, Cheryl; Ferreira-Meyers, Karen; Rigeade, Anne-Laure; et Al Dakr, Lilas. Montréal: Presses de l'Université de Montréal, 2023, pp. 95–104.

Stern, Ernesta. "Quelques souvenirs intimes sur l'impératrice Eugénie." *Revue Politique et Littéraire. Revue Bleue,* no. 14, July 19, 1924, pp. 489–496.

Taylor-Leduc, Susan. "French Empress Eugénie: Patron and Collector." *La Gazette Drouot,* February 10, 2021, pp. 1–7.

Vasseur, Édouard. "L'Exposition universelle de 1867: apothéose du Second Empire et de la génération de 1830." *École nationale des chartes, PSL,* 2001.

Vidler, Anthony. "Reading the City: The Urban Book from Mercier to Mitterand." *PMLA,* vol. 122, no. 1, Special Topic: Cities (Jan. 2007), pp. 235–251.

Vidler, Anthony. "Researching Revolutionary Architecture." *Journal of Architectural Education,* vol. 44, no. 4, August 1991, pp. 206–210.

Vidler, Anthony. "The New World: The Reconstruction of Urban Utopia in Late Nineteenth Century France." *Perspecta*, 1971.

Archives

Archives du château de Compiègne, cartons Impératrice Eugénie, cartons Prince Impérial.

Archives Frauenfeld, Switzerland:
  Sign 7 ' 702, file 012171
  F 1 ' 0, $^2/_1$
  Sign 7 ' 702-File 012115 1

Archives Nationales de Paris:
  Private Archives: Fonds Napoléon-400 AP/52 to 79
  Fonds F15 (maternal societies, philanthropic associations)
  Fonds F16 (prisons)
  Fonds F20 (philanthropic associations, 1858–1861)

Great Britain:
  Archives of Baring Bank: https://baringarchive.org.uk/ and https://baring.access.preservica.com/
  Journals of Queen Victoria available online (upon request): http://proquest.libguides.com/queenvictoria

University of Pennsylvania, Philadelphia: Kislak Center for Special Collections, Rare Books and Manuscripts, Van Pelt Library.

INDEX